Geor:

From one baseball
fan to another.

Best wishes,

Bob Wirz

The Passion
Of Baseball

Bob Wirz

THE PASSION OF BASEBALL

by
Bob Wirz
Copyright © Bob Wirz 2016
Cover Copyright © Laron McGinn 2016
Published by Veritas
(An Imprint of Ravenswood Publishing)

This book is a work of non-fiction based on the personal experiences and knowledge of the author.

Ravenswood Publishing
1275 Baptist Chapel Rd.
Autryville, NC 28318
http://www.ravenswoodpublishing.com

Printed in the U.S.A.

ISBN-13: 978-1536989618
ISBN-10: 1536989614

DEDICATION

My parents, R. A. and G. Marie Wirz, who provided wonderful parental support from the very beginning. I believe they would be proud.

Foreword

By Denny Matthews
Radio Voice of the *Kansas City Royals*

Baseball is a unique game, and everyone who knows and follows this great game has their own unique perspective. Everyone sees the game differently. I have known Bob Wirz since 1969. We reached the major leagues together with the Kansas City Royals. I would come into his office and do my pre-game preparation on the edge of his desk in the old ballpark—Municipal Stadium.

I always enjoyed his perspective and opinions on the game—very knowledgeable and insightful. We have had some great baseball conversations. Bob was terrific in his first major league job—Director of Public Relations, Kansas City Royals. Very organized—perfect disposition and temperament for that post. Patient and understanding—sometimes in the middle of some mild chaos.

Bob set up the Royals' first media guide, programs, and yearbook—I still have my own set of originals. Bob's memories of the Royals' early years (1969-74) in the book unlock a flood of memories for me—he remembers things that I don't, and I remember incidents he might or might not recall. Yes, the early Royals years were ... those were definitely good times.

Knowing his personality and work ethic, I knew that Bob and his talents would be in demand wherever he went. It would be someone else's gain and the Royals' loss. We were all very proud of him when he landed in the office of the Commissioner of Baseball. While there, he saw and participated in some of the historic moments of the game. He has run his own business; he has had part ownership in a minor league team. He has truly been invested in the game of baseball.

1

This book chronicles the life of Bob, and what a rewarding journey it has been. Doing work and working in the game you love. What a wonderful combination. The game of baseball has been good to Bob, and Bob Wirz has been a terrific asset to the game. So sit back and enjoy the book—I sure will.

(Denny Matthews, who has been a major part of Kansas City Royals radio broadcasts continuously since the first season in 1969, was elected to the broadcasters' wing of the National Baseball Hall of Fame—Ford C. Frick Award—in 2007. He has co-authored three books with the Kansas City T-Bones' Senior Director of Media Relations, Matt Fulks. They are *Play by Play: 25 Years of Royals on Radio; Tales from the Royals Dugout;* and *Hi, Anybody.*)

Preface

I am alternately staring at my computer screen and gazing out the window on an abnormally mild late autumn day. The World Series has been over only a short time, the remaining colorful leaves will soon have fallen on the 18th fairway that I face, and I know that it will be more than 100 days and most likely several New England snowfalls before pitchers and catchers gather in the warmth of Florida and Arizona to start another beautiful baseball season. Somehow, I will get through these days until mid-February. I always do.

I understand only about six percent of the general population end up working in the field we were originally attracted to as youngsters. A good many young athletes believe they will be major league baseball players; perhaps as many youngsters want to be actors or president of the United States.

I am clearly in the six percent category. I did not know what avenue would eventually open up, but there was no doubt whatsoever or any wavering at any point along the way that I wanted to work in major league baseball. I can remember saying on many an occasion "I don't care if it is selling peanuts or cotton candy, I want to work in major league baseball."

So there.

My sole objective from the tender age of eight—maybe even earlier—was to find a way to this magnificent, utterly frustrating, financially questionable profession.

I hope to be able to string together enough of my memories of these past 65-70 years of baseball to provide some worthwhile reading. It was supposed to be 60 years, but since I have procrastinated so long in getting finished, it is now much longer than originally intended. "Oh my," a friend of long ago, the noted sportscaster Dick Enberg, might say.

I am doing this little project essentially for myself. I do not know how many others will enjoy my personal journey, but it is here if you so choose. I like to joke, and it may not be too far from the truth, that if this lad who is no longer quite so young were to slide off the face of the earth, today a dozen people might show up to pay their respects. If word reaches others across this land, they likely will sigh, maybe offer a smile (or frown) from some long-ago incident, and then keep reading their newspaper.

Oh, no. I've dated myself already. "Reading the newspaper?" More likely, it is whatever type of electronic device that is in their hands at the moment.

I do hope my family will want to read it at some point, and share a copy with the grandchildren, who may not fully understand my baseball journey.

I have no idea exactly when—or why, for that matter—this eternal passion for baseball started. And I doubt there is anyone around who can explain.

What I do know is that it was long before August 16, 1949, which was the day this soon-to-be-12-year-old saw his first major league game. The historians will recognize that was one year to the day after the great Bambino, George Herman "Babe" Ruth, passed away. I have so many vivid memories of that day although they have to wait their turn.

I lived every one of my days until college in the "metropolis" of Halsey, NE, which is tucked away on the Blaine and Thomas county lines along Highway 2 in what we consider the beautiful Sandhills.

It sometimes takes outsiders a while to agree about the "beauty" of mid-Nebraska since the more citified people sometimes consider the area to be an endless stretch of rolling hills more heavily populated by cattle than by people. If given a chance, the area will win even most of the non-believers over because of the gentleness of both the scenery

4

and the people. The worries of the real metropolises of our country do not exist, which is not to say Sandhills people do not have reason for a troubled brow from time to time. Their worries most likely stem from whether there is too little moisture, whether the summer will be too hot to allow a good hay crop, or whether cattle prices will be reasonable when it is time to take the yearlings to the sales ring.

When one rode down Highway 2, the two-lane road that runs through Halsey, the population sign read 141 for most of the time those of us in the Class of 1955 were growing up. That is 141 people. Yes, 141. Many of them, probably a near majority, were relatives since both of my parents came from large families. The village is much smaller today although, thankfully, still breathing.

How in the world does a young lad among those 141 fall in love with baseball? There is no easy explanation. We played baseball in school, and we had a Town Team for a few Sunday afternoons in the summer. The World Series had some meaning to a good number of the men, and they would listen to games on the radio, but only if they were not feeding or moving the cattle from one pasture to another and only if the reception was strong enough to bring in some distant signal. I can tell you no one else fell so deeply into the throes of Mr. Doubleday's game.

Why me?

Dad, a highly popular man who was known as R. A. or his longtime nickname of Fat (which he wasn't), liked baseball. He even managed the Town Team at times, perhaps because he lived in town, instead of on a ranch, where it would not be known until the last minute if the Sunday afternoon game was high enough up the list of priorities to go play. But even with his interest, I have no recollection that Dad ever sweated out every pitch of a Cardinals game day after day like his son did.

5

Mom, or Marie to her legions of friends, did not seem to pay great attention to the games, although in later years, she surely enjoyed watching the Atlanta Braves when their games became available by satellite in Halsey or in my parents' winter oasis of Mesa, AZ. Mom never stood in the way of me listening to a game, even if the static prevailed for hours on end. She never, ever discouraged me.

The other member of the family, my sister, Bev, grew up to be a pretty good baseball fan, but I am quite certain she was more into cutting out paper dolls in those days than straining to see if Sam Hairston could double in a key run to give the Pueblo (CO) Dodgers the run they needed to edge the Sioux City (IA) Soos. These Class A Western League teams weren't within hundreds of miles of our doorstep next to Highway 2, so how much could it matter to a teenage girl even if her brother considered it of paramount importance?

Our little village of Halsey was best known as home to the largest man-made forest in the country, aptly named the Nebraska National Forest. The forest had been started in 1902 when, according to popular legend, a University of Nebraska nurseryman, Dr. Charles Bessey, wanted to prove he could grow trees in the sometimes fertile, many times sandy soil of the area. He proved the point with this 90,000-plus acre layout, which stretches from the Dismal River on the south to the Middle Loup River on the north.

Bessey Nursery became such a thriving undertaking that virtually every evergreen tree planted in Nebraska or in several neighboring states was shipped out of there. I believe it ships millions of pine, cedar and spruce to these states to this day.

You can imagine how important the Nebraska National Forest became. Ranchers leased some of the acreage to summer their cattle, and hunters enjoyed tracking down deer among the mature pine trees whenever a season was opened up to them. Tourists made the drive to the lookout tower, where they could climb the 60-foot structure to gaze

6

at the 360-degree panorama while the ranger explained his role of watching for fires, which could—and did, at times—devastate the area. And the forest became the largest employer in this area for both adults and teens, except for those who grew up on a family ranch.

Your humble writer spent several high school and college summers watering, counting and weeding, on bended knees, the tree beds which were home to those baby evergreens. They were pampered nearly as much as any other newborn.

The forest also was home to picnic grounds and the largest swimming pool in at least a 100-mile stretch —an unfathomable situation for today's MTV-, iPad-, SUV-oriented young people and probably for most of their parents.

My hometown itself consisted of roughly eight blocks of single- or two-story homes located on one side or the other of Highway 2, and along the Chicago, Burlington and Quincy railroad. We had passenger trains in those early days, and the CB&Q also was important for the delivery of coal, which most homes used, and cattle cake, which added valuable pounds for the mostly Hereford cattle herds. The days when the public could ride the rails in that area have long since disappeared, but the railroad now has two sets of tracks because of the stunningly heavy schedule of 100 car freight trains going east and west. Travelers to those parts will be shocked to see how much coal is transported out of Wyoming to points east. The average of one train an hour, 24 hours a day, seven days a week is not an exaggeration, so the light sleepers among visitors to Halsey and the other villages will have a haunting feeling of trains rumbling through the bedroom all night long.

Our red-brick schoolhouse was very sufficient for Grades 1-12. However, in my high school days, a wood-frame building—an extravagance at the time—was moved to town so that we could take shop class. The wood-frame building had been a one-room schoolhouse several miles north of town, and, in fact, the then-named Rose Hill School was where my mother got her education.

Halsey's footnote to history may only be its forest and the surrounding sandy hills, but its defined existence away from more populated areas made it all the more removed from baseball in the 1940s. Perhaps my geographic separation from areas more involved in baseball made my interest all the more daring and exciting, and my determination all the stronger.

I love recalling the details of this area since I don't get to Nebraska as often these days and I don't always like the changes I see in these tiny towns.

Special Thanks to So Many

It is dangerous to start thanking staff and friends who helped me research a detail, find a photo, discuss promotional avenues or proof this memoir because I know I will be forgetting the contributions of others, but here goes anyway.

Longtime public relations friend Margaret Durante was an excellent editor, making so many good suggestions and catching my long sentences.   Laura Abbott added her meticulous editing skills. The original members of a little group we call the Writer's Bloc (Julian Padowicz, Doug Hearle and Ken Koprowski) continually lent me publishing's nuances I likely would have overlooked. Interns like David Gissel, Jason Leone, Justin Mensceli, Mike Nelson and Jack Newman never flinched when I needed help pinpointing the date of an event. Chris Rice helped me when a Kansas City Royals name might have been forgotten.

The public relations directors of every major league team and the American and National League offices taught me so much, which gave me the confidence to eventually undertake a project of this nature. They also endured the lengthy PR meetings and equally tedious memos I considered were for the good of the game, and (mostly) put up with my countless suggestions whenever their team was hosting an All-Star Game or World Series.

And I would like to thank what I call My Dandy Dozen from among literally hundreds of friends and associates along my journey who played major roles for countless reasons. This group is made up of Buddy Blattner, David Carpenter, Fred Claire, Bob Fishel, Lou Gorman, Bowie Kuhn, Monte Irvin, Bob Lemon, Denny Matthews, Perry Pilotti, Cedric Tallis and George Toma.

I am so blessed to this day for my immediate family of my wife Maybeth; sister Bev Jefferies; sons Jeff and Brad; daughters-in-law Antonia and Eileen; stepdaughter Amy Matton (and husband Craig Edwards); stepson Peter Matton; and beloved grandchildren Matthew, Lucas and Diego Wirz and Maddy and Samantha Edwards.

Bob Wirz Celebrates a Birthday
(Not his 21st or 50th; Just Another Milestone)

The song which follows was written by my wife, Maybeth, with more love than I probably deserve. It was too precious, as is she, not to be included in this little memoir. Naturally, it is to the tune of "Take Me Out To The Ballgame."

Bob Wirz really loves baseball, he's obsessed with the game!
The strike-outs the hits and the RBIs,
Statistics line up to put stars in his eyes!
So it's read, read, read all the box scores
that come in the paper each day.
And he knows, knows, knows all the numbers,
in his head they stay!

Bob Wirz really loves baseball, he's obsessed with the game!
It's three-three in Boston, six-two in L.A.
with so many scores, he keeps busy all day.
So he'll watch, watch, watch on the TV
or tune in XM in the car.
And he'll search, search, search for those numbers
wherever they are!

Bob Wirz really loves baseball, he's obsessed with the game!
He loves keeping score with his pencil in hand;
his happiest moments are in the grandstand!
He will mark, mark, mark all the plays down,
and keep track of all of the game!
And he loves, loves, loves knowing
it's never the same.

Bob Wirz really loves baseball, he's obsessed with the game!
The friendships he's made and the people he knows
meet him and greet him wherever he goes!
So he's kept, kept, kept all his stories
of things that he's seen and he's done.
Please Bob, write, write, write all them down
so we can share the fun!

Infatuation Before the Age of 10

The Early Years (Pre-1950)

I know that I had not reached my 10th birthday when I first fell in love with baseball because that would have been toward the end of the 1947 baseball season. The Class A Western League was founded that year, and it played a big part in my initiation.

Sam Hairston, the first of the parade of Hairstons who have carried on that significant name in baseball ever since, was a sturdily built catcher who did, indeed, seem to double every time his team needed a rally. Sam did not get to the majors, which in those days required a player to climb through the ranks of imposing farm systems from Class D to Class C, then B, A, AA and AAA before getting his name on a major league lineup card.

We were located between Western League teams, such as Lincoln and Omaha (NE) and Denver, and with relatives in the Mile High City, I eventually got to a handful of games.

I also remember, with a tad of help to guarantee accuracy from *The Encyclopedia of Minor League Baseball*, that Les Peden was an all-star third baseman at Des Moines, IA;, and future Chicago White Sox second baseman Nellie Fox was a standout for Lincoln, as were diminutive but highly successful southpaw Bobby Shantz and a scantly recalled outfielder with the lovely name of Rocky Ippolito.

Some of those names will never fade for yours truly.

The opportunities to see a game in person were rare. A couple of times a summer made it a banner year. But I had radio as a companion all season long. No, kids, there was no television in the Sandhills until considerably later.

13

I had three possibilities for hearing games on the radio. The upright (perhaps a Philco) in my tucked-away upstairs bedroom in our modest but comfortable two-story house (hey, we had indoor plumbing for most of these years) was my regular hideaway. It gave me privacy for my daydreaming.

I could lie on my bunk bed or sit on the floor among my tiny collection of baseball treasures as I listened to a game. There were choices, if the weather cooperated, to bring in a radio signal. The major league Game of the Day probably was the favorite, but we also could sometimes get KMA from Shenandoah, IA; WHO in Des Moines (Ronald Reagan's play-by-play haunt for a time); the Cardinals' station in St. Joseph, MO (for day games only); and various Western League broadcasts from Topeka, KS, Des Moines or Sioux City, IA. KMOX, the 50,000-watt St. Louis powerhouse, was a possibility on the rare evening when weather conditions were perfect.

We thought we were pretty good, pre-high school. Budding author (5) along with best buds Nick Rodocker (8) and Joe Miller (6)

The other options were the family radio in the living room but next to the kitchen entry in case it was my turn to dry dishes, or the car radio, and I don't believe I even needed a key to Mom's and Dad's Chevy. I cannot over-emphasize the daily battle with static as to whether I would be able to hear a game or even a few pitches.

Atmospheric conditions made it easier to listen to football and basketball games in the non-baseball months, and even to be introduced to hockey. I knew absolutely nothing about hockey, but there were only six National Hockey League teams, and how romantic it sounded to hear someone cry "GOAL!" or "SCORE!" The penalty box was a complete mystery to this lad.

While Bob Devaney had not yet landed in Lincoln to create the University of Nebraska football powerhouses, the Cornhuskers still meant a lot to all of us in the state, and

Bill Stern's broadcasts of important national collegiate games made the fall Saturday afternoons a joy. We cheered for the Huskers in basketball season, of course, but my memory bank seems to bring up more Kansas and Kansas State games because of the strength of the teams and the powerful signal coming out of WIBW Radio in Topeka.

My baseball appetite also could get a boost if we went 50 miles east to Broken Bow, NE, on a Saturday shopping excursion. While Mom and Dad took care of the more important shopping needs, young Bob would hustle off to the Rexall Drug Store on the south side of the square of this 3,000-person community to see if any new baseball magazines had arrived.

The photos alone were treasures to improve my image of the "heroes" I heard about on the radio. And the best treat of all was if I could find a *Baseball Digest*. April was the best month of all because that issue had the full 40-man roster for all 16 major league teams. I still have a number of those issues, complete with my pencil markings as I learned the names of players sent to the minor leagues or of an occasional addition. Subsequent issues of the *Digest* normally had smaller versions of active rosters. It is nearly impossible to explain what all of this meant, and I do not expect my baseball-loving grandsons to understand since their updates are up-to-the minute on the gadget of the day today.

I created my own ways of getting more enjoyment.

One creation—and this from one of the least handy people I know—was a scoreboard I built from a piece of one-inch wood no more than a foot wide and less than that in height. I had nails for each inning and for the R-H-E portion of the scoreboard. It seems to me I used white circular reinforcement tabs to hang for each half-inning, but for the life of me, I cannot recall what I designed if either team scored.

16

I also used numerous notebooks because it was fun to post the scores half-inning by half-inning as I became aware of results. I would write down the batteries, as well, when I knew who the pitchers and catchers were for each game. But I daresay it would be a hodgepodge of incomplete information at day's end. Still, I found satisfaction from what I had done.

As I grew into my teens and girls became part of my life, during my workdays at the forest, I would establish two women's baseball teams and have the Hollywood Starlets oppose the Local Lasses (I don't believe they had special team names) to compete. A friend suggests this was the original fantasy baseball game.

I suppose it depended on how my dating life was going as to whether the Sandhills gals or the Janet Leighs, Debra Pagets and Jane Powells of movie fame were the more successful on any given day. Trust me, it did keep me thinking about baseball, which made the workday go much faster.

When I could drive and was going somewhere on our roads less traveled because of the sparse population of Central Nebraska, if I met a car while the speedometer mileage went from one to five (in tenths of a mile), it meant a run was scored by the visiting team. The home team scored from six to zero.

If I saw a flock of geese or a batch of sparrows sitting on telephone lines, I would count them, then use the number to create a make-believe roster limit for that day's game or for a weekend series. If there were 18 birds, I might have seven pitchers, a spare catcher, infielder and outfielder. The designated hitter was still years in the future.

I believe you grasp that the point is so much of my life was built around baseball. Always has been, always will be.

I know there are shortcomings by having any one topic be so dominant. So be it. This goes a long way toward explaining why any number of my lifetime friends may scoff at allowing anything to dominate to such an extreme. You know what: Just as many seem to admire the career I've enjoyed for all these decades.

So this is intended to set the stage for the chapters that follow, each detailing at least one incident or personality— often both—that has impacted the life of this long-ago lad of the Nebraska Sandhills as he has moved through the years to today's, well, let's say more advanced part of life where age exceeds the speed limit, even on the more advanced four-lane highways.

Savoring the First Game Forever

1949

As surely as we know Barack Obama's presidency ends January 20, 2017, I can tell you nothing but nothing has any chance of ever exceeding my very first opportunity to see a major league baseball game.

It was August 16, 1949, a date easy to remember and not merely because I was a month to the day shy of my 12th birthday. No, it was the first anniversary of the death of Babe Ruth. I will get back to the Bambino in a bit.

A trip from Nebraska to Chicago and on to Cleveland and Niagara Falls was no little undertaking for Mom and Dad. Neither the highways nor the automobiles were in the same strata as today.

But the Wirz four plus Uncle Gerald and Aunt Margaret Rodocker packed our way into the car and headed East, with the primary destination—except for young Bob—to see Mom's (and Uncle Gerald's) sister, Vi, and family in Thompson, OH, a long daily commute from Uncle Joe Nagy's job in Cleveland.

The highlight of the entire trip for me, as much as I loved Aunt Vi, was to go to Wrigley Field, where, wouldn't you know, my heroes, the St. Louis Cardinals, were visiting.

I showed my persistence about baseball, perhaps for the first time but certainly not the last, as we traveled through Iowa because I knew from my trusty radio before we left home that the Western League's Des Moines Bruins had a game on that very evening at Pioneer Park. What a thrill it would be to attend!

I was in the minority among the travel party, but it did not keep me from persisting. I imagine I was a royal pain in the a__, to tell the truth. Making matters worse, every mile or so (at least as it seemed to an 11-year-old) in this corn belt, there were signs stating "PIONEER." While they were promoting Pioneer seed corn, it seemed they were rubbing salt in my wound about not getting to Pioneer Park that night.

On the day we were to be in Chicago, we arrived at Wrigley Field hours before the Cubs and Cardinals were to get down to business. What a wildly anticipated event it was, and not just for me! I do not believe any of us had seen a major league game; or a big stadium, and Wrigley Field already had a grand reputation since it was a "mere" 35 years old and the Cubs played every one of their 77 home games in daylight.

Wrigley Field had been the scene of six World Series from its debut in 1914 to 1945, all losing battles, as I need not remind the Cubs' loyalists.

We soaked in every ounce of atmosphere we could before the gates opened, which I vaguely recall included one or more adult-beverage parlors. And when we got inside and could see that now-ancient scoreboard in centerfield, where every inning of every game continues to this day to be posted by hand, and could study every pillar and the beautiful green grass ... well, it was breathtaking.

Our seats were on the first-base side—and quite decent, as I recall—and it was not long before we could see firsthand how the Northsiders loved their Cubbies. It was Ladies Day, a popular event of those days, and there was a moment of silence to remember the great home-run champion Babe. Yes, they paid tribute one year to the day after his passing.

I admit I cannot remember many specifics about the game, except that my No. 1 hero, Stan Musial, had a couple of hits (a single and triple plus two walks in a perfect day at the plate, I learned recently via the Internet). The Cardinals rallied in the eighth and ninth innings, but the Cubs put up three runs in the bottom of the ninth to win, 5-4. I still have two scorecards from the day to help my memory, one with my hand-printed names of the starters and everyone who got into the game. I must have been too busy taking it all in to keep score after the top of the first, when Red Schoendienst led off with a hit and an eventual run while Marty Marion followed with a hit and Musial with a walk.

The Cardinals' lineup, all too familiar, was Schoendienst, Marion, Musial, Slaughter, Northey, Nelson, Garagiola (whom I would get to know and work with many years later), Glaviano, and pitcher Max Lanier (who I would learn much later may be best remembered as one of the major leaguers who had to be punished for jumping to the Mexican League).

The Cubs started Jeffcoat, Mauch, Reich, Cavarretta (I spelled it Caveratta), Ramazzotti, Pafko, Owen, Smalley, and Dubiel. I still remember most of those players now 60-some years later, although the programs only listed the last name, uniform number and position.

To digress briefly, I used the free scorecard for my lineups as opposed to the four-page, 10-cent version sold to the public. It could be that the smaller freebie fit my size better. I do not believe it would have meant anything that it was provided by Chicago's striking printers, who advised everyone, "Don't buy the SCAB *Herald American, Tribune, Daily News, Sun-Times.*" Those newspapers were being published during what the handout proclaimed was "against Chicago's papers, their first strike in 97 years." That's pretty amazing, when we think about it.

The official scorecard has double value to me today anyway since the projected starting lineups were printed and I have the autograph of future Hall of Fame pitcher Grover Cleveland Alexander in the slot where the St. Louis starting hurler was intended to be listed. I vaguely remember getting that autograph years later during an amateur game in Broken Bow. Only some type of fate would allow for me having the scorecard with me when my path crossed with the great one.

We would have paid 15 cents for "spicy" red hots (Oscar Mayer variety, no less) that day; 20 cents for an egg sandwich; 10 cents for a soft drink; and a whole quarter for a Pabst beer. A Cubs jacket was advertised at $5.95, or a quarter more by mail. Those were the days.

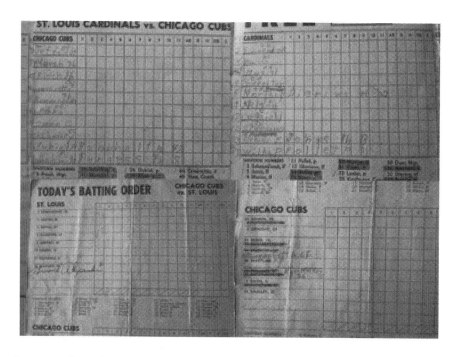

Scorecards and my youthful penmanship help me remember that very first Major League game on August 16, 1949

An official program from that first game in 1949

Our day was far from finished when the last out was recorded. Now, we started a vigil outside of Wrigley Field because we could see each Cardinals player look out from the second floor and eventually emerge to the outside. I can remember very nearly touching some of these heroes in the crush of other adoring fans. Uncle Gerald nearly got crushed himself at one point when a group of fans thought he was umpire Frank Dascoli.

I must have floated for days because of this total experience, even though we had additional thrills during our trip, such as touring an empty Notre Dame Stadium and later sitting in a box seat Uncle Joe got through his municipal job in Cleveland to watch both the Yankees and the Washington Senators play games against the Indians.

We saw Satchel Paige, whom I would interview years later in Kansas City, pitch for the Indians, and we were there when Ohio native and former Indians outfielder Gene

23

Woodling was honored with "Gene Woodling Night" even though he was now in his first year with the mighty Yankees. Bob Feller was among those to hit a home run. I believe it was his first after his return five years earlier from wartime duty. And it was my only opportunity to see the graceful Joe DiMaggio play. His Hall of Fame career ended two years later, although I was fortunate enough to meet this often-shy man a few times later, especially during Hall of Fame events.

Another meaningful baseball highlight during this trip was to watch games on television at Vi's and Joe's home, which was so rural we could romp through the yard and among the fruit trees. Some Indians games had made their way onto the black-and-white screen, a treat that would not come to my Sandhills hometown for several more years.

Add in the majesty of Niagara Falls, including a walk under them on the Canadian side, and a trip upstream on the Maid of the Mist, and it should not be difficult to realize how this was a trip not often exceeded to this day.

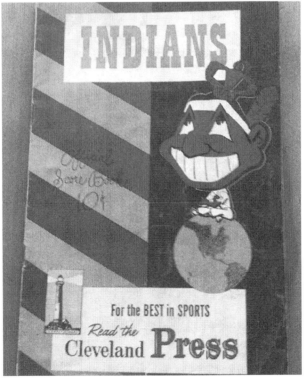

What joy to see the Indians and Yankees with the likes of Rizzuto, Henrich, Lopat, Gordon and Feller on that same trip in '49

25

Where Were You When Bobby Thomson Homered?

1950-55

The basic premise of this book is to write about a few significant baseball events or personalities every year. However, I have already captured the essence of what was taking place through my early teen years with so very many games on the radio and an occasional trip to Denver, so I will merely hit some highlights for the first half of the 1950s.

We played sports in school, with softball in the fall, basketball in the winter, and track and a bit of baseball in the spring. Softball was important since we did not have enough high school boys to field even a six-man football team. As I recall, softball was not entirely for the boys, and it certainly was not limited to the four years of high school or we would have had to forgo this sport, as well.

I know our first "organized" basketball team was in fifth grade because my cousin, Nick Rodocker, and I truly dominated the scoring. We beat Dunning (NE), our rival 10 miles to the east of Halsey, thumping the Tigers, 5-2, with Nick scoring three points and yours truly the other two.

My mind is not quite as clear as to when we first took to the softball diamond, but it certainly was well ahead of high school (1951-52 was my freshman year), so I was one of those blessed to get to play at a very young age. I may have been the only lefty around, so I got to stake claim to first base.

I have one very clear recollection of the fall of 1951 because we played a game at Bingham, NE, another tiny town nearly 100 miles to our west on Highway 2. We did not travel that far very often, but one must remember the towns in this Hereford cattle-raising area of the Sandhills were separated by 10 or more miles and seldom had population signs reading more than a couple hundred people. That is it, folks. Dig out an old atlas.

I do not know if we won, 22-18, or lost by a similar margin, but my memory is that on the way home, we learned on the car radio that Bobby Thomson had hit what has been known as the "Shot Heard 'Round the World" ever since that very day, lifting his New York Giants into the World Series with a heart-pounding playoff victory over the rival Brooklyn Dodgers.

I doubt the news of Thomson's homer even meant a great deal to most of my teammates, who probably were much more concerned about what ranching chores might still remain for them when they got home. I was the "pampered" city slicker who lived in town and knew something about the Giants and Dodgers.

How often I have thought of that day in Bingham, especially when I worked my way into professional baseball and a job in New York City more than two decades later. I would have a flashback whenever I was fortunate enough to meet either Thomson or Ralph Branca, the man who threw the "Shot Heard 'Round the World" pitch, at a baseball event or a pro-am golf tournament.

In the really-small-world department, I eventually had the opportunity to work alongside Hall of Fame outfielder Monte Irvin for more than 10 years. Irvin will get more attention as we go along, but how could I have imagined that October day in Nebraska that I would be sharing office space with this caring man who lived through the Negro League days to eventually get an opportunity to make his mark in the National League?

Our high school baseball was very limited each spring by a combination of the un-spring-like weather of March and April and the disappointment to this lad that very few schools fielded teams. Track and field was easier because it did not require a lot of bodies to throw the shot put or run

27

the 100-yard dash. Virtually every school could put together a four-man relay team.

We had a baseball team, especially since my Class of 1955 featured a male dominance of seven people. There were five girls until the popular Teaford Twins moved away after our junior year.

I'm pretty certain my memory is correct that one year we went to the district tournament, a qualifier for the state tourney, without playing a single game beforehand. The only practice or two that we managed were literally with snowflakes falling. You have guessed correctly that we did not reach the state tournament. We were humbled something like 10-0 in the distant town of Guide Rock, NE.

My fondest memory of high school baseball was a 2-0 defeat at Cairo, NE. Cairo was some 115 miles east of Halsey, again along Highway 2, and the pain and joy (believe me when I say there was some of each) of that game was brought back to life numerous times every year when we drove through Cairo on the way to the State High School Basketball Tournament in Lincoln and later when I was a student at the University of Nebraska.

The reason I can remember that we lost 2-0 was the role I played. I was at my usual first-base position (although I did a fair amount of pitching in my upper-class years), and it was my overthrow of third base that allowed one of the two runs to score. On the opposite side of this mostly embarrassing day was the fact I got to third base, then got picked off.

Now I was not a total klutz, as it may seem, but I remember those two plays vividly, sometimes with a smile, all these years later.

We drew Cairo for a district tournament game later in the spring, and we were hopeful because we would be on a neutral diamond in Ravenna, NE. The picture got considerably brighter when we scored twice in the first inning. But the situation reversed quickly. Final score: Cairo 16, Halsey 6. Oh, my!

The state tournament was not in the offing; we were not even close. We did not make it in basketball, either, although the Halsey Hawks did plenty of damage on the hardwoods (and tile floors, which were not rare in those days).

I need to set the stage for basketball since it would have to be considered the major sport at that time in our area, and the state tournament was quite a festival. Anyone who knows much about the State of Nebraska and its sports history realizes everything revolves around the University of Nebraska football team. The Cornhuskers; Huskers, if you prefer. Even in the '40s and '50s, Husker football games in the capital city of Lincoln stood far above everything else. Bob Devaney and Tom Osborne had not yet brought the glory days to the state, but it still was the best we had to offer. Since the teams were often so-so, the games were embellished with statewide participation in events like Band Day, when the football field was packed from end zone to end zone and thousands of high school band members could participate.

Halsey did not participate because the only music class our school had except for chorus consisted of a rhythm band, where people played the triangle, tambourine or sticks. That must surely have ended in grade school, too.

The State High School Basketball Tournament was played over a four-day span from noon or even earlier each day. There were four classes of competition, later on expanding to six, and spreading from having all games in the Coliseum on the NU campus to other Lincoln sites.

I do not believe I am overstating the importance of the tournament because tiny schools like Halsey could qualify in Class D. Class A consisted of the big boys from Boys Town and Creighton Prep and the public schools in Omaha and Lincoln, with out-state hopefuls like Scottsbluff and Alliance occasionally qualifying. These were pre-television days, of course, but the statewide daily, *The Omaha World-Herald,* and various radio stations gave big-time coverage.

The *World-Herald's* prep icon, Gregg McBride, was like a god to every rancher and farmer throughout the 93 counties as he issued his weekly Top Ten rankings for each class all winter long. Come state tournament time, McBride and a cadre of the newspaper's writers and photographers chronicled everything from the games to how Mom and Dad had saved to be able to come watch Johnny play, to which cheerleaders exerted the most pep. It was page after page of colorful coverage.

Young Bob Wirz would have died to play rather than be a bleacher creature along with Dad and however many schoolmates made the 230-mile trek from Halsey to watch all day long.

With our Class of '55 playing a major role, Halsey had at least a slight chance. We won our District Tournament as juniors. That got us within two games of a state tournament berth. I was thrilled that we got to play our Regional in Broken Bow. Broken Bow was almost big-time to me, a Class B school. We were outmanned in our Regional opener, ending what I believe was a 20-5 season.

I may be reversing the records of the two seasons, but I believe we were 17-8 as seniors. The classifications had changed, expanding to six, and we, naturally, were in Class E since it was the smallest of the groups. I don't believe we had to win as many games to get to State, and we started our last run in Valentine, NE, some 80 miles from Halsey. We were only allowed 10 players on the roster—it was the same in every class—so there was not much we could do to keep from overwhelming our initial opponent from Brewster, NE, a town of perhaps 50 people. We won something like 113-25, establishing a state scoring record for the new Class E.

Can you believe, we lost the next night? That was it. Our high school careers were over without making it to the State Tournament. I don't even remember the opponent that night. My one recollection is that I decided to go down fighting; not literally, mind you. I picked up my fourth and fifth fouls in a very short amount of time late in the game— my very first time to foul out.

I also know there were a great many tears from many of us after that defeat. It was too much to endure. I guess everything was not cast aside, though, because I still have my No. 11 jersey, the one in white with blue trimming. It is in one of the dusty boxes I have moved all over the country.

We had one other outlet for playing baseball in those days. The general idea was that each village had a Town Team. Games were played on Sunday afternoons from May-July, which meant nearly 10 games in a season. The good news, especially for someone like me, was there was no age restriction. I am pretty certain I first played for the Halsey Town Team when I was 14, and some of my teammates may have been in their 50s. We needed every player we could find on most Sundays in order to field a team.

In digging through my boxes of mementos, I realize the league was once known as the Sandhills Baseball League, although my primary recollection is that of the Grassland Baseball League. I even found a cardboard-like schedule for 1955, which listed six teams. It may be the NBA and NHL patterned their playoffs after Grassland because four of the six teams qualified for the playoffs!

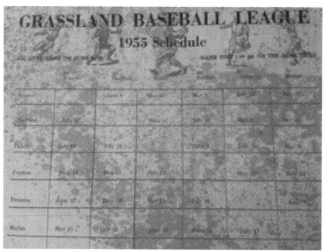

Town Team games were limited to Sunday afternoons in the Sandhills, but they provided great enjoyment

Every diamond had a skin infield, and a virtual requirement every Sunday morning was for someone—often my dad or uncle Pete Rodocker—to attach their pickup to the heavy drag made of railroad ties and make numerous trips around the infield to get rid of the weeds. Sandburs were especially troublesome. No one wanted to reach down for a grounder or run the bases and have a sandbur cling to his pants (whether a standard baseball uniform or work jeans) or puncture a finger. I'm sure most mothers would cringe today, but our drinking water for these often intensely hot afternoons would come from a common 10-gallon milk can which someone would drop a heavy block of ice into and fill from the garden hose.

Rules may have been made to be broken, but the bylaws I uncovered on onion skin paper for the Sandhills League emphasized rosters had to be sent to the league secretary in advance although "players coming home from service by discharge or on leave shall be excluded" from the necessity of being reported 10 days in advance of playing. "No uniforms shall be necessary to participate" was stated as part of Rule 7.

The financial statement for 1956, distributed prior to the next season, showed revenue of $99, mostly from the $15-per-team entry fee, and expenses of $97.98, with the notation the balance ($1.02) would be "used to offset (the) deficit in 1955." I guess the league was pretty well protected from any shenanigans.

While I was an emergency fill-in at 14, it was not long before I became a regular. I preferred to play first base or pitch, but we learned to play where we were needed because the bench was pretty limited on most Sundays. Young Bob even was the winning pitcher in one All-Star Game in about 1955 or 1956, and thanks to a remarkable mother who put together numerous scrapbooks for my sister and me, it can be told with decent accuracy that the East bats came alive while I was pitching to help us to an 18-5 victory. The box score shows eight errors for each team, and indicates I gave up three runs on three hits, but does not specify how many innings I pitched. It appears three of us may have worked three innings apiece.

It probably seems an 18-5 score was pretty outlandish for an All-Star Game, but one story in the *Omaha World-Herald* pointed out 94 runs were scored in three games one weekend, with four of the six teams tallying between 16 and 27 runs. We dropped into the basement in the regular season when Seneca ran past us, 16-8.

The transition from playing to watching sports was pretty swift in mid-1955 because I graduated from high school and soon found myself starting my freshman year at the University of Nebraska. The disappointment of not being good enough to play except for intra-murals was that I was on a campus of about 8,000 students instead of being in a class of 10 and I could watch all sorts of sports events.

While there were some successes for certain Cornhusker sports teams during my years on campus (1955-59), the basic tone of mediocrity may well have been established about 48 hours before I attended my first class.

The Nebraska football teams of those years were far from the powerhouses we have grown accustomed to over much of the last 50 years, but the Huskers still provided enough success for statewide pride since the gridiron heroes were the closest we had to a major league sport.

The Huskers had a solid season in '54, winding up with a 50-0 shellacking of the University of Hawaii in Honolulu and a trip to the Orange Bowl since the Big Seven Conference could not send champion Oklahoma to a bowl two years in a row.

Hawaii provided the opposition for the Huskers again when the '55 season started in Lincoln, and most everyone had visions of a repeat of that 50-0 romp of the previous fall. Many of the Nebraska players were imported from eastern states like Pennsylvania in those days to round out a roster loaded with homegrown talent from both 11- and six-man high school squads.

A romp on my first Saturday as a college student? No way. At least a victory, right? Not exactly. The undersized, undermanned Rainbows slipped into Municipal Stadium and snatched a 6-0 victory. Impossible, we thought. But not so, and the first of my four student years of sub-.500 football and nearly a coach a year was underway.

Watching Dr. Strangelove's Majestic Shots

1956

The reality that my personal athletic playing accomplishments were not going anywhere ended in my freshman year at the University of Nebraska (1955-56). I am virtually certain I realized my limitations when I enrolled, but I had to make one effort. I went to a tryout for the baseball team. I could not run, throw or hit with anything resembling the necessary talent, even for a mediocre team. That dose of realism certainly encouraged me to start thinking about other avenues if I was going to be involved in baseball.

That freshman year was far from being a total loss. I never missed a Cornhusker football or basketball game, and when spring finally came around, I could go see Tony Sharpe's NU baseball team as well as our minor league baseball team, the Lincoln Chiefs.

Professional baseball right in my town. That was something new to relish. And did we ever! One of my buddies had a car, and we could get to Sherman Field in a matter of minutes. It was not exactly a showpiece stadium, even for that era, but we did not care. The mostly wooden structure with clubhouses on the third-base side and a press box perched on top, and with visiting teams representing the likes of the Dodgers (Pueblo, CO); Cubs (Des Moines, IA); and Giants (Albuquerque, NM), was nothing short of amazing to me.

The Chiefs represented the Pittsburgh Pirates, the first organization to require players to wear batting helmets. I squeezed in as many games as possible in the first few weeks of the season because I would be going back to Halsey as soon as school got out early in May.

Lanky Bennie Daniels hurled a one-hitter on one chilly evening. I recall he had a no-hitter later in the season, and Lincoln had a true star in the making in first baseman Dick Stuart, who later during his major league days had such nicknames as Dr. Strangeglove because of his many misadventures in the field.

By the time the season ended, Stuart had hit 66 home runs and driven in 158 runs, with many of the round-trippers majestic shots beyond the left field fence and not far from the railroad tracks that were busy throughout games.

It was the first professional season when I got to experience wallowing in the ups and downs of a team, even if it was the Class A Western League, and a star was being born right in front of my pals and me. Stuart was only 23 at the time, was rumored to be competing with Nebraska quarterback Don Erway for the attention of a Lincoln lovely, and seemed likely to have a future as one of the game's bright attractions. As *The Encyclopedia of Minor League Baseball* reminds us today, only sluggers (Joe Bauman, Bob Crues and Joe Hauser) had ever recorded greater home-run totals than Dick Stuart in a single season.

The 6-foot-3 righty gave this young hero worshiper and Chiefs fans the thrill of another 31 homers in '57 before the Pirates moved him on to Double-A Atlanta and Triple-A Hollywood for another 14 blasts the last third of the season. Stuart was playing first base for the Pirates the second half of 1958, and before his career was over, he had 228 home runs, including highs of 42 home runs and an American League-leading 118 RBIs for the Boston Red Sox in '63.

He also drove his managers crazy by sharing or leading league first basemen in errors for eight consecutive years, although Dr. Strangeglove never quite equaled the 30 errors he posted that first season in Lincoln.

36

My 27-Strikeout Catcher

1957

With the advantage of being able to look back nearly six decades, I can report that a high point in 1957—although I couldn't possibly realize it for about a dozen years—was to get familiar with the Lincoln Chiefs catching tandem of regular Marcus Cobos and his backup, Harry Dunlop.

Cobos was a colorful and competent catcher, who got the bulk of the work. Dunlop was listed at 6-foot-2, but he seemed taller, which did not help at all when he got to home plate with a bat in his hands. He hit a "mighty" .198 with one home run in 252 at-bats, but before anyone thinks I am reporting this in a derogatory manner, I hasten to remind that I consider anyone capable of donning a professional baseball uniform at all to have God-like characteristics. Remember, this hopeless dreamer might have stretched to 5-foot-8½ and had my playing career end in a tiny high school.

Dunlop played for three major league organizations and amassed 980 games from 1952 to 1968, with most of his time with teams in Classes A-B-C-D, which would be the equivalent of high and low Class A leagues today.

His best brush with fame came in his rookie season of 1952 when he caught three no-hit games in a 14-day span for Bristol, VA, of the Appalachian League, including one contest when Pittsburgh prospect and eventual major leaguer Ron Necciai registered 27 strikeouts. While one hitter was retired on a groundout, Dunlop let a strikeout pitch get past him one inning and Necciai ended the frame with four K's.

Dunlop and I never met until 1969, when, hallelujah, we both became part of the American League expansion team in Kansas City. He had proven himself not only as a player, but also by managing in the minor leagues for eight years and twice being named California League Manager of the Year when his Stockton and San Jose teams won championships. Joe Gordon, now a Hall of Famer for his sterling career as a second baseman, brought Dunlop on board as one of the Royals coaches.

We spent the next six years together with the Royals, Harry a loyal soldier to our bevy of managers and yours truly as the publicity director. He was the down-to-earth, appreciative type I could go to for any of a publicist's needs, and even though I often teased him about being the backup to Cobos in Lincoln, he never even threatened to punch my lights out.

The gentle man from Sacramento, now retired and in his 80s went on to manage for several more minor league seasons and to coach, largely under Jack McKeon, for 20 major league seasons.

Broadcasting Via the Heating Pipes

1958

By my junior year at the University of Nebraska, I was able to start getting my sometimes-timid feet wet in the journalistic world, both in newspaper work and in broadcasting. I would not get paid as I did while still in high school when I wrote for five cents an inch for the weekly *Thomas County Herald.* Of course, I was graduating from writing community briefs such as "Mr. and Mrs. Dana Harsh had Sunday dinner at the home of Mrs. Harsh's brother Gerald Rodocker" or an occasional high school game story.

There was some competition for opportunities, as I recall, to cover Nebraska athletic events for *The Daily Nebraskan*, but I found very few people interested in trying their hand at doing play-by-play for the campus radio station, KNUS.

If anyone ever heard the broadcasts, it was likely their unsophisticated radios were picking up the signal off of the heating pipes in the dormitories, such as Selleck Quadrangle, where I spent all four years since I had chosen not to go through the pledging system and possibly joining one of numerous fraternities.

The lack of listeners did not deter me or my cohorts from wanting to learn the broadcasting trade. This was an OPPORTUNITY not to be missed. We did not even have much day-to-day supervision at KNUS, but off we would go with our bulky equipment to set up right on broadcast row for Cornhusker basketball games at the still-functioning Coliseum or in the press box at Memorial Stadium, which seated something like 35,000 compared with the more than 90,000 who pile into the oft-expanded edifice these years on autumn Saturdays.

We had access to all of the notes and stats, limited as they were in those days, that were provided for the big boys from *The Omaha World-Herald, Lincoln Star* and *The Lincoln Journal,* as well as to the popular radio voices on KFAB or WOW from Omaha.

I promise every game was a thrill for this 20-year-old, who felt like he had been living with such a dream for nearly half a lifetime. It was big-time sports to me even if the Huskers seldom were among the nation's elite. But to be able to call the plays as the Huskers went up against the likes of Oklahoma's Bud Wilkinson or Syracuse's Ben Schwartzwalder was special.

With baseball running so deep in my blood, I also took advantage of an opportunity to set up right behind the home-plate screen or in the limited first-base bleachers to broadcast Huskers games. We were the only people doing baseball broadcasts because Nebraska did not stand out on the diamond and college baseball was not all that important nationally, especially in the often-frigid Midwest in April and early May. I doubt there was even newspaper coverage by an on-site reporter unless it was by *The Daily Nebraskan.*

When I did some research to be certain my mind was not straying, I learned that anything over 20 games was a bonus for the team. The Huskers had what must have been a huge season in 1958, going 17-10 for Sharpe, who had a 31-year run as head coach.

Details are fuzzy (and the Nebraska media guides of today do not even make a mention), but I know as sure as I am able to hit this keyboard that I broadcast a no-hit game one day. I have no idea of the score and I had to have research help to find out the Oklahoma Sooners were the opponent, but the no-hitter was thrown by Dwight Siebler, a right-hander who had my attention for the next decade and whose name never escapes me to this very day.

I cannot prove it, but I may well have done double duty on that feat, perhaps also writing about it for *The Daily Nebraskan.*

Siebler was a native Nebraskan, having grown up in the northeastern part of the state at Columbus, not far from Norfolk, which later got tremendous national attention because of its own local hero, a fellow named Johnny Carson. What made Siebler's feats live on for me as well as for *The World-Herald* was that he became a major leaguer five years later, and that was nearly as rare as a snowless winter for Nebraskans of those times.

Siebler probably never got close to a no-hitter in the American League, but he was in 48 games for the Minnesota Twins from 1963 to 1967, winning four times (three losses), starting eight games, and putting up an earned run average of 3.45, which would earn a part-time major leaguer hundreds of thousands of dollars today.

Nebraska's basketball history is a blip on any radar screen compared with its rich life on the football field, which is easily certified by the fact the Husker men have never won a single game in the NCAA tournament. However, I was witness as a fan to two major basketball events which occurred within weeks of each other late in the 1957-58 season.

Wilt Chamberlain, 13 months older than this typist, set the collegiate basketball world on its ear when he joined the often-powerful University of Kansas the same year (1955) as I enrolled at Nebraska.

While the Philadelphian was an unquestioned superstar from that time until his professional career came to an end in 1973, I am not certain the sports world was ever more intrigued about this 7-foot-2 player than in his initial season in Lawrence, KS.

There weren't many 7-footers 50 or more years ago. Who else could stand flat-footed and reach nine feet, six inches into the air? Had anyone seen a reverse dunk? With freshmen not eligible for varsity play in those days, the initial game pitted the KU freshmen against legendary Phog Allen's varsity, favored to win another conference championship.

All "Wilt the Stilt" did was score 42 points, pull down 29 rebounds and block four shots. Add in tales of Chamberlain's off-court activities, including a white convertible, and the fact Lawrence still was a segregated community, and the legend grew almost overnight.

My sister, Bev, and I were among several I've-got-to-see-him-myself students who trekked from Lincoln to Lawrence when it was Nebraska's turn to play freshmen and varsity games against KU. We were not disappointed in the ways Wilt could amaze.

By the time in late season of 1957-58 (Chamberlain's third and final season with the Jayhawks) when Kansas came calling to Lincoln, there was no question what team was considered the best in the land. Our Cornhuskers probably should not have been in the same league.

One of the joys of sports, of course, is that the victors are decided on the court, gridiron or diamond and not by the polls. Unranked and unappreciated, Nebraska beat mighty KU, 43-41, when popular but undersized two-handed set-shot artist Jim Kubacki drilled a long one to seal the victory and send everyone into a frenzy.

We had a chance to relive the event weeks later when Kansas State, now ascended to No. 1 in the nation behind a Nebraskan named Bob Boozer, visited the Coliseum. Same result. The Huskers may not have any NCAA wins, but they made a name for themselves in that short span, and I got to witness it all.

Victimizing the Sooners

1959

I had a major breakthrough during my senior year at Nebraska, and it certainly did not take place in the classroom, where I tease sometimes in speeches about my four-point grade average with the kicker being that we were on a nine-point scale.

The opportunity came about to get valuable, real-world experience by working at *The Lincoln Journal*, the afternoon partner to the morning *Lincoln Star*. I had spent the previous summer writing and laying out the sports page at *The Alliance (NE) Times-Herald*, which ranged from eight to 24 pages a day depending on whether it was grocery-ad day.

In effect, I was the sports editor, as well as covering a local beat of the police and fire departments. I have often said that I learned more about journalism that summer than I had in three previous years at the university. While I virtually believe it to be true, there was no way I could have succeeded without the foundation established in my J-school and English classes.

The Journal experience was two-fold: I spent half of my dozen or so hours of each week's part- time job on the rim of the news desk, editing both local and wire stories, writing headlines, and proofreading each page after it was set in type. The other 50 percent was in the sports department, where I worked alongside Sports Editor Dick Becker and full-time staff members such as Del Black, Bob Munger and Bob Martel, a Huskers classmate even though he was older and much more advanced.

I was largely assigned to cover the Lincoln high schools in whatever sport was in season, but that in itself was a meaningful opportunity since the preps drew a lot of daily space. Schools were out for the summer when I was in

43

Alliance, so this was my first solid chance to make a mark with my game coverage and feature stories.

As low man on the totem pole as a part-timer, I also drew a neat assignment on some of the home-football afternoons. The newspaper published a special edition even though the Huskers still had a struggling program. It was a four-page supplement wrapped around the regular afternoon paper, and was printed in pink.

One has to remember how important newspaper coverage was. The Huskers were well established on radio, but live television was an unknown. Our office was roughly the equivalent of half a dozen blocks south of Memorial Stadium, and the goal was to have the pink version of *The Journal* available on the street by the time fans would walk downtown after the game ended.

The front page would carry brief accounts of some of the important Eastern football games since they started an hour earlier, but the banner headline and major story, win or lose, would be a recap of the Nebraska game. I would listen to the radio broadcast, using a headset, and do a modified play-by-play summation of each important drive by either team. Then Becker, the lucky guy with the responsibility of writing the lead story on the game, would dictate one paragraph from the press box to serve as the lead under his byline.

I will never forget this one afternoon (my files show it was Halloween of 1959) when mighty Oklahoma came to town. One must remember that this was a few years before Bob Devaney came in from Wyoming and rescued a mediocre Nebraska program, and many years ahead of the autumn afternoons when Tom Osborne-led Huskers teams might make the annual battle against Barry Switzer's Sooners the best game of the entire collegiate season.

Nebraska stunned Oklahoma, 25-21, before about 34,000 faithful.

I got to write the initial story of that legendary contest except for that lead paragraph, so anyone who scrambles through files of microfilm or weathered newspapers will not find my name.

I did not get the byline, but I wore a headset in our downtown Lincoln, NE, office and wrote most of the early-edition story of this historic Cornhusker upset of mighty Oklahoma ('59)

How important was the event?

Don Bryant, who was Becker's counterpart with *The Lincoln Star* —yes, the same lovely man who became affectionately known as the Fat Fox years later as one of the more colorful sports information directors on the national landscape —wrote the lead story for the next morning's *Sunday Journal and Star.* It recapped the significance of the NU victory:

"Yes, it really did happen.

"Coach Bill Jennings and the superbly valiant Nebraska Cornhuskers stand proudly today as the toast of the Big 8 Conference—the first conference team to defeat Bud Wilkinson's Big Red since 1946.

"A Wilkinson-coached team had never lost a conference game in 74 previous outings."

I got my first chance to cover a professional baseball game a few months later. Everyone else was probably resting after a day on the golf course or perhaps even preparing early-season football sections in pigskin-crazed Huskerland, but this was big-time importance and pressure for me, no matter how significant the game.

"With two regulars out of action indefinitely and a 3rd ejected, the (Lincoln) Chiefs dropped a

7-4 decision to Sioux City before 470 fans at Sherman Field Wednesday night. This closed out the worst home stand of the season," I wrote.

Future major league pitcher Joel Horlen played right field after the ejection, and future big-league manager Dick Howser was Sioux City's leadoff hitter in what no doubt was a routine contest except for the rookie scribe.

The companionship of *The Journal and Star* staff also proved important as I went about emerging from my somewhat sheltered life. One event still reverberates to this day.

Larry Shepard had managed the Chiefs prior to this season. I did not know him, but the veterans of the newspaper staff obviously thought highly of Shepard, who was on his way to eventually leading the Pittsburgh Pirates. The Shepard Family was building a new home in Lincoln even though Larry was out in Utah as skipper of the Triple-A Salt Lake City Bees.

He would be home soon, and the guys knew that while the house would be finished, the lawn was full of weeds and dandelions from the summer of baseball many hundreds of miles away. Talk about Midwestern friendliness, the sports staff decided to have a Schlitz-a-weed on the Shepard's lawn.

As you may have guessed, Schlitz was a leading beer of the time. So, with a couple of cases to urge the gang on, we embarked on hands and knees to get rid of those nasty dandelions. If you are thinking it did not take a great deal to get me to feel psyched about being included as one of the sports staff regulars, well, you are right.

My First Career Decision

1960

I had my first career decision to make as 1959 was winding down. With my new bachelor of arts degree in hand at the end of summer school, I had three options to get started toward my goal of being in the major league baseball world. Each was a stepping-stone type of opportunity with modest pay for those days, but it was nice to be able to weigh the choices.

I could stay with *The Lincoln Journal's* sports department, already a joy as a learning experience; become sports editor of a daily newspaper somewhat outstate in Nebraska; or give the broadcasting world a full-time try. You will notice I was still at least another step from anything involving professional baseball.

I opted to join KHAS Radio in Hastings, NE, a town of 20,000 or so, and went that direction because the station was the most active in the entire state in doing live play-by-play of sports. We primarily covered Hastings High School, St. Cecilia High School and Hastings College.

I believe to this day I may have had more enjoyment in the next three years of broadcasting an absolute ton of football, basketball and baseball games than in virtually anything I have done, even though I have actively worked something like 150 World Series games, a wonderful experience I will share later.

My experience at KNUS during my University of Nebraska days had given me the basics, and it was not long before I had pretty much total confidence in my ability to call a good game for our listeners.

My biggest hurdle on many occasions, especially for road games when I usually worked alone, was to locate the pre-ordered telephone line, set up our remote broadcast unit and make connection with the person on duty at KHAS. Simple enough, right? Most of the gymnasiums and baseball facilities did not have a press box, so the search for the phone line—I mean, a line to which two wires would be connected—was very much like the proverbial quest for a "needle in a haystack." I cannot tell you how relieved I would be to find it and make contact with the telephone company or our station.

Doing the game was, pardon the expression, a "piece of cake" compared with setting up.

The job was a delight for this aspiring Mel Allen or Ernie Harwell, even though my duties at KHAS also included serving as news director, delivering the sports news, handling a two-hour disc jockey stint (in which I could select my own Glenn Miller favorites to play for the student nurses I knew would be listening during their shift at the nearby state mental hospital), and some days hosting hour-long sports talk shows.

But my decision to give broadcasting a try was a good one in that I would handle up to 150 live events in a 12-month period, including more than 20 football games, about 50 basketball contests and up to 80 baseball games. The baseball was exclusively American Legion games, but Hastings was a hotbed, the program was envied throughout the state, and I was getting a world of experience.

I would be less than honest if I had not wondered for the last 50 or so years how my career might have worked out if I had had the patience to stay with radio long enough for a major opportunity to come along to broadcast University of Nebraska sports or to latch on at some other college or professional job.

Much like the movie *Summer of '42* stood out for the social life of 20-somethings, the Summer of 1960 was one sensational opportunity behind the microphone for me. While broadcasting Hastings College football and basketball and doing the same among top-level high schools in the

49

state no doubt made those events more elite, once again, it was my passion for baseball that highlighted my work.

Baseball is by far the most difficult of the three sports because of the airtime one has to fill, so I probably did a better job with the other sports at that point in my career. We knew where the '60 season would end up because Hastings was assured of one of the eight spots in the American Legion World Series as the host city. It was reaching that revered week in late August that was the real adventure.

We traveled from Oklahoma to North Dakota during the schedule leading up to the World Series. The team was on a bus, and I sort of rode shotgun behind it in our KHAS Radio station wagon.

The station wagon saved the day early in our longest regularly-scheduled road trip, a week or so traveling through Kansas and Oklahoma. Salina, KS, was our first destination, and not an easy one to begin with because Salina's Legion program was pretty much the Sunflower State's standard bearer, just as Hastings was in the Cornhusker State.

Wouldn't you know, the bus broke down something like an hour before we would have reached Salina. Our coach, Earl Applebee, a magnificent baseball teacher and an equally respected human being, decided the only way the Hastings team could make it to the field on time was if we piled 10 players—one to serve as our "bench" for the night—into the KHAS station wagon with yours truly at the wheel.

I was essential, of course, because the fans back home were eagerly anticipating the broadcast.

Oh, how the players came through, winning despite being without their coach, who arrived with the rest of the team and the now-repaired bus, almost simultaneously with the end of the game. I shudder to think about the liability the station had with me carrying so many young lives, but we made it on time in those pre-cell phone, pre-GPS days.

Hastings played virtually a professional-paced schedule in that compact season, being at home one night, then traveling two or three hours to Lincoln or Omaha with some regularity. I doubt that I could have handled my disc jockey duties more than a couple of times a week.

Our last trip prior to the World Series was the regional tournament in Bismarck, ND, several hundred miles to our north. Hastings won in Bismarck, too, and the team was greeted royally with a homecoming celebration leading into the World Series.

My microphone sent these jubilant words back to Hastings, NE, when our American Legion team won the regional tournament in Bismarck

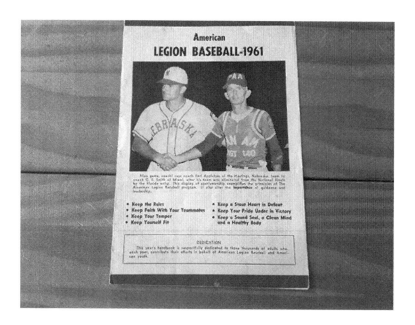

Hastings, NE Legion coach Earl Applebee, left, was a great friend to this eager young broadcaster

KHAS went all out at tournament time, thanks to our ambitious general manager, John Powell, broadcasting not just the Hastings games but every contest in the eight-team, double-elimination World Series. As we did for many a basketball tournament, that meant doing as many as three or four games in a day. I had some relief for an inning or so, but really did not care to give up the microphone all that often.

The American Legion World Series, a neat event to this day and often the launching pad for some would-be major leaguer of the future, proved to be tremendous. Three future major league stars were involved: dazzling shortstop Mark Belanger with Pittsfield, MA; power-throwing southpaw Dave McNally of Billings, MT; and Rusty Staub, the more talented of the two Staub brothers the Houston Astros signed in tandem a short time after the World Series.

It was two-and-out for Belanger and his mates, but Billings and Staub's Crescent City Post 125 out of New Orleans battled their way into the finals. I believe most thought McNally would carry Billings to victory, but the future Baltimore great was wild that day, and New Orleans went home happy.

Hastings won once, which was respectable, and I had experienced the thrill of broadcasting an American League World Series from start to finish.

Cardinals and Student Nurses Sweeten My Army Summer

1961

I missed taking part in the next season of American Legion baseball, but it was for a very good reason and I certainly was not without baseball.

The military draft was still part of every healthy young American male's life in those days, which meant a minimum of a two-year commitment. This may have been a good option because of the

post-service educational benefits, especially for anyone who did not have a career path. My specific path into professional baseball was not an obvious one since I did not have any inside connections.

Still, there was no question this was my goal, and I had made strides in both the newspaper and radio fields. I thought for some time about officer candidate school, and went so far as to be accepted by the Navy, which even gave me a reporting date when I would show up in the Groton, CT, area, ironically little more than an hour from where I have lived for many a year.

My decision, which did not come without some agonizing, was to join the Army National Guard, which meant a six-year commitment, but only six months of active duty unless war broke out. I also had to attend meetings, which, as I recall, included one night a week, one weekend a month and an annual two-week summer camp. This was much better because I could maintain my regular life except for the one six-month period.

I had a busy basketball season behind the microphone, then headed off in March to Fort Leonard Wood, MO, or Fort Lost in the Woods, as I would eventually know it to be called. Now I can tell you, I was not the best soldier around,

54

particularly during our eight weeks of basic training. I did not really care for the bivouac sessions out in the wilderness; my weakling shoulders always proved an embarrassment when it came time to do pull-ups, and I did not especially enjoy overbearing, grown men (sergeants) yelling out orders.

I know they were only trying to toughen us up so we could defend the country if we were called upon. I've always taken the position—an excuse, I guess—that if we were in a war, I would have had a better attitude about the whole experience of crawling under barbed wire, marching to a cadence and doing KP.

Nevertheless, after basic training, we got to go home on furlough, and when I returned for advanced basic, I would be able to have my car, even though it had to be parked in a dusty field off of the Fort Leonard Wood grounds. If memory serves, I still had my first car, a black 1950 Chevrolet. It was not a charmer, but it had four wheels.

My assignment in advanced basic, which was scheduled to run another eight weeks, was to attend clerk typist school. I guess the Army brass had decided it would be best to keep me out of the trenches. I was not opposed. So I worked on typing half of each day, even though I already had 60- to 70-word-per-minute skills. I had even taken part in typing competitions in high school, where my speed might have been good enough to place if I could have stayed away from typos. The other half of my workday was to study English, which certainly could use steady review even though I had a minor in this field from the University of Nebraska.

Mercifully (probably for all parties), I was taken out of this often mindless work after about two weeks. I was assigned to on-job-training, with my specific task largely to write up reports on court-martial cases, which often involved young men not so fortunate as to have a university degree or the type of upbringing as the Wirz Family offered.

They would go absent without leave (AWOL), be hauled in front of the authorities and possibly spend time in the brig, which may not have been the best solution for getting them trained and productive.

One joyous part of on-job-training was that I did not have any weekend duties. No guard duty, no kitchen work. And my Chevy awaited.

Fort Leonard Wood was located in South Central Missouri, near the beautiful Ozarks and only 30 miles north of the modern-day resort destination of Branson with all of its country music theaters. It also was near the sprawling Mark Twain National Forest, which I have zero recollection of from my sometimes steamy summer in the Army.

I started my 100 days and a wake-up countdown for finishing my active-duty stint much earlier than practical, most likely still during basic training. But once I started my on-job-training stint, my total weekend focus was on one of two destinations. My favorite was the 100 miles or so to St. Louis, although I can tell you that if the Cardinals were not home, the trips with my buddies to Springfield, MO, and then south toward Arkansas were not half bad. We had gotten acquainted with a group of student nurses out of Springfield. Enough said, I think.

I imagine Bull Shoals, AR; Rockaway Beach and environs were a poor man's Ozarks, where lake life is highly popular to this day. Army pay was not extravagant, but somehow we managed. A six pack; a hotel room where we could rest our Army-weary bones, if that was actually the case; and seeing the nurses made those weekends more than acceptable. I do not recall that I had a girlfriend back home, anyway.

St. Louis weekends were completely different. The Muny Opera in Forest Park, with Broadway-like performances that changed every week or two, were new experiences for this Sandhills boy, and the city had a wonderful zoo.

Stan ("The Man") Musial and his St. Louis Cardinals mates were the highlight, of course. Yes, they were my favorite, even over the nurses, although I am not certain my traveling companions always felt that way.

I must have started following the Cardinals when I was around eight, which would have been in the mid-1940s. I do not have specific memories of 1944, when the Cardinals and the American League's St. Louis Browns played their only World Series against each other, or even of the Cardinals beating the Boston Red Sox in '46 on Enos Slaughter's Game 7 dash from first base all the way home.

Suffice it to say I had already started wrecking my hearing from pressing my ear against the old upright radio in my bedroom at night to listen to Harry Caray's wildly enthusiastic broadcasts for a number of years before I ever saw Sportsman's Park, the Cardinals' home, which I thought surely had to be one of the best places on earth.

Musial, the man with the coiled swing and my absolute hero, had already passed the 3,000-hit mark and was only a couple of years away from ending his 22-year career. But St. Louis had a wealth of other stars, with Bill White at first base and Ken Boyer at third, along with a coveted pitching staff that included Nebraskan Bob Gibson, Larry Jackson, Curl Simmons, Ray Sadecki, Ernie Broglio and Lindy McDaniel, in whose hometown area of Hollis and Altus, OK, I had broadcast an American Legion game a year earlier.

Just walking up the street toward Sportsman's Park gave me a thrill. I could actually get a scorecard on the street, watch the progress of the other games on the scoreboard and truly live out my childhood dreams. For the first time, I even saw Willie Mays—probably the most exciting player I have ever seen. It was an easy summer to cherish.

My Brush With Fame

1962

It was back into the radio booth once my Army obligation ended in September, 1961. I could not wait. Little did I know, however, that television would draw me away within a number of months.

KHAS-TV, the NBC affiliate in Hastings, was a sister station to KHAS Radio in that they were both owned by Fred Seaton, a successful local businessman who by that time was serving as President Dwight Eisenhower's Secretary of the Interior.

The radio station was located downtown, and the TV station was a few miles to the north, probably enhancing its ability to cover the tri-city market, which also included the larger city of Grand Island, NE, and the college town of Kearney, NE. Local television coverage meant a great deal because it had not reached the point where the larger markets of Lincoln and Omaha were beamed into every home. KHAS-TV largely was it when it came to area news, weather and sports.

It would have been ideal for me if the two stations had shared staffs, but there was very little overlap and I was still new enough and sufficiently shy that I was not going to press to be sports director of both operations.

My routine at KHAS-TV was to do two sports news shows a day; fill in occasionally on the weather (for which I was totally lacking in training); and be the voice on an increasingly diverse series of sports specials that our aggressive general manager, Duane Watts, would set up.

This was a major reason for me to switch from radio to TV. The television industry was just beginning to evolve, and our abilities were Stone Age in comparison with present times. We could not do live remote broadcasts of sports

58

events, and every interview outside of the studio was on film. Yes, film. The 16-millimeter film had to be delivered to a separate facility for development, as I recall, so if there was a great sports event or even a minor fender-bender that the station considered worthy of covering, we were not able to show the footage in anything approximating the "Breaking News" hysteria we see today. Come to think of it, our audience was probably much better off because of the slowness of those times.

Watts, a short man with a tidy mustache and considered to have a temper that could easily be ignited, loved sports. We got along fabulously. He certainly seemed to like me, and I enjoyed breaking some new ground for our viewers.

I spent less than two years in TV, but in that time, in addition to my sports news telecasts during the 10:00-10:30 slot leading into *The Tonight Show,* I got to host a weekly sports talk show, a season of Nebraska football play-by-play, a regular bowling program, and a show covering my very first professional sport. Well, some called wrestling a professional sport.

For the Huskers games, we would travel to Lincoln or wherever they played, film the entire football game in play-by-play fashion, have the film developed, and put it on the air the next day. It may sound primitive—and certainly qualified as such in some ways—but while the big boys in Lincoln and Omaha had more regular access to Coach Devaney, we showed the game from start to finish. It was unique for those times. What a thrill to do a game from atop Memorial Stadium in Lincoln or from Columbia, MO, or Norman, OK!

The bowling show was filmed on Sunday mornings in Grand Island about a half hour away, and played back that night. As we were the only local station, if a dreaded winter storm forced people indoors, it was quite a treat to see local lanes action, even if the host barely knew the sport beyond a 7-10 split.

Hosting the wrestling shows was a once-in-a-lifetime experience. Once was enough, in some ways.

"Channel 5 Wrestling" came as close to giving me "celebrity status" as anything that I have done to this day, even though if you keep reading, you will find much more appealing roles in events of far greater interest.

The hour-long wrestling shows were televised live every Thursday evening, just ahead of NBC-TV's prime-time schedule. The ring would be driven in from Omaha early in the afternoon and set up in our studio, which barely had any spare space beyond our humble news, weather and sports desks.

I was the host, and famed wrestler-turned-promoter Joe Dusek was my partner. The Duseks — Joe, Emil and Ernie —had been hated in such famous arenas as Madison Square Garden in New York City, where they were known as "the dirty Duseks."

Ernie still did occasional stints inside the ring, I suspect largely when a wrestler had to cancel at the last minute. Joe and I sat ringside in suits and neckties. I never knew what was going to happen during our show except that it would be over within 60 minutes. We might have two matches, perhaps even a three-set affair, but, miraculously (wink, wink), everything would be decided before it was time to say good night.

When a match was over and I interviewed one or multiple participants, it was entirely possible I would get yelled at or made the butt of some joke. A Frenchman once picked all 150 or so pounds of me up in the center of the ring and, in front of both our TV and ringside audiences, kissed me on both cheeks. I have joked many a time in the 50 years since that that event was the back-breaker in getting me out of the sport.

Joe Dusek made one promise—and kept it. No matter how much yelling was done and how many threats were made by one of the demonstrative wrestlers, I would never be harmed.

My "fame" emerged because of the popularity of the sport, and the fact that many a Saturday night, I would be out in a nearby town—virtually all within the KHAS-TV signal—as ring announcer. "In this corner, weighing 245 pounds, the reigning Midwest heavyweight champion, please welcome the Kansas Mauler." The cheers or boos would rain down, depending on whether I was introducing the hero or the villain, but before the matches, TV Bob (yes, me) would be asked to sign autographs for some who watched our Thursday night shows, which invariably set the stage for the major match for that night.

Wrestling gave me one other slight advantage. Because of my identity with the TV shows, I delivered (I'm not sure how believably, either) commercials for Verne Gagne's Gera Speed. Most times, the commercials were done live. I believe I got $10 per commercial, and if I did two or three in a week, it was a great supplement for someone whose salary was around $120 a week. I also got $10 each time I made a mention of a future wrestling show during my regular sportscast. Somehow, I frequently worked it in, whether the FCC knew about it or not.

Gagne, who came from the Minneapolis area and somewhat amazingly made personal appearances ringside in Hastings during hunting season, was considered World Champion. I have never completely understood whether he was World Champion when he appeared at some of the nation's major arenas or if he was basically the Midwest's World Champion. He was a nice man in addition to being quite a physical specimen.

As anyone can imagine, when I got into my major league baseball career a few years later, it was seldom that I talked about having been a ring and television announcer for wrestling.

I have to laugh that one time my cover was broken. I had written a story for the October 1963 issue of *Wrestling Review* magazine. The editors called it "Sizzlin' Nebraska" with a subhead which pretty much told it all that "when that bell rings, Nebraskans forget all about corn husking and square dancing as they cheer the hero and hiss the villain."

Some proof I actually handled professional wrestling shows and wrote about them for this national magazine

I was sitting in the press box in Seattle minding my own business one day when a Mariners writer, J. Michael Kenyon, who was big enough to be in the ring himself, sauntered over to talk about "my wrestling days." I believe he either had a copy of *Wrestling Review* or possibly just referred to it. So much for my fame.

A Year of Excitement and Transition

1963

Everyone has transitional years. This would be a major one for me. I got married and moved back into the newspaper world all in a span of three or four months.

But before any of this happened, I had a pair of red-letter experiences. I actually got to my very first professional baseball camp, and I interviewed Cassius Clay or Muhammad Ali, as he has been known as perhaps the world's most celebrated athlete for most of the last 50 years. What thrills these were!

I will take them in order.

Earl Applebee, our highly-respected American Legion coach in Hastings, had as an assistant before I moved to town another Nebraskan, Dick Cecil, and Dick had moved on to become assistant farm director for the Milwaukee Braves. Remember them? The team had started as the National League team in Boston, the Braves, then moved to Milwaukee and eventually became the Atlanta Braves of today.

With my role as sports director at KHAS-TV, Applebee's friendship with Cecil, and willingness on the part of General Manager Watts, it was set up for us to spend a few days in the Braves' minor league spring-training camp near Waycross, GA.

I was beside myself with happiness, but also nervous because of the unknown. How would this TV crew so far removed from Milwaukee and with an eager but untested reporter be received?

The task was to develop enough interviews and stories that could hold up long enough for us to return home, edit what we had shot, and work the features in for my regular sports reports and my sports talk program.

I am still grateful half a century later to Braves Farm Director John Mullen; Director of Minor League Operations Jim Fanning; Cecil; and the various managers, coaches and players who endured everything I asked of them.

Mullen, Fanning and Cecil all went on to distinguish themselves in greater ways. Ironically, years later when he was a major league executive and I was in the major leagues in public relations, I would see John Mullen again. He often would entertain at the piano if one could be found at a Winter Meetings hotel, displaying both the keyboard and singing talent that had gotten him onto one of the early-day television talent shows. It probably was either with Ted Mack or Major Bowes. Houston General Manager Spec Richardson was Mullen's foil as baseball people gathered for a little down time, which probably would not be possible today because of the 24-7 player negotiating at these December gatherings.

Finally, getting to visit a professional baseball camp.
Atlanta Braves minor leaguers trained at Waycross, GA

Fanning eventually became the first general manager of the expansion Montreal Expos, then moved into the managerial chair and led the team to its only postseason in 1981.

Cecil became a vice president of the Atlanta Braves, but he really made his name as a pioneering soccer executive, not only in Atlanta but throughout the country.

For those of you who are thinking about the sprawling facilities minor league spring training consists of today with the clover-leaf set of diamonds, weight-training rooms and whirlpools ... well, this was not the scene at Waycross, which, by the way, borders the Okefenokee Swamp rather than today's desired vacation destinations of Savannah or Sea Island.

This was a former military base with barracks for the players to live in. I cannot remember how many diamonds there were, but I know the word "fancy" would not be used in any manner. The major league team was starting a long run of spring training at West Palm Beach, FL, some 350 miles to the south, so future Hall of Famers Hank Aaron, Warren Spahn and Eddie Mathews and superb catchers Del Crandall and Joe Torre were not in Waycross.

The best prospect, as we understood it, was 19-year-old outfielder Bill Robinson, who reached the major leagues three years later and had a more-than-respectable career (1,472 games with 166 home runs and a .258 batting average), although he ended up playing a mere six games in the Braves' organization before going on to the New York Yankees, Philadelphia and Pittsburgh. Still, it was fun for this cub reporter to think how it must be to be looked at as a prized prospect as he shagged fly balls, ran and took his turn hitting.

Applebee, our talented photographer and I made the 1,400-mile trip in KHAS-TV's station wagon.

We concentrated on baseball fundamentals for most of our stories, which usually had to be two minutes or less so as not to ignore the top sports stories of the day. The Braves instructors guided us with tender loving care. One story I remember almost as if it was yesterday featured the bazooka gun which fired pop-ups for the 18-to-23-year-old catchers to learn the skills they would need whether they played on the lowest rung of the minors or in a crucial National League game at County Stadium.

Once back down to earth in Hastings, I tried juggling my TV duties with being prepared to get married.

Little could I imagine that the summer also would give me the opportunity to interview Cassius Clay, along with golf legends Arnold Palmer and Gary Player.

A call came in one day that Clay and his entourage had stopped at a truck stop just outside Hastings. To say that celebrities passed our way every day would be an exaggeration of major proportions.

We were lucky enough to get a film crew together and scramble to the truck stop before Clay's bus headed west toward Denver. My mind is a blur as to how to ask the 21-year-old, already known for his brilliant work inside the ring and his talent for reciting rhyme, if he would do an interview with this greenhorn sports reporter. But it did not seem to be difficult as it would become a few years later as Clay became Muhammad Ali and was the darling of the Howard Cosells of the media world.

The author interviewing Cassius Clay in 1963 as he prepared to fight Sonny Liston (Photo converted from a 16-millimeter videotape)

We stood next to his bus, and this is a transcript of much of the interview, likely with me trembling on every word:

Question: You've become famous for not only your fist work, but with your poetry. Do you have any poems for us today about the big ugly bear (Sonny Liston)?

Clay: Yes, for those of you out there in the listening audience who won't be able to see the Clay, Liston fight, here is the eighth round exactly as it will happen. Clay comes out to meet Liston and Liston starts to retreat. If Liston goes back an inch farther, he'll end up in a ring side seat. Clay swings with a left, Clay swings with a right, look at young Cassius carry the fight. Liston keeps backing, but there's not enough room. It's a matter of time. Clay lowers a boom, now Clay lands with a right, what a beautiful swing and the punch raises the bear clear out of the ring. Liston is still rising and the ref wears a frown (inaudible few words) counting until Sonny goes down. Now Liston disappears from view, the crowd is getting frantic, but our radar stations have picked him up, he's somewhere over the Atlantic. Who would have thought when they came to the fight that they witnessed the launching of a human satellite? Yes, the crowd did not dream when they laid down their money that they would see a total eclipse of the Sonny. That's exactly what's gonna happen.

Question: Is there a chance Sonny could go in less than eight?

Clay: Well if he keeps talking jive, he'll go in five. If he makes me sore, I'll get him in four. If he keep talking about me, I'll get him in three. If that don't do, I'll cut it to two and if he runs, he'll go in one.

Clay: Thank you and I want all the people out there who are betting on Sonny, a lot of people are betting on Sonny. I want all of you to know; if you like to lose your money, then be a fool and bet on Sonny.

Approximately half a year later on February 25, 1964, in Miami Beach, boastful Clay became the youngest boxer, at 22, to take the world heavyweight title. It was a TKO when Liston did not answer the bell for the seventh round.

I still have the original 16-millimeter film of that interview, and enjoy occasionally showing it to friends and, of course, my grandchildren since Cassius (later Muhammad Ali) became the most recognized athlete in the entire world. It is surprising how little of the brash Clay's amazing poetry has survived.

Palmer and Player were much more advanced in seizing the lion's share of the golf spotlight than Clay then was in boxing when they came to Hillcrest Country Club in Lincoln

68

on July 30, 1963, to give a clinic and play an 18-hole exhibition.

Once again, KHAS-TV gave me the rare opportunity to take in a good portion of the day's activities, which I know through the press pass I still have was for the benefit of the Lincoln Children's Zoo. While fans paid $5 to take part, I went looking for a chance to interview Palmer and Player.

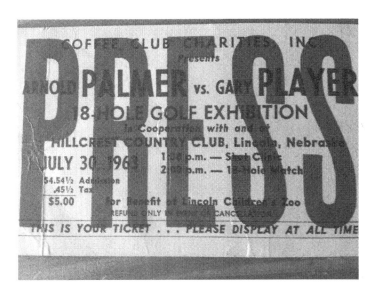

What an opportunity to interview major personalities, such as Arnold Palmer and Gary Player

The three of us sat side by side, with Palmer on my right and Player on my left. The filmed interview, still in my possession, indicated the questions were far short of compelling, but the golfers were ever the gentlemen and did not embarrass the eager, young reporter.

Portions of the interview with naive question after naive question:

Question: What are your future plans?

Palmer: Well, thank you and I'm going to play some exhibitions for the next few weeks and also get some rest.

Question: And, of course, you're still hoping to earn a slot in that big championship, the World Series of Golf in September.

Palmer: Well, I'm gonna play in the playoff. Just on a Tuesday before the American golf classic in Akron, yes.

Question: Arnold, in the next few years because of the current mounting pressures there, is there likely to be any curtailment of your tournament activity to any major degree?

Palmer: Uh, no. I have every intention of continuing to play tournament golf.

Question: Gary, you came in here to Lincoln today and what are the immediate golf plans from this point?

Player: Well, I have to play 10 exhibitions in the next 12 days so I have quite a full schedule ahead.

Interviewer: Looks like you do. Are some of those with Arnie?

Player: Yes, four of them with Arnold and four with Jack Nicklaus and two of them on my own.

Question: When back on the tour for you?

Player: Not for quite a while. I've got another month, I think. In fact I might only play two more tournaments this year the way things are going.

Question: Any major immediate goals for you Gary?

Player: Oh well, I'd just like to win the U.S. Open and I'll be a very happy man.

Interviewer: I'd think that you would.

Question: Do you feel there's a possibility of anyone winning the grand slam of golf?

Palmer: Well there's always the possibility. I would never say that someone can't win and I'm certainly going to continue to try, and I'm sure Gary is, and I know that Jack is also, so like I say, I think it is possible; whether it'll happen or not is another thing.

The duo showed off their shot-making talent during the clinic, and I clearly remember the final setup when the two right-handed heroes said one would hit a hook and the other a fade at the same time with the balls crossing and striking at a midway point well down the fairway. I can tell you the balls did not collide, but from the naked eye, it certainly appeared they were close enough to have easily done so.

After my brushes with these famous celebrities, I was more certain than ever of my choice of a career in sports. Perhaps one day it would be somewhat of the norm to interview noted athletes, even though the transcript of the Clay and Palmer-Player chats showed how much work my interviewing skills needed. For now, I needed to get thinking about wedding plans.

I had met Julie Anne Rhea, a student nurse from Salt Lake City who was in town for three months of training at Ingleside Hospital, a state mental institution, early in my time in Hastings. The rotation of student nurses from Nebraska and elsewhere was not a bad thing for my crowd. I actually dated Julie's roommate during part of her time in the area, but Julie and I gradually became friends, and on her very last day before going home, she took the bus from the hospital just out of town and we spent an afternoon in conversation. It was a mutual feeling that we wanted to stay in contact.

Julie left nursing a short time later, which I always felt was too bad even if she did not want this as her career choice. She became a stewardess for United Air Lines, coincidentally a field my sister, Bev, also entered. Julie was based out of San Francisco once her training ended, but we remained in touch either by telephone or letter. Today's young people would almost certainly scoff at such "old-fashioned" habits, but they were the only two logical paths of those days.

She would bid for a flight schedule each month, but being junior with United, it was iffy what she would get. She found one less-than-ideal route which would allow us to see each other. I doubt anyone else wanted such a schedule. Julie would fly from San Francisco to Omaha, arriving late in the evening, and would leave around 8 a.m. the next morning, fly to Chicago and back to San Francisco.

I would finish my evening sports news at 10:30, hop in the car and drive the 150 miles to Omaha, arriving at nearly the same time as she got to the hotel.

She knocked my socks off. I had my share of girlfriends throughout high school and during the summer when home from college, but when I saw her for the first time after her time in Hastings, I was, I don't mind saying, dazzled. The cute, pixie look I had remembered had been replaced by a trim, beautiful, San Francisco-sophisticated young woman. Her personality and mine seemed to fit, as before, but how could she be interested in me?

Now this was 1963, friends. It was nothing like the movies draw us in today when boy meets girl and sizzling romance takes over. We would spend the next few hours after meeting in Omaha in conversation, probably in my

72

room, because her fellow stewardesses were trying to get a few hours of sleep before the grueling Omaha-Chicago-San Francisco day that followed.

It is a wonder either of us survived those few meetings with only two or three hours of sleep. The trips may have always meant a Saturday-night arrival, because I usually had to drive another 150 miles as soon as Julie left for the airport in order to get to Grand Island, NE, to host Bowl-a-Rama, a 33-week competition among many of Central Nebraska's top bowlers.

I had to do a quick study to learn how to call a weekly bowling show in Grand Island, NE

I hoped she could turn on the charm for her airline passengers even though tired. That was much of being a stewardess in those days. United would stand for nothing less. For my part, the wonder is that I never ended up in a ditch when I would doze at the wheel. I was excited for seeing Julie, but not as alert as one should be to drive Highway 2, let alone to host a TV show.

We decided to get married during one of those Omaha visits. I believe it was in January, and we eventually established a late-August wedding date. Julie quit United, even though she had been offered a supervisory role in Chicago, quite a tribute for less than two years of flying.

73

Stewardesses could not be married in those days, so the end of her time was coming. She moved to Hastings, found a part-time job, and waited an exasperatingly long time with only three dresses while her trucking company took its sweet time delivering the trunk with the balance of her belongings.

The wedding was to take place in Salt Lake City, and just before it, I had to spend two weeks in what now was Air Force Reserve training summer camp at Camp Ripley, MN. We had just purchased a brand-new 1963 Chevrolet Impala in what they called Anniversary Gold. It was a proud moment. The first new car for either of us.

To make everything work, Julie took on the not-so-attractive a task of driving the car from Nebraska to Utah while I was finishing my military stint. Then I would fly out, and the wedding would take place in front of both of our sets of parents, a few other relatives, and friends. It was modest to say the least, but Julie looked gorgeous and I was thrilled beyond words.

We flew to San Francisco right after the reception for our honeymoon, and were greeted on board United with a surprise wedding cake since my brother-in-law, Harry Jefferies, also worked for the airline and could pull off the surprise.

I swear to this day I was not aware of this when we set the wedding date and honeymoon destination, but the St. Louis Cardinals, my baseball pride and joy, were playing the Giants at Candlestick Park. By now, I had a terrible cold. Wind-swept Candlestick was not the place to shake it.

Regardless, we spent two days during our trip of less than a week watching baseball games. If Julie did not have the message by now of my "other passion," she had to understand before the honeymoon ended.

I'm pretty sure I had only seen major league games in Kansas City and St. Louis in addition to that early trip to Wrigley Field and Cleveland, so getting to see another stadium was a treat. We enjoyed Fisherman's Wharf, eating at (Joe) DiMaggio's Restaurant, the Golden Gate Bridge, Lombard Street, cable cars, the glass elevator to the Top of the Mark, and seeing where Julie had lived and worked. Sharing all of this with my beautiful bride was special. But come on. I mean, baseball had me hooked long before I dreamed of experiencing everything else that San Francisco had to offer.

Willie Mays gave us—well, me, at least—an added thrill in that "The Say Hey Kid" cracked his 400th career home run during our visit to Candlestick Park.

We lived in a little second-floor apartment in Hastings after we got married, and it was there on November 22, 1963, that Julie and I heard the awful news of President John F. Kennedy being shot in Dallas. I usually did not go to the television station until around 2 p.m., and I seem to remember I had gone in early for something, then come home for lunch.

The news came to us via a table-top radio, probably tuned to KHAS Radio, my former employer, although we joined everyone else in the United States in turning on our TV to see what more we could learn. News was not nearly 24-7 back in '63, so I cannot say for certain how soon we saw photos or the terrible scenes from the motorcade, hospital or LBJ's swearing in. I do remember as clearly as if it was yesterday that we were at my parents' home in Halsey that weekend and saw live when Lee Harvey Oswald was taken out. That would be pretty dramatic today even considering all of the "Breaking News" craze we see on television.

Julie and I probably were in Halsey for a temporary goodbye weekend since I had accepted a job in the sports department of *The Wichita (KS) Eagle*. I would never return to either radio or television, as it turned out —a decision I still think about on occasion, especially since I can see myself enjoying the thrills of that type of career.

I had enjoyed my time with *The Lincoln Journal*, and *The Eagle* was Kansas' largest newspaper so I considered that I was moving to a higher level. My immediate assignment with the newspaper was to take over the prep beat, which included covering games, handling a feature page once a week and doing the statewide rankings for football and basketball. I'm sure that opportunity was appealing because of what I had seen in Nebraska, especially with high school guru Gregg McBride. He clearly was Mr. Nebraska when it came to prep coverage; a Mount Rushmore in that arena.

Wichita did not have professional baseball in those days, but I was impressed that the newspaper covered Kansas, Kansas State and Wichita State, all national basketball powers at the time. The non-pro National Baseball Congress, with its three-week powerhouse tournament in August, would allow me to continue with some baseball coverage.

We Almost Overlooked Jim Ryun

1964

I was sitting at my desk at *The Eagle* one day, probably working on that week's high school feature page, when I answered the telephone for what often was an off-the-wall question to settle a bar bet or to give out a score.

"I want to tell you about this young man at Wichita East High School who probably will break the four-minute mile this year," the caller said. "Oh, sure," I was thinking. Four-minute miles were about as routine in those days as a four-home run game. But I listened. The caller, listener, viewer, reader or whatever deserves nothing less.

I am going to continue this saga by saying he (it might have been a woman; I cannot say for certain) told me enough that my antenna went up. This might be a one-in-a-lifetime story that we were not on top of, even though we tried to be fair in giving attention to the Kansas Relays or whatever track and field event had merit.

Looking into this tip was the way our newspaper learned about lanky Jim Ryun, who later that summer did, indeed, become the first high school student to break the four-minute barrier. Ryun's time was 3:59.

The Topeka (KS) Capital-Journal was well ahead of us in knowing about this emerging "Pride of Wichita" runner, almost certainly because of the talented photojournalist Rich Clarkson, whose career included many a *Sports Illustrated* or *Time* cover, in addition to the local reputation he helped our in-state rival newspaper develop. While most newspapers, *The Eagle* included, ran mostly two- or three-column photos, our rival might use half a page for one photo. The Topeka newspaper gave major coverage to Kansas and Kansas State events, as well as to the major league sports in Kansas City, but the breadth of its statewide high school and small-college coverage was well off our pace.

Ryun, as handsome and smooth a runner as could be found, turned not only Wichita and the state of Kansas on its ear with his feats during 1964, but dazzled the nation as well. As a 17-year-old, he made his Olympic debut that same year. He went on to break the world mile record (3:51.1) two years later, and took part in three consecutive Olympics.

He had a frustrating Olympic career, finishing last in his 1,500-meter semifinals in Tokyo in '64, and he was a victim to a furious early pace in the high altitude of Mexico City four years later, settling for a silver medal. That happened even though by this time, Ryun had become the world's premier middle-distance runner, with world records in the mile, half-mile and 1,500 meters. In the '72 games in Munich, he tripped (was jostled, some felt) in his 1,500-meter heat and was denied a re-entry by the International Olympic Committee.

Other feats by this remarkable runner included winning the NCAA mile for the University of Kansas in 1967, a career of his own as a photojournalist, and 10 years in the House of Representatives as a Republican for his home state.

How red-faced would we have been had much more time elapsed before we caught up to this story in the early part of Ryun's career? Looking back, it still was a thrill that I helped introduce Ryun to our readership. We never ignored his feats from that point forward, although since he was such a world-class athlete, the national stage often carried the day with its coverage. He would fit right up there with Bryce Harper or Mike Trout or any other sudden hero today.

A healthy share of my baseball in these days came from an old favorite—the radio. Since *The Eagle* was a morning newspaper, there were many days when I did not go to work until 5 or even 6 p.m. This meant if the Kansas City

Athletics had a day game, I would often find a way to do two of my favorite things—be in the sunshine and listen to a game.

These were the Charles O. Finley A's, so they might be hugging last place, but that was not a deterrent to me. I fed off of being able to immerse myself in that day's game, and to learn all I could from the announcers because I so hoped my day would come. I wanted to know everything I could. Merle Harmon, whom I got to know later on, was the lead announcer. Great voice and pace. I would work the lineups in my head so I knew what options the managers had for pinch hitters. This feel for the game and its intricate workings made my daydreams come to life.

I would second-guess with the best of them. No one else knew my opinion, although there were nights at work when fellow baseball addict Bill Kentling, whose dad was a scout, might trace what went right or wrong or what might have happened had the "idiot manager" been thinking as we were.

Another joy was to listen to Bruce Rice's sports shows on KCMO in Kansas City. Bruce had a magazine-type show that was well ahead of its time. I believe it was 15 minutes long, but that was good compared with most radio rip-and-read sportscasts. Bruce was what they called a "pros pro," with a wonderful sense of humor which also made him one of the region's best masters of ceremonies. A heart attack took him away much too early, although that was years later when I was working in Kansas City and we had become good friends.

If I could get in an afternoon listening to a game and to Rice, I would be ready to put in a good night at *The Eagle.*

Re-Seeding Teams Was a Reality
For Hap Dumont

1965

I earned a promotion by this time; two, I suppose, in reality. I was promoted to *The Eagle's* Sports News Editor, the No. 2 person, behind veteran Sports Editor Bill Hodge. The fact Hodge wrote a lead column most every day and often was out covering an event gave me a great deal of leeway for an editor and decision-maker still in his leadership infancy. This was real on-job-training, and an important role since we had 150,000 to 200,000 subscribers.

The second promotion was that when not saddled to the news slot to put together that night's two editions, I was able to move from covering mostly high school sports to some coverage of the Big Eight and Missouri Valley conferences in basketball and football, and periodically a major college track and field meet.

Regular baseball coverage was limited since we did not have a professional team in Wichita and the heyday of the Wichita State program was well down the road. But I made out most of the weekly assignments, so I made absolutely certain I was at the forefront for the semi-pro Victory League and the respected National Baseball Congress tournaments, which accounted for much of July and August.

I was enamored with Ray "Hap" Dumont, the P. T. Barnum of the NBC tournament, a reasonably important event of considerable national reputation in those days because it would corral the top 32 semi-pro teams in the country for a double-elimination tournament played exclusively at Lawrence Stadium (now Lawrence-Dumont Stadium) for a morning-to-night, three-week baseball festival. Morning to night is not an exaggeration, either, because games were scheduled at that pace since there was only one diamond in use. When extra innings or rain delays showed up, play might continue virtually all night.

A few things about the entrepreneurial Dumont stand out to this day.

He had a gruff appearance, which no doubt kept many more than an arm's distance away from his office. Once inside, it was a total jumble of papers; no, boxes of papers. Hap scrambled to make the event work and pay out, selling rulebooks and scorebooks and whatever else he could, and the remnants of his mass mailings could be found all over the floor and shelves.

We got along famously, probably in part because he understood how I loved baseball and realistically, I imagine, because he knew I would give him many an inch of coverage in *The Eagle.*

Dumont truly was the Barnum of this time in sports, perhaps rivaled only by eventual Hall of Famer Bill Veeck, the maverick owner of such often-struggling franchises as the St. Louis Browns, Cleveland Indians and Chicago White Sox. Dumont would dream up an off-the-wall promotion that would attract attention, and this was years ahead of professional baseball embracing the promotions and marketing schemes of today.

The Fairbanks (AK) Goldpanners, headed up by Red Boucher, who eventually became governor, were the darlings of many an NBC tournament, including those I covered. Well in advance of the tournament, fans would hear of Boucher's own promotional propaganda, such as playing a game at midnight because of the virtual round-the-clock sun on certain dates in Alaska.

Primarily, though, the Goldpanners were eagerly awaited each season because they would come to town with rosters made up of future major leaguers who would spend the summer in Alaska after their collegiate season was over and before they became draft-eligible. One time, Rick Monday, who was to become the No. 1 draft choice in the entire country, was with the Goldpanners but was not active because the roster was too loaded with more experienced talent. It may have been the same year Tom Seaver was pulled after what I recall were five perfect innings. Boucher might well have made that move, of course, to allow the future Hall of Famer more rest so he could take on another opponent in a couple of days.

The most bizarre part of Dumont's tournament—a facet more dangerous than I could imagine in my straight-laced mind—was that he would re-seed the teams after each round of play. He did not necessarily want Fairbanks to win, especially since Wichita had not one but several teams from the summer-long Victory League capable of taking the championship, but he wanted the 'Panners and other teams he could promote to be around as long as possible. So, if a relatively unknown team came in and showed surprising strength, Dumont would make certain it did not run head-on into the Alaskans for fear either might be eliminated early.

Many an out-of-town manager or sponsor might get upset at the schedule, but you know what: This was Dumont's event, and he was going to have it played out in the most dramatic way possible.

Another favorite team of both Dumont and the baseball-crazed fans who watched games nonstop came from the Kansas State Penitentiary. I kid you not when I say fans would line up along the infield fence to get a closer glimpse at these prisoners. The players had talent, too, so Dumont wanted them competing for more than a couple of games, and I cannot imagine these were the worst afternoons and evenings of an incarcerated man's life.

Summertime games in the local semi-pro Sunflower League were fun, as well, because the Wichita companies that sponsored teams did not want a dud. Onetime Dodgers infielder Charlie Neal was a favorite well after his major league days; so was Bob Boyd, known as "Frozen Rope" because of his advanced-age ability to still hammer constant line drives.

I sometimes received another bonus in that baseball's bible, *The Sporting News*, would give me some national exposure—and a few welcome bucks—to recap highlights of the NBC tournament for the baseball world at large. Dumont also would have me write the lead story for the next season's tournament booklet, one more item to litter the floor of his office.

This was such a rich year for me. I got to fly around the Midwest on a chartered airplane with much-better-known writers and broadcasters on what was known as the Big Eight Conference Skywriters Tour to preview every one of the football teams. I also traveled to such college campuses as Oklahoma State, where the legendary Hank Iba still was the head coach; covered the coveted end-of-season Big Eight Basketball Tournament in Kansas City; and interviewed the likes of baseball's ageless wonder Satchell Paige.

Becoming a Dad, Seeing Yankee Stadium, and Another Career Move

1966

As I look back now, this had to be one of the most important—and transitional—years of my life, even though it had to unfold in stages and much of it could not have been forecast.

I knew, of course, that I was going to become a dad, although all of the details and obligations may not have been sufficiently implanted into this Nebraska brain. The happy day when Jeffrey Alan Wirz arrived at Wesley Medical Center in Wichita was April 6. The last 24 hours were an endurance test for Julie, with me having it so much easier with juggling some office time and trying to grab a little sleep in a not-so-comfortable hospital chair.

We were thrilled, as one would expect, although the first-time dad was concerned about the bruise under one of Jeff's eyes and especially with the soft spot on top of his head. Hey, I never said I knew what bringing a new little guy into the world was all about.

Grandparents soon arrived from Utah and Nebraska to help us adjust. I learned how to change a diaper and a few other little essentials, along with trying to help our dachshund, Brer John, get over the shock that he was no longer the most important "baby" in our family.

Little did I know that within the next seven months, I would make my first trip to New York City and see Yankee Stadium, or, on a grander scale, that Julie and I, along with Jeff and Brer, would transition from Wichita to Denver, where I would take a job in the sports department of *The Denver Post.*

But between Jeff joining us and the move to the Mile High City, there was a summer in which I got the thrill of covering a few Kansas City Athletics games to do features or columns; another NBC Tournament; and a regular beat, covering the Kansas State Wildcats in football.

K-State was the weak link of the Big Eight Conference in those days, winning once or twice a season in a "good" year under Coach Doug Weaver. But it was a nice assignment, nevertheless, allowing me to regularly cover an important conference and travel to road games in such varied areas as Albuquerque, NM, and West Point, NY, home of the fabled Black Knights of the Hudson. That is Army, to the uninitiated.

Albuquerque gave me my first real test of hot Mexican food, as well as my initial look at the stucco houses that dominated the city. For some of Kansas State's home games in Manhattan, KS, or the shorter junkets, we occasionally took *The Eagle's* plane, which, as I recall, was a four-seat Cessna (manufactured in Wichita). The pilot, a staff photographer and I could get to our destination; see the game; and, in some cases, return to the office in time for me to write my story.

But the bonus for that fall's football schedule was flying into New York City and driving up along the picturesque Hudson River to cover Kansas State's opener, a 21-6 loss at Army. The Cadets still were pretty competitive nationally at that time, and Army had all of the tradition anyone would want. It was many years later when I had a greater opportunity to soak in all of the atmosphere surrounding an Army football game, which included watching an impressive parade by most of the cadets, touring the campus to see where the top brass lived, tailgating and enjoying the beauty surrounding Michie Stadium.

The real treat was my first visit to The Big Apple, and Julie provided a bonus by sending a telegram which was awaiting me at the hotel that Jeff, now at six months, had cut his first tooth. Two of them, I believe.

Bob Hentzen of *The Topeka Capital-Journal*, who had been covering the Kansas and Kansas State sports teams for years and knew the traveling routine much better than I did, was my companion for dinner at Mama Leone's Restaurant, where my biggest recollection was needing to ask for a glass of water. I'm sure we did not request sparkling water.

I knew the Yankees were in town that Friday night, and how could I possibly not go to the game? I went alone, and I have no idea whether I got brave enough to try the subway or if I took a taxi. Either had to be accompanied by some stress, as unfamiliar and untested as I was in such environments.

I almost sat in on history that night. The Yankees were not very good in those pre-George Steinbrenner days, laboring well under .500, as difficult as it might be for those who became fans anywhere from the '70s to today to believe. The visiting Minnesota Twins were vastly superior. Ralph Houk's Yankee starter was Jim Bouton, who was laboring at 2-7 after standout seasons in 1963-64, and would not make a great many more headlines until he wrote the tell-all *Ball Four* years later.

He was exceptional on this particular evening, however. And how! He carried a perfect game and a 1-0 lead into the eighth inning, when Don Mincher got to Bouton for a one-out single to center. I've remembered all this time that Bouton came within five outs of the perfect game. One of today's great research tools allows me to tell you the shutout was still in place when the ninth inning opened. But Zoilo Versalles hit a ground-rule double, and Sandy Valdespino pinch-hit and was struck by a pitch. Cesar Tovar, a pesky hitter his entire career, was called on to sacrifice, and when Yankees third baseman Mike Ferraro threw the ball away, both runners scored. The Yankees lost, 2-1, but this young chap had experienced his first night in "The House That Ruth Built."

I don't believe I knew it at that time, but within weeks, the Wirz Three—plus Brer—would be moving from Wichita to Denver. Bless this mind of mine, but I do not have a clear recollection of how the opportunity came along to join *The Denver Post.*

I had learned so much in those three years in Wichita. How to lay out a sports section, and how to handle a staff (since I had become the No. 2 man in the department and my boss was often traveling or tied down with his column). I also learned how to tiptoe around a union back shop, where I had to hover on many a night to make certain a story made its way into type and into the individual page form in time to stay on deadline. I feel certain many of the people considered me a royal pain in the a__ as I tried to squeeze every state college story into that first edition so it would reach the outlying subscribers the next morning.

But Denver was appealing, with larger newspaper circulation, to say nothing of being able to look out the window of our modest apartment in Littleton and see the majestic Rockies. We also were closer to Julie's home in Salt Lake City and no farther away from my parents.

Another issue, which surely could not have been overlooked, was the fact Denver had a Triple-A baseball team. In fact, the Bears were a model minor league franchise in those days, built largely through a previous relationship with the New York Yankees. This is where Tony Kubek, Bobby Richardson and so many other future Yankees stars cut their teeth.

Some felt the powerhouse Denver teams might have challenged for a first division finish in the American League because this was long before free agency and potent organizations could stockpile talent.

The record books show that one in-season visit by the parent Yankees to Denver in 1964 drew 25,832 fans. An astonishing number, as were the 300,000 and 400,000 attendance seasons for the Bears in the '40s and '50s when Bears Stadium was a new minor league showpiece.

Our move to Denver was one to remember. Extra cash was not always our friend, so there were Julie, 7-month-old Jeff, Brer, and the head of this household in the cab with all of our earthly possessions in the back of the U-Haul truck.

Hey, how much had we stepped up in the three years since moving to Wichita? We had pulled a U-Haul trailer behind the '63 Chevy for the move to Wichita, and had arrived in the middle of one horrific ice storm, which had the trailer swaying back and forth as we slid down Kellogg Avenue toward our apartment.

The truck trailer for our move to Denver was attached to the cab, and I would estimate it was 12 to 15 feet long. That was progress!

My job with *The Denver Post* could have been looked at as a step back, I suppose, since I was purely a staffer; a newbie, at that. They had me work on recreational sports because of a weekly tabloid insert to various parts of the metropolitan area, and I was often assigned to a high school or college game or to editing.

What a year, though, from becoming a father to the New York-West Point trip and the move westward to Denver.

The Denver Post Turned Out To Be Only a Nice Pit Stop

1967

How could this possibly match last year? Not so fast, buddy.

The Post had a veteran staff, and most people had their own beats, but they gave the new guy a chance. I distinctly remember being assigned to cover a two-game weekend hockey series between the University of Denver and Boston University. What little I knew about hockey I had most likely gleaned from my early teen years in Halsey, when I would search for any sports event I could find on that upright radio in my upstairs bedroom. I tried to understand the games in the six-team National Hockey League, but knowing more about a clothesline than a blue line and understanding an offside penalty in football was much easier than comprehending an offside call in hockey.

College hockey was limited to a few parts of the country, but the Northeast and Rocky Mountains were two of the good ones; hotbeds, one might say.

I have always felt I did an especially good job covering those games—though a hockey expert might find my terminology lacking—because I had to work extra hard to do justice to the series.

I also was assigned to cover the NCAA Basketball Regional in Corvallis, OR, which was a special treat in so many ways. First, *The Post* trusted me enough, and, secondly, I believe it was only the second time I had traveled that far west, the first being for a trip with my family way back when I was about eight.

We covered the tournament primarily because Wyoming was one of the four teams involved, but the real plums for me were that Texas Western, a surprise champion the previous season under Don Haskins, was back to try to defend and UCLA was participating, featuring a very youthful Lew Alcindor. We have known this all-time great for so many years now as Kareem Abdul-Jabbar.

The John Wooden-coached Bruins ripped through Wyoming, 109-60; Texas Western was upset; and UCLA took care of Pacific, 80-64, to advance to what we know today as the Final Four. In looking back, only 23 teams were in the tournament in 1967. I'm sure I took extra pride in having written about UCLA and Alcindor since they went on to finish a 30-0 season and win the first of seven consecutive national titles. Alcindor was named the Most Outstanding Player for all three of his championship runs with UCLA.

It turned out that was one of my final assignments from *The Post* because the Denver Bears were looking for a new public relations director. I was interested even though it had only been six months since we moved from Wichita. The staff at the newspaper, including some above the sports department, were baffled. Why would someone leave the relative comfort of being a part of a major newspaper to join a team that had fallen well off its attendance pace and the prestige of being at the pinnacle of the minor leagues?

Much of the issue for the Bears was that the American Football League had been established with the Denver Broncos very much a part of this upstart undertaking. The Bears had quickly become the poor stepchild, and Bears Stadium's seating had been vastly increased, partly for the AFL and because longtime Bears boss Bob Howsam was involved in trying to start the Continental Baseball League. Several thousand seats were added beyond right field for that never-off-the-ground operation.

So, even if the Bears drew 4,000 to 5,000 fans, which wasn't often at that time, the stadium seemed empty. That was not attractive to the fans.

But this was a professional baseball opportunity for me. Need I remind you that was my goal from the very beginning.

I had developed a great friendship by this time with longtime *Post* writer Frank Haraway, a beloved and energetic man considerably older than I. Haraway had walked with the help of crutches for a long time, but he could out-walk most everyone. Frank's beats were the University of Colorado for football and basketball, and the Bears. Our mutual interests in sports were totally compatible, and he loved the Bears—so much, in fact, that there was a cowbell attached just outside of the modest Bears Stadium press box, and at the end of every inning in which the team scored, Haraway would stand up, lean out and ring the bell once for each run. Haraway, along with *Rocky Mountain News* Sports Editor Chet Nelson, were largely the identity of baseball in Denver to everyone still following the Bears or fondly remembering their dominant years.

I have to believe Haraway put in many a good word for me with Bears General Manager Jim Burris because he knew my love of baseball, and, I would like to believe, he felt I had some talent for publicizing the Bears.

The Post insisted I take a leave of absence from my job instead of totally cutting myself off in case my new venture did not pan out as I hoped. I have joked for years that I wonder if the leave of absence is still in effect.

It was April 1 (yes, April Fool's Day) when I started with the Bears, mere days before the Pacific Coast League season started. I was beyond excited. I couldn't wait to meet Manager Cal Ermer, a wonderful career baseball man, and the players and to be able to test my skills in the public relations field. I believe I had every confidence in the world in my basic baseball knowledge, but publicizing a team was new to me.

It was not an easy task, either. The Bears had become the stepchild to the Broncos and University of Colorado teams.

The season was so-so at best, with a 69-76 record, and with Ermer being promoted to take over the parent Minnesota Twins less than halfway through the schedule. He was replaced by another mild-mannered manager, Johnny Goryl, a player-coach when the season started after a decent major league career as an infielder with the Chicago Cubs and the Twins.

Both managers were a delight to work with, but when Jim Mooring led the team with 13 home runs in the light air of the Rockies and Andy Kosco was tops with 67 runs batted in ... well, I'm sure you get the picture. Our only league leader was in runs allowed by a pitcher.

I could feel the struggle, although I had a great amount of liberty as I tried to develop more media support for the Bears.

I did see my first World Series games that fall in St. Louis (versus Boston), and Julie and I managed a trip to the Winter Meetings in Mexico City, a neat experience to start getting a tiny taste of what major league life would be like. I sent some stories back to Denver, and sidelights of the trip were highlighted by attending our first—and last—bull fight and Julie trying her hand at bargaining with the street vendors.

As a postscript to being a part of the Winter Meetings for the first time, I never missed another of these annual gatherings for more than 30 years. I believe the run was from 1967 through 2003 with a few additional scattered visits in recent years.

The Story Keeps Getting Better

1968

The offseason can get very long, although my first winter in baseball was quite eventful.

My office was under those South Stands, as they were known for football and in case the Continental League ever came to life, because the regular office atop Bears Stadium barely had room for selling tickets and for my boss, Jim Burris, and his secretary.

The South Stands may have come to life for Broncos games, but from October to March, I was a lonely soul in a chilly setting. It was there that I painstakingly pieced together a greatly enhanced Bears Media Guide, frankly, the type of challenge I enjoyed. I can hold my own as a scavenger, especially when it comes to digging into forgotten storage areas, and the personal libraries of Frank Haraway and Pacific Coast League historian Bill Weiss to search for yearly rosters, records, and notes. After all, who wouldn't want to know which Bears player has hit the most sacrifice flies or hit the most batters in a season? A sense of humor really helped at times that winter.

Because of Denver's rich minor league history, I could bring back to life the feats of such notables as Marv Throneberry, Norm Siebern and our current hitting star Bo Osborne. Throneberry was especially prolific, driving in 117, 145 and 124 runs from 1955-57. And that was well before he became the lovable Marvelous Marv of the bumbling, win-starved early-day New York Mets.

When I finished my 40 pages of work, which does not sound like much alongside the computer-driven mountains of specialized statistics of today, I had to rely on our secretary to read my notes, sometimes in longhand, to convert them for our printer. The first draft resulted in numerous misspelled mentions of Ralph Honk, who had managed the Bears to three consecutive winning Triple-A seasons. I never could clearly print a lower case and distinguishable u or n. Yes, in reality, it was Ralph Houk, the Major, who later managed the Yankees, Detroit and Boston for 20 major league seasons.

My first professional team. That's me, left, upper row, with the 1967 Denver Bears. General Manager Jim Burris, right, gave me this opportunity

A side job also developed. *Denver Post* Sports Editor Lee Meade and I took on the task of serving as the official statisticians for the first year of the American Basketball Association. Sounds like fun, right? Keeping track of scoring champion Connie Hawkins and that crowd?

The ABA, which was under early-day all-America George Mikan as commissioner, knew it had to be novel to draw

94

attention, so it introduced a red, white and blue ball and a three-point shot. Where would basketball, either college or the pros, be today without the three-pointer?

The trouble for us was that the teams were responsible for keeping the official stats for home games and forwarding them to us (by regular mail since this was before fax machines), and we would compile everything into a weekly report and mail it back to the teams and the media.

Record-keeping on field goal attempts had not been prominent for long, and now the teams were responsible for breaking down both two- and three-point attempts. The Denver Larks (now the Nuggets), Indiana Pacers, San Antonio Spurs, Kentucky Colonels and everyone else managed it, but that was too much for Barney Kremenko, a New York writer of some note, who was working for the New York Americans (soon to become the Nets, who played on Long Island).

So let it be told, we occasionally had to make up the shot attempts for the "official" stats in that first 70-game season.

We thought the Bears would be better in 1968 with the addition of 23-year-old third baseman Graig Nettles (although the Twins were not certain he could handle the position where he eventually became a major league Gold Glover), 1965 second base hotshot Frank Quilici, former Husker right-hander Dwight Siebler, and ageless reliever Art Fowler (45 at that time).

I got to preview what our team might look like with a few days in Minnesota's minor league camp in Melbourne, FL. It was not much of a facility, probably the norm for these times, but it still was a thrill for this guy to get a peek at what spring training was like.

Johnny Goryl, who eventually was to manage parts of two seasons with Minnesota and then spend decades helping the Cleveland Indians in whatever role they needed, continued to be one of this typist's favorites. But he did not last long as Denver's manager, and he was replaced by feisty Billy Martin. This has allowed me to joke forever that I was the first PR man for Martin as a manager.

Martin and Jim Burris got along famously, partly because the boss could go around town telling Martin stories. One favorite involved Clint Courtney, with whom Martin had clashed several times during their major league playing days. Martin would always say something like "and the next time I see him, we will fight again."

"Martin has showed them (players) a few new wrinkles with his unorthodox lineups and gambling approach to the game," popular *Rocky Mountain News* columnist Bob Collins wrote when the parent Twins were coming to Bears Stadium for an exhibition game. "He's had the Bears running hard, forcing the play and taking the extra base at every opportunity. We've had a lot of men thrown out and a few rallies killed. But we also have won several games we wouldn't have without pressing the other team into errors."

In other words, Denver fans were seeing the same traits Alfred Manuel Martin would show during his 16 major league managerial seasons, which started the very next season (1969) when he led Minnesota to a 97-65, first-place finish. Then it was Detroit, Texas, the New York Yankees several times, and Oakland with his sensational results— and his flops—through 1988.

We finished the season a mediocre 73-72, but the Bears played at a .565 pace under Martin, the best mark since Denver entered the Triple-A ranks. The team was even better at .631 from July 1-September 1, and it could have been slightly better at the end except for a team party he put together the night before the season finale in Indianapolis. I understand it was a rouser, maybe Denver's version of the Copacabana, which Martin had been part of during his Yankees playing days.

I had many an encounter with Martin through the years because of his off-and-on managing career with the Yankees, although nothing sticks out like one night at Shea

96

Stadium in the early '70s when we both were attending what the New York chapter of the Baseball Writers Association of America called its Pre-Dinner Dinner. It was mostly a casual evening for the writers and New York teams a month or so before the annual black-tie awards dinner at the Americana Hotel in midtown.

I was out in the hallway when Martin came through, probably from a pit stop because he certainly had been at the bar at least a few times that night. When he spotted me, he stopped and said something like, "Bob, I just put in a good word for you a few days ago with George (Steinbrenner)." While working with the two of them in New York could elevate any PR man's visibility instantly, it also could ultimately shorten a baseball career. Thankfully, I never heard another word about this so-called "good word" to The Boss.

Nettles did not disappoint, becoming the most successful of the '67-68 Bears teams when it came to playing in the majors. He was called up to the American League team in early September after hitting 22 round-trippers and flirting with .300, and he whacked four home runs in one three-day span against Detroit and jump-started what turned out to be a 390-home run, 22-year career, mainly during the Bronx Zoo days of the Yankees in the '70s and early '80s.

I still remember what a thrill it was to have Nettles or any of our other players get a major league opportunity. It was such a long way from dreaming of such things in Halsey.

I felt relatively satisfied with my second professional season since I had made strides with the media, and helped orchestrate a wives-players game (Julie hit well, and little Jeff ran head-on into one of the pipes separating one home plate area box seat section from another to give us one of his many scares). I also spearheaded creation of an Old-Timers Game featuring Hall of Fame southpaw Warren Spahn, who was managing visiting Tulsa.

The Bears were tabbed as the Pacific Coast League nominee for the Larry MacPhail Trophy, which represented promotional excellence, and I knew I had a hand in giving us that honor.

It turned out that the Wirz Family's year was far from over. There was not going to be a second chilly winter under the South Stands.

I always tried to have my eyes open to any crack that might get noticed by the major leagues. It was good fortune that Charlie Metro, well respected throughout the game for his judgment on players, lived nearby in Golden, CO. He had been named Director of Scouting and Instruction for the expansion Kansas City Royals, who would begin play in the American League in 1969. Charlie often scouted the Bears and the visiting teams since his home was so close to Bears Stadium.

I had made it my business to get to know Metro during the season, and despite a sometimes gruff exterior, he always was warm to my overtures.

When the American League held its expansion draft to supply the Royals and Seattle Pilots, Kansas City played right into my hands by selecting three Bears. They were slick-fielding shortstop Jackie Hernandez, first baseman-outfielder Bob Oliver and speedy centerfielder Pat Kelly.

I quickly put together a feature story on the trio, extolling their virtues (and probably overlooking any possible flaws) and shot it off to Royals General Manager Cedric Tallis and Metro. I made it known the organization was welcome to use the story if it was beneficial. This is what I wrote.

This Story May Have Made
A Difference in My Career

It's no secret that an interesting winter is ahead for baseball fans as they try to piece together in their own minds the most likely lineup for the Kansas City Royals in their initial season.

The guessing game will encompass everything else from A to Z including to name the starting rotation and to select the most valuable and the most exciting members of Kansas City's new American League entry.

Chances are the more familiar names such as Hoyt Wilhelm, Wally Bunker, Joe Foy or Jerry Adair will be pegged the most frequently in these discussions, simply because they are the best now.

But what about the newcomers, some of whom will even need an introduction to a majority of their teammates?

A good bet, especially in considering candidates who have exciting qualities and are likely to catch on as fan favorites, is a trio of draftees who need no introduction to each other as they were minor league teammates last summer.

The threesome includes shortstop Jackie Hernandez, outfielder Pat Kelly and outfielder-first baseman Bob Oliver, who played for Denver in the Pacific Coast League.

All three have the potential to be outstanding and to provide those long-remembered special thrills.

But it must be said that all three still have to prove themselves at a major league level. Hernandez, a 28-year-old Cuban with cat-like movements, has logged the most major league time—better than two seasons and 176 games. Anyone who has ever seen the 6-foot, 170 pounder for very long will praise him as one of the few shortstops anywhere who can make all the plays.

It's likewise true that he has some history kicking routine plays, and he has a questionable bat although his plate work most likely is sufficient in this era. Jacinto Hernandez got his first major league opportunity with the California Angels late in 1965, then he rode the bench the entire 1966 season in which he batted just 23 times.

Bill Rigney reluctantly gave him up in the spring of 1967 as part of the five-man swap which saw Dean Chance land in Minnesota.But Hernandez went to Denver where he started slowly at bat. All of a sudden fortunes changed. He began to develop rapidly, with the help of a new bunting skill taught to him by manager Cal Ermer.

When Ermer became the Twins' manager, he wasted little time calling Hernandez and his .269 batting average to join him, although Zolio Versalles still held the regular job during the stretch drive which saw the Twins lose the pennant to Boston on the final day of the season.Versalles was traded during the winter, and Hernandez found himself on the hot seat months before the 1968 season started. He was the most likely successor to Versalles, the onetime most valuable player, and shortstop was believed to hold the key to the Twins' hopes to play in the '68 World Series.

Less than four months into the season, Hernandez was back in Denver. But to his credit, he didn't let the demotion stop him. If anything, he was more determined. His hustle was more evident. He made all the plays again. He batted .287 for 51 games, and provided the all-around spark necessary to lift Martin's club from last place to within range of second when the season ended.

Certainly Martin's inspirational leadership had been a factor, but so had Hernandez's inspirational play.

Kelly has all the natural talent, too, but the flychaser is four years young than Hernandez, and has more time to make good. He gave indications last summer that he may be ready, even though his major league experience is limited to 20 games. The southpaw batter hit .306 at Denver, second best in the Pacific Coast League, even though military duty kept him out of the lineup at frequent intervals all summer.

Kelly doesn't have a lot of power. He has just 31 home runs in six pro seasons. What he does have is blazing speed. His 109 thefts the last three seasons figure out to one for every 2.6 games in those minor league campaigns. Kelly logged his high of 52 thefts at Charlotte in the Southern League in 1966.

He comes by the speed quite naturally. His older brother is Leroy Kelly, the Cleveland Browns back who led the National Football League in rushing in 1967. Harold Patrick Kelly could have chosen football after being acclaimed as Philadelphia's best high school athlete one year, but he decided on baseball and it appears the decision will pay off.

Actually, Kelly doesn't have sole claim to speed among the Denver threesome which Kansas City shelled out $525,000 for in the expansion draft. Hernandez, a more skillful base-runner at this stage, swiped 13 bases in his short stint at Denver last summer, and Oliver logged a career high of 17.

Just as Hernandez is at his best in the field and Kelly on the basepaths, Oliver has his greatest moments when runners are in scoring position, and what greater asset can a hitter have? It's often stated that all the 6-foot-3, 210 pounder does is drive in runs. He isn't showy. He had averaged 76 RBI in five previous seasons as a pro, but he topped it all last year with 93—just seven shy of the Pacific Coast League lead. Oliver did that despite missing a week with pneumonia, and struggling for several more weeks to regain his full strength. Oliver, a right hander, hit .297 and collected 31 doubles, 8 triples and 20 home runs while finishing in the top seven in eight different offensive categories. Another "plus" for the 25-year-old, who toiled in the Pittsburgh chain until he was obtained by Minnesota for its Denver farm in an offseason trade last year for veteran reliever Ron Kline, is his versatility. He's supposed to be a first baseman by trade, but he's seen little of that post the *last few years while doing an adequate job at third base or any of the outfield posts and even filling in at second.*

Oliver will be getting his first real shot in the majors in 1969 (he batted twice for Pittsburgh in 1965), but don't count him out. Remember, he stepped up to Triple-A for the first time on a regular basis last season, and all he did was improve on every one of his offensive statistics over his previous high. None of the three is resting on his laurels this winter while waiting for February and the shot at a regular job with Kansas City. Hernandez is striving for still more proficiency as a member of the Ponce team in the Puerto Rican Winter League, while Kelly is with Magallenes and Oliver with Lara, both in the Venezuelan League.

Kansas City had hired a publicity director, but as luck would have it, he ended up being short on baseball knowledge. I will never know what lit a candle for the Royals—likely Metro's kind words and an assist from my story—but it was only a few days until I was on an airplane to interview for the job.

A major league opportunity. Wow and double wow! I had just turned 31, and I did not need an airplane to get back to Denver.

Julie was about five months pregnant with what would turn out to be our second son. But this move had to be made. I was to make the princely sum of $12,000. It may have been $12,500. We rented a town house and made the move from the Denver suburb of Lakewood to the suburb of Overland Park, KS, something like a 30-minute drive to the Royals' first offices in downtown Kansas City.

I knew mom and dad were happy for us, realizing how long I had dreamed of this type of opportunity. Mom's letter written the night before I started work in Kansas City proudly told of the various stories that had been written about me in the newspapers. The story was even on mid-Nebraska's only television station, in North Platte.

My work in developing that Denver Bears Media Guide paid off. One of the myriad of tasks at hand shortly after the November start in Kansas City was handling the Royals' 1969 media guide. We eventually had 62 players going to spring training, they had come from all over the baseball landscape, and there was no such thing as statistical uniformity with the player biographies. One team might not list walks and strikeouts for hitters, another wouldn't have stolen bases, and there was no rhyme or reason to the order in which the statistics were laid out in the previous major or minor league team's media guide.

With only my secretary to help, this was my constant task most every night after I had put in a full day of writing press releases and getting acquainted with the Kansas City area and its media.

There would be no complaints, unless it was a murmur from a now full-figured wife who was trying to get to know another new neighborhood with a lively 2½-year-old at her side, because we were in the major leagues.

The Royals Come to Life...
And a Second Son

1969

Where do I start? Every day in my initial major league season was a joy. That is not to say it was easy. I had so very much to learn and to decide on since Kansas City had been without a team for one year after Charlie O. Finley moved the Athletics to Oakland after the '67 season, just as his bonus babies were starting to mature.

The city had the A's for 13 seasons after they moved from Philadelphia, but not a single one of the teams in KC played .500 baseball. The closest was a 73-81 record in the fourth season (1958), and the last eight years the team lost an average of 96 games.

Finley had jerked everyone's chain with his zoo beyond the right-field fence at Municipal Stadium, 10 managers in the 13 years with no one lasting two full seasons and general interference. While major league attendance in general was far below today's numbers when 2 million or 3 million fans are not uncommon for a home season, Kansas City only reached 1 million in its first two summers and the norm in the later years of the Athletics seemed somewhat encouraging if it reached 700,000. The average crowd of 8,000 or 9,000 a game meant neither the locals nor vacationers were excited to come see the team.

It hurt to know that fans from Kansas and Nebraska and other nearby states would drive through Kansas City to go see the established and successful St. Louis Cardinals on the other end of Missouri.

The initial enthusiasm for the expansion Royals had to be built with positive play on the diamond, although it was refreshing for Kansas Citians to know there was local ownership from self-made drug magnate Ewing Kauffman and his family. Kauffman's Marion Laboratories was a proud local entity which would grow even more as this generous businessman poured money and time into the franchise.

It was up to General Manager Cedric Tallis, who had come from the California Angels (now the Los Angeles Angels); Farm Director Lou Gorman (from Baltimore); and Charlie Metro to build the team and get the public more interested. History would go on to show they did a great job for an expansion franchise, finishing fourth in the six-team Western Division of the American League in the inaugural season of 1969 although the record was only 69-93. The Royals finished second and climbed above .500 (85-76) in our third season, and reached their first of a string of postseason appearances and divisional titles in Year 8 (1976).

But I am getting ahead of myself. The expansion draft in the fall of 1968—and before I was hired—set the initial tone. Tallis and Company went mostly for younger prospects while Seattle leaned toward proven—and older—talent. Tallis turned out to be the wiser of the two leaders.

These were the first 15 of the 30 Kansas City selections:

No.	Player	Pos.	Previous Organization
1.	Nelson, Roger	RHP	Baltimore
2.	Foy, Joe	3B	Boston
3.	Rooker, Jim	LHP	New York
4.	Keough, Joe	OF	Oakland
5.	Jones, Steve	LHP	Washington
6.	Warden, Jon	LHP	Detroit

7.	Rodriguez, Ellie	C	New York
8.	Morehead, Dave	RHP	Boston
9.	Fiore, Mike	1B	Baltimore
10.	Oliver, Bob	OF-1B	Minnesota
11.	Butler, Bill	LHP	Detroit
12.	Whitaker, Steve	OF	New York
13.	Bunker, Wally	RHP	Baltimore
14.	Schaal, Paul	3B	California
15.	Haynes, Bill	1B	Chicago

Note: Oliver, #17 OF Pat Kelly, #22 SS Jackie Hernandez had been on our Denver team that season (1968).

The expansion draft selections were expected to form the nucleus of our Opening Day 25-man roster, although with some of them still untested at high levels, the Royals brought in another 22 non-roster players. This list included veteran major leaguers such as powerful Dave Nicholson, and pitchers Orlando Pena, Larry Sherry, Tracy Stallard and Dave Wickersham. They had one thing in common. Unfortunately, it was they had not been in the big time the previous year.

Nicholson, Sherry and Stallard all had resumes that gave someone like myself the opportunity to give some cautious buildup to the media. Nicholson had so much raw power, but was also known for his frequent swings and misses. Sherry had starred in the 1959 World Series for the Los Angeles Dodgers, getting two wins and two saves. Stallard had given up Roger Maris' record-shattering 61st home run at Yankee Stadium in '61. Wickersham, a very religious

106

man, had won as many as 19 games in a major league season (Detroit, 1964). It turned out he would be the only one of the group to appear in regular-season games for the Royals.

Once I completed the media guide and some work on our first game-day program, it was off to spring training in Fort Myers, FL.

I cannot begin to explain how much I had thought about being part of spring training, listening to games from Al Lang Field in St. Petersburg and elsewhere and seeing newspaper and magazine photos with the palm trees swaying behind the action or the staged photos that were very much a part of those years.

Dilemma!

Everyone has to confront them at various points in their life. I was up against a major one. Julie was now eight months pregnant and fast-moving Jeff was nearing three. I really had no choice but to go to Fort Myers if I wanted to be in this job, and I was leaving a wife, son and dachshund Brer John for six weeks or so.

With her parents in Salt Lake City and mine in Halsey, we had no one to help out except for the wife of our traveling secretary, who lived in the same complex in Overland Park.

It was tough on me; perilous for Julie. Three or four weeks into camp and nearly a week into our exhibition season, I went back to Kansas City, arriving the evening of March 12. I learned at the airport in Kansas City that Julie had gone into labor and had been driven to Shawnee Mission Hospital. I was not there to do this normal husbandly job.

I did arrive a few hours ahead of Bradley Scott Wirz, which was some type of blessing. Brad was a blondie from the beginning, and a joy to all of us. I stayed for the better part of a week. Julie's mother arrived, and I headed back for another chunk—but not all—of spring training.

They did not tell me for a short time, but Julie had gone back into the hospital some time after I left. Thankfully, she recovered, although the guilt lingered for a time.

"It's a Boy" (Brad) and a proud dad returns to the Kansas City Royals' spring training camp to pass out cigars to the likes of Syd Thrift, left, and Tommy Henrich

Fort Myers, on the west coast of Florida and well removed from all other spring training camps at that time, was pretty much of a sleepy community. I hardly recognize it now because of the immense growth. We followed the Pittsburgh Pirates to town, and got a warm reception although there was some fence mending to be done to get spring training totally embraced once again.

The Fort Myers News Press gave us lots of coverage, thanks to gentlemanly Sports Editor Len Harsh and competent photographer Dick Byland, who I was able to hire to do most of the photos we needed for our season-opening game program and our yearbook. We also could count on a beat reporter from *The Kansas City Star* being on hand virtually full time. But since we were about 130 miles removed from the west coast media hub of St. Petersburg and Tampa and they had the established big city teams to cover, it was very difficult to get even The Associated Press to send a photographer our way. I had to be pretty cunning to get photos back to Kansas City so our fans could see what our players looked like or to see the staged family-on-the-beach pictures that often came with spring training while everyone up north was still in winter. Sometimes, we might luck out and get a wire photo transmitted from one of our road games.

The Kansas City television stations often paid us a visit, but it would only be once each spring training with a backlog of interviews they could put into a sportscast. We broadcast a number of our Grapefruit League games, but I'm not certain we ever had a televised game in spring training during my six years with the Royals.

The two most memorable events of that first spring training probably started with the very first exhibition game, which brought Montreal and its French-speaking media to our little press box, and even smaller lunch room, where we provided a very modest fare that usually included make-your-own-sandwich makings for the visiting teams and our media. The Expos also were a first year team, coming into the National League with the San Diego Padres.

Our guys collected 16 hits, but we lost that first game, 9-8, and had to wait two more days for our very first win, a 2-1 triumph in Fort Myers over Ted Williams' Washington Senators when Pat Kelly and Chuck Harrison both homered. I wish I could say I remember all of the details instead of relying on one of my Royals media guides, which were pretty much my pride and joy.

The second "happening" was the trade during the final week with Seattle which made rookie Lou Piniella our left fielder, and, with little doubt as the season unfolded, the closest we had to a star. "Sweet Lou" joined the Royals for their final Florida exhibition, and all he did that day against the Philadelphia Phillies in Clearwater was go 4-for-4.

I had gone back to Kansas City by that time to get ready for two scheduled weekend exhibitions against the Cardinals and our American League debut two days later on April 8.

The Royals' second-year media guide (1970) explained how Piniella became a favorite:

"He had a double his first time at bat in the regular season as the Royals' leadoff man and scored the first run. The next three times up he singled, then flied out and finished with a walk. He drove in the winning run with two out in the 17th the next night, later collected Kansas City's first triple and first two home runs in Municipal Stadium."

While not that prolific every day, the 25-year-old (when the season started) hit .282, with 21 doubles, six triples, 11 home runs and 68 runs batted in, and the Baseball Writers Association of America (BBWAA) voted him American League Rookie of the Year. The Kansas City Athletics never had a player so honored.

Piniella, as well as wife Anita, a former Miss Tampa, were such a photogenic couple, and I could count on them any time we needed to set up an interview or a photo shoot to promote the Royals. The only thing I had to do was remind Lou a little ahead of time, and he would graciously rush off to mow his heavy whiskers, which might otherwise have grown for a day or two.

The Royals' first manager was Joe Gordon, one of Finley's parade of managers, who was better known as a power-hitting second baseman for the New York Yankees and Cleveland Indians for 11 seasons from 1938 to 1950. It took more time than many thought was fair, but "Flash" eventually was elected to the Hall of Fame for his playing skills.

110

Joe was the warmest of people, loved by all who knew him. He was a delight to travel with on our preseason caravan through several states to promote the return of baseball to Kansas City and equally fun to be with when not at the ballpark. He loved to hold court at a place like the original Trader Vic's in Oakland, where dark rum could be lethal if one was not prepared to handle something with a kick.

It did not get much better than watching Gordon and Williams, who managed the Washington Senators in 1969, square off to discuss hitting. They could pull in a crowd of players and writers, who loved the give and take between these marvelous hitters now in their early 50s.

Joe Gordon would not have been enshrined at Cooperstown for his managing, but he did pull many a right button for these newly-born Royals.

This was the first year of divisional play in the major leagues, and Minnesota won the Western Division (our bracket) with 97 and 98 victories in the first two seasons behind the likes of eventual Hall of Famers Rod Carew and Harmon Killebrew and a certain Hall of Fame hitter in Tony Oliva, if not for his bad knees, but the Royals opened the season acting like world beaters.

In the 12th inning of the opener at Municipal Stadium, Gordon summoned Joe Keough from the Kansas City bench to pinch hit, and the fresh-faced young outfielder made the Royals a 4-3 victor with a slicing single past Oliva in right field. The next night it took 17 innings to produce the same result with an identical score.

Somewhat disappointedly, the two games combined to draw only 31,428 fans, fewer than Municipal Stadium's capacity of just over 35,000, even though we had established an American League record with 6,805 season tickets.

When I say Gordon pushed the right buttons early on in that maiden season, how else could an expansion team have broken exactly even in its first 42 games, collecting 11 of our 21 victories in the team's final at-bat?

Another of the most memorable victories came later in April when Bob (Hawk) Taylor, a bonus baby a dozen years earlier with the Milwaukee Braves but a mediocre major leaguer at best, crushed a three-run homer in the bottom of the eighth inning to treat our largest crowd of the entire season (a near-capacity 31,872) to a come-from-behind, 7-5 victory. What made it particularly sweet was that it capped a doubleheader split against Oakland, the former residents of Municipal Stadium.

KANSAS CITY ROYALS 1969 BASEBALL CLUB

Some memories never fade, such as mine of that very first Kansas City Royals team

The All-Star Game and World Series were among the other magical events for me in 1969.

Washington, DC, was the site of the All-Star Game. I was in a cab from the airport in the nation's capital when word came of the first steps being taken on the moon by Neil

Armstrong, and that was only the start of a three-day whirlwind. Baseball honored its Greatest Team Ever, stars of the first century of the major leagues, at a black-tie dinner, and it would not be an overstatement to say I was starry-eyed. What a gathering!

Then came the game, which was accompanied by a monsoon. We were in a massive tent enjoying a pre-game feast when it hit. I'm somewhat in disbelief to this day that the tent did not collapse. The game was postponed, then played the next afternoon with Vice President Spiro Agnew standing in for President Richard Nixon, who had left to be on hand for the splashdown of the Apollo 11 crew.

It was during the All-Star Game that I first saw security people occupying every aisle near the dugouts and facing away from the diamond in the event anyone tried to get close to the presidential box.

The 1969 World Series was especially memorable in baseball annals because the New York Mets, behind the strong arms of Tom Seaver and Jerry Koosman, stunned the Frank Robinson-Brooks Robinson-Boog Powell-Dave McNally-Jim Palmer-Mike Cuellar-led Baltimore Orioles in five games, giving the New Yorkers their first championship. Baltimore's only victory was in Game 1.

I did not have any assignments, and was attending primarily through the graciousness of the Royals. It was a chance to relax, enjoy and think about how it would be if I did have a role.

My memory of that trip always goes back to two primary events, neither involving a turning point in a game.

With World Series games still being played in the glorious daytime, we got on Kauffman's private jet late on Sunday afternoon after Game 2 and headed to New York City. I could not have imagined the thrill that awaited this still-starry-eyed young PR man.

I had only been to the Big Apple a couple of times, first for that Army-Kansas State football game at West Point and earlier in the '69 season when I made a Boston-New York swing with the Royals that included another memorable stop since Kansas City started the trip with an exhibition game in Pittsburgh. That was the only time I got the thrill of seeing Forbes Field.

As we were approaching New York, Mr. K's captain, Rick King, sent word for me to come up to the cabin. Rick and co-pilot Frank Reamer obviously were aware this major league rookie had not been to NYC often. They pulled a seat across and behind them—I believe it was not much more than something like a smooth 1-by-10 board—and motioned for me to strap myself in.

Well, it was right at twilight with one of those beautiful sunsets on the horizon. I feel I can still see it nearly five decades later. The lights in the city were just coming to life, as were the nighttime views of the bridges. Sorry to say, I cannot specifically remember the view of the Statue of Liberty, but it had to have been stunning. What an amazing, once-in-a-lifetime opportunity to have this view that pilots surely cherish whenever the timing and the sunset are just right! This one seemed perfect.

The twinkling of the NYC lights was in stark contrast to the scene a few days later at Shea Stadium as the Mets were putting the finishing touches on their amazing World Series triumph.

Our seats were in the lower tier, something like just beyond first base. The field had been torn up about three weeks earlier when the Mets clinched the National League's East Division title and fans stormed onto the sod, tearing up any souvenir they could find. Another such scene was anticipated at the end of the World Series, and I believe the open gates had allowed people without tickets to the game to get in and virtually fill the aisles. Not everyone was an everyday fan.

I don't mind admitting this 30-something who had grown up in the serenity of the Nebraska Sandhills was not at ease. Bedlam was not part of our regular vocabulary. It was difficult to enjoy the last inning or so as much as one would like, although I may have been less out of sorts than the fans of the shocked Orioles.

We survived just fine, despite the scene at game's end, as described by *The Official Baseball Guide*, the must-have annual of those years, published by *The Sporting News:*

"All hell broke loose on October 16 soon after 3 p.m. Every conceivable Met fan who could get onto the field did so. They feverishly dug up the sod by the handfuls. Thousands of grass toupees were held aloft triumphantly and the fans all seemed to face the stands as though asked by the numerous TV cameras busily recording the holocaust."

Once the World Series ended, I finally had some time to slow down a little from the nonstop pace of nearly a year. It would be the first opportunity to really reflect on what life in the major leagues was like and to have some time with our growing family that now included two sons.

Fort Myers Beach, Here We Come

1970

The casual fan always wanted to know "What do you do in the offseason?" I believe many of them thought it was a four- or five-month vacation. Hardly. We could get away some, especially since the boys were not yet in school, although a PR man's salary was hardly lucrative enough to go wild. And, baseball tasks never ended.

My office time was taken up trying to drum up some feature stories or photos since the Kansas City media could easily get caught up in the other sports seasons and forget about the Royals for weeks on end. We see lots of baseball coverage in the offseason now as talk radio brings on constant chatter and newspapers are fueled by free-agent speculation, but it was not so 40 or so years ago. We couldn't even get a Sunday notebook in *The Kansas City Star,* so we had to generate whatever we could.

There also was preparation for the winter meetings in December; our press caravan for a couple of weeks in January or early February; advance planning for next year's yearbook and program; and, of course, the media guide. It became known around our house as the G__ D___ media guide since I was often working on it in evening hours.

This was the first year my family would be joining me for spring training in Fort Myers. We set up shop at Fort Myers Beach, which meant I would have nearly an hour's commute each way to Terry Park, but Julie and the boys could be on the beach.

It was a great spring for pictures, with those I most remember being of 1-year-old and fair-colored Brad getting sunburned and eating seaweed. I guess we did not win any

Parent of the Year honors. There also was one of those photos that survive through time of the boys and me.

Our offices were barracks-like at Terry Park. Nothing fancy, to be certain, but serviceable for the seven or eight of us who made up the entire off-the-diamond contingent at our home away from home.

One day, photographer Dick Byland of *The Fort Myers News-Press*, perhaps on assignment from me to get shots to send back to Kansas City for both team and media use, posed Jeff, now nearly 4, and Brad atop my desk. They appeared to be sorting through media guides when, in fact, it probably was a miracle they stayed still long enough for the shutter to fire. Both had KC caps on although Brad did not appear to like his. The picture was used in the annual *News-Press* section about the team, and it sentimentally is featured in our den at home, and in at least one of the boys' homes more than four decades later. One never knows when that one-in-a-million picture is taken.

An all-time favorite with sons Jeff, left, and Brad in my spring training office in Fort Myers, FL

We were lucky if we had one or two days off in the six to seven weeks of spring training, but there was an occasional evening event, whether with Fort Myers businessmen, sponsors visiting from Kansas City, or merely the staff.

One dinner during this spring training was especially memorable. Tallis had arranged for the staff, spouses and probably any Kansas City media in town—no more than 20 people at most—to go out to Sea Grape Island.

Sea Grape is one of the tiny islands in the Pine Island Sound portion of the Gulf of Mexico. I don't believe it could have been much more than an acre in size. One could only reach the island (unless it was by boat) via the type of one-car dirt road I knew so well from my Nebraska upbringing.

Tallis loved to have a good time, and to have others share in it. He also was known to push the pedal when he was behind the wheel. We got to experience his driving this special night because everyone was seated at one time for the single item on the menu. You dare not be late, and if anyone wanted a cocktail—what baseball person didn't?—it was only to be consumed in a small waiting area just outside of the quaint dining room.

There was charm in the fact Sea Grape was only operated about six months of each year, and the owner/host operated a similar facility the rest of the year, as I recall, in Michigan; maybe it was Wisconsin. He was beyond middle age, with white hair and a Hawaiian-type print shirt unbuttoned pretty much to the navel.

The conversation of the evening has long since left me, although baseball no doubt was at or near the top, and the single item featured for dinner was not red snapper or some other Florida fish, but rather pork chops. Thick, juicy pork chops.

I can still visualize much of the setting all these years later.

Fort Myers still was isolated from any other Grapefruit League city, so the team spent anywhere from 90 minutes to nearly four hours each way on the bus for road games. I was normally in a car, often driving or riding with the one or two writers we were lucky to have in camp from Kansas City or Topeka. We would be behind the bus both in arriving at and departing from our destination of the day.

We got very familiar with the back roads leading to Bradenton or St. Petersburg or wherever because Interstate 75 was still years from being built. The Tamiami Trail—Highway 41—was too agonizingly slow because, well, it only had one or two lanes, went through some of the towns and was primarily patronized by the not-so-young snowbirds who populated the area.

This particular spring, we had two games scheduled in Cocoa, FL, against Houston. Keep in mind that as a second-year team, we were not considered a huge draw. Neither were the Astros, so fans were not knocking down the gates to see these two teams. We were matches because we both needed a full schedule, not the defending World Champions against their toughest foe.

Through the generosity of our owner, chartered flights were set up because Cocoa, near Cape Canaveral, was a good 3½ hours away. It was virtually clear across the state and well north of Lee County.

These turned into two never-to-be-forgotten trips because of threatening wind and rain. On one occasion, while loading the traveling party of 30 or 40 plus all of the baseball gear, the plane completely tipped nose up. Some serious adjustment of the total weight had to be made. Then, we were advised there would be a weather delay. We eventually took off, but once in the air were advised the weather had worsened again and we would be diverted to Miami, where we would be met by buses to take us back to Fort Myers.

That is well over 100 miles and across Alligator Alley, the laborious 80 or so miles from Fort Lauderdale to Naples. It was not a joyous trip.

What do they say about lightning never striking the same place twice? Now don't take this literally, but once again on our next trip to play the Astros, Mother Nature scheduled identical weather. This time we waited through what was to be the worst of the weather, then took off for what probably should have been a 50-minute flight in our prop plane.

It was the worst flight I have ever been on. The seasoned travelers among the players agreed. I have no idea how many airbags were used or how long the flight ended up taking, but my wife told me later she could see a plane she suspected was ours, circling Fort Myers Beach, which was well off any direct flight path and at low altitude. We landed safely, but spring training was getting to be a bit long.

It looked for a time like the Royals were going to rival Finley's days in Kansas City in the number of managerial changes that were made.

Gordon resigned a few days after the '69 season ended, admitting in the press conference "it is a lot tougher now to handle the players" than it was when he last managed eight years earlier. Metro moved from leading the scouting department to replace Gordon. That job lasted only until June 9, when Metro was fired and Bob Lemon, our pitching coach, took over.

No one questioned that Metro knew the game inside and out, but, among other things, he could be rigid with players. I made about half of the trips with the Royals in those days, and I was on the disastrous nine-game junket to Washington, New York and Boston in which we won only once. Several of the losses came in the late stages of the game, sometimes in bizarre situations.

The firing took place the first day of the next home stand, which went somewhat better against those same teams plus Minnesota. Lemon was a sweetheart of a man, who already was so well known for his 207 pitching victories, mostly with Cleveland, and he later guided the Yankees to some of their storied modern-day success. I will have much more to say when we get to 1978, the fabled Bucky Dent-playoff-home run season.

"Lem" brought the Royals back to expansion-team respectability in his nearly three years of guiding them. I would forever be indebted from a PR standpoint because he was a gem to work with, win or lose. For the entire Wirz Family, he became a wonderful friend for the rest of his life, sprinkles of which you will read about later on.

The best two parts of 1970 for the team might well have been the opening of a unique Baseball Academy in Sarasota, FL, and the first year in Royal Blue of smooth centerfielder Amos Otis.

The concept behind the Academy was that athletes from other sports with natural athletic talent and great eye-hand coordination could be developed into major league baseball players. For two examples, consider runners and basketball players.

A certain percentage of the Royals' staff and, importantly, Kauffman, loved the idea. Others were loath to it, especially if it cut into the normal scouting and development budget organizations had depended on throughout history.

Baseball lifer Syd Thrift headed up the Academy staff, and we reported in the 1971 Royals Media Guide that his staff, including the team's regular scouts, looked at nearly 8,000 athletes in tryout camps held in 41 states before selecting the first class of 43, who were to train and attend college classes year-round.

The Academy, which lasted for a few years and probably would have lived on had the Royals been a profitable operation, produced one outstanding major talent in Kansas

121

Citian Frank White. He became an all-star second baseman on the championship teams the Royals would field over many of the next 15 years.

Otis was acquired in one of the numerous magical trades pulled off in the first few years by Tallis. The 22-year-old and pitcher Bob Johnson, who would become the best strikeout pitcher the Royals had seen, were obtained from the New York Mets in a Winter Meetings swap that sent instinctively-talented third baseman Joe Foy to the National League team.

Otis was silky smooth in centerfield if a bit shy of outfield fences, and with Piniella manning left and lefty-swinging Ed Kirkpatrick or slugging first baseman-outfielder Oliver in right, the Royals would be ahead of any other third-year team in outfield talent.

While not ideal for a PR man because Otis was anywhere from reluctant to unpredictable when it came to the media, he performed well beyond the skill level of his limited major league experience (67 games) and hit .284 with 36 doubles, nine triples, 11 home runs, 91 runs and 33 stolen bases (in 35 attempts) in his first season at Municipal Stadium. He led all major league outfielders in putouts and total chances.

With Oliver driving in 99 runs and Piniella 88, there was encouragement despite a 65-97 second-year record.

I had some tools for offseason publicity leading into 1971.

Son Brad's Haunting Episodes
And a Winning Season

1971

I feel pretty certain that any baseball family taking young kids to spring training for six or seven weeks can tell stories good and bad about the experiences. While there are benefits like keeping the family together, to be sure, the youngsters are uprooted from their home environment, their friends, even the comfort of their own beds.

Brad would turn 2 in mid-March, but the whole experience of driving from Kansas City to Fort Myers Beach and living in out-of-the-ordinary surroundings was too much. He could not settle into a routine. There were tears almost constantly, so it seemed, at least to his mother, who was alone with Brad and Jeff for long hours each day. The players' families were all around, but they could connect much more easily with one another than a staff wife and a player's wife. So many of the players were still facing the uncertainty of whether they would make the team.

I have one vivid memory during spring training. We planned a party for our fellow staff members and for Lem and the coaches. Can you believe we only had three coaches, Galen Cisco, Harry Dunlop and George Strickland? Major league teams have about eight plus multiple trainers, lifting instructors, videographers and a cadre of others today.

Dunlop, whose own family would stay home in Sacramento until school was out, was especially sympathetic to our dilemma with Brad. When it came time to put Brad to bed, which was no easy task in those days, Harry laid down on a bed next to him and kept Brad entertained until both of them went into a deep sleep.

As a postscript to what otherwise was an evening filled with laughter, when the group left for home, Lem backed into a light pole, bringing some damage to the rented car. I would hate to think we had "over-served" our lovable manager.

Brad did not totally settle down until we were back in our Independence, MO, home (yes, the hometown of President Harry Truman) and ready to start the season. I can still see Brad going into his room when our long drive from Florida ended and virtually falling asleep while leaning against his mattress. He had missed his home surroundings, as most any 2-year-old would.

Brad, who thankfully has been a highly-successful marketing specialist for a number of years, does not seem scarred from that long trip to Fort Myers Beach or from another of those memorable family trips that took place after the season.

The exact day in November is easy for this sports-crazed person to recall. We had been with my family in Halsey for an early Thanksgiving, then headed out early Thanksgiving morning for a two-day drive to Julie's family home in Salt Lake City.

We had what many call the college football Game-of-the-Century to entertain us on the radio. This was the epic back-and-forth struggle between archrivals Nebraska and Oklahoma, ranked Nos. 1 and 2, respectively, in the nation. With Jeff Kinney scoring four times, the Huskers eventually won, 35-31. I was a happy guy.

As day turned toward evening in Wyoming, all of a sudden as we entered a mountain pass east of Laramie, we found ourselves battling an ice storm. It was not fun. Thankfully, we were on divided highway and we could see cars and trucks sliding all over on the eastbound portion. It was one slow, hold-your-breath drive into Laramie, where we were able to get a motel room.

We were not certain what was ahead of us the next day because Wyoming has long stretches between towns of much size and plenty of room for storms to roll in. We wanted to get a decent start, with thoughts we would return to Laramie for another day if the icy conditions continued. We only got a few miles back on the highway, which thankfully was surprisingly clear, when Brad was doubled over in pain.

It would be a couple of hours, even if the roads stayed clear, before we would reach Rawlins. What to do? It was not an easy choice.

I had a hunch our little blond-headed guy needed to relieve himself of some liquid. Call it male intuition. Julie had a pint jar with us for this type of emergency. It works for boys, right? The jar was brought out, and Brad tried. Not a drop.

We were steadily getting farther away from Laramie; more into the middle of nowhere, as someone who grew up in the sparsely populated Sandhills of Nebraska understood. Brad's pain was getting more intense.

In a few minutes, I suggested a second try with the pint jar. Well, it would have been better if it was a quart. The pain disappeared just that quickly.

It turned out that the Gatorade we had in the motel room that tasted terrible to Jeff and his mom and dad had been largely consumed by Brad.

The rest of the trip to Salt Lake City was a breeze.

Oh, I almost forgot the '71 baseball season, which would be a shame since it was easily the best in Kansas City history. The 85-win summer (85-76) eclipsed the previous best in the city by 11 victories. The third-year Royals made a statement to the major leagues they were on their way, even though we finished 16 games behind Oakland in the American League's Western Division. We had the fourth-best record in the 12-team league.

Speed actually could have been the theme for the entire year since 5-foot-4 shortstop Fred Patek, obtained in a major trade with Pittsburgh, joined Otis in stealing 101 bases, a total the American League had not seen in 54 years since Ray Chapman and Braggo Roth stole 103 for Cleveland in 1917. Otis stole 52 times, Patek 49.

Patek, easily embraced since he was the major leagues' smallest player and a dazzling fielder, and second baseman Cookie Rojas teamed as a double-play combination for five full years, as well as part of '76 and '77. They were at their best when one would glide behind second base and make a glove-hand flip to the other, who would complete the twin killing.

Winning and all-star caliber players made my job so much easier.

Introducing George Wallace
And Embarrassment in Honolulu

1972

I am not certain I realized it at the time, and my confidence had to be pretty solid since this would be my fourth major league season. But 1972 would need to be a year in which I stepped up the depth of my non-game-related work since the Royals were one year away from opening the long-awaited Royals Stadium and hosting the All-Star Game.

One never could fully predict what a day with the team would be like because I might find myself suddenly writing a release about a player trade—at least drafting something on the prospect it was in the works. One day in spring training suddenly called for some swift thinking because Alabama Governor and Democratic presidential hopeful George Wallace was going to be in our camp at Fort Myers.

I do not believe we had much advance notice, but all of a sudden there he and his entourage were near our No. 2 diamond, where we often took batting practice if we did not have a game.

The edginess for me was that I was asked to introduce Wallace to some of our players, and he was widely known at that time for his segregationist attitudes. I had to take into consideration the feelings of the players if I ignored them, and I was not certain how Wallace would react to being around such African-American players as Otis and Oliver, two of our everyday players.

I had confidence Oliver would be a gentleman, and we had an excellent relationship going back to our Triple-A days in Denver. Big Bob, listed at 6-foot-2 but always appearing taller, wielded an important right-handed power bat while playing either first base or the outfield. That bat, in fact, could have put my career on hold a couple of years earlier when he whistled a batting-practice liner into our leftfield bullpen area, taking yours truly on my side when I should have been watching out for such an incident.

On this morning, I found Oliver near the visitor's clubhouse, mere steps away from the batting cage on Diamond 2. I cannot remember if there was time to talk with him in advance, but I got him and Wallace together for an introduction. No sweat. Both were perfect gentlemen, no matter what either might have been thinking.

My hope, as always, was to give the Royals a good image, and to do everything in my power to get us as much publicity as possible, especially given the remoteness of Fort Myers to the national media and limited daily coverage in our camp.

I don't believe this quick stop netted either the presidential campaign or the Royals any major headlines. Nor were there any headlines saying "Baseball Publicist Screws Up in Introducing Black Player to George Wallace."

It was only a couple of months later on May 15 when Wallace was shot while campaigning in Laurel, MD, with bullets striking him in the abdomen and chest and leaving him paralyzed from the waist down for the rest of his life.

Ironically, Oliver only hit one home run for Kansas City that season—he had hit 27 two years earlier—before being traded to the California (now Los Angeles) Angels.

The All-Star Game was in Atlanta that year, and I went there all eyes and ears because the task of preparing for the 500 or so media members who attended these major events every July would be left mostly to me and my small staff— primarily one part-time assistant and a secretary—one year later.

It is important to remember that while today, Major League Baseball has a sizeable contingent devoted to the All-Star Game and every minute detail and brings in many of the team PR directors to assist with interviews, press conferences and game notes, it was not that way in '72-'73.

The host team was pretty much on its own, and, frankly, the game meant more to the well-being of the sport than it does today. It always drew the best—certainly one of the best—television ratings of the entire summer.

Thank heavens for Bob Hope, my counterpart, but much more experienced and worldly, who was with the Braves. Hope (no relation to the comedian and a friend to this day—and my son Brad's first employer other than his dad after graduation from Syracuse—)not only was hospitable but he also made certain I had a good view of the game and all of its activities from the main press box. He even prepared a three-ring binder with copies of all of his major correspondence in preparation for hosting the All-Star Game and made certain I got a copy.

It served as my blueprint for the next 12 months.

The Royals, dropping to 76-78, did not have a sterling follow-up season to the 85 wins of 1971. However, we were well represented at the All-Star Game with Otis, Piniella and Richie Scheinblum as outfielders; second baseman Rojas; and our skipper, Lem, as one of the American League coaches.

Otis was injured and did not play, but I have distinct memories for diverse reasons about the other three players.

Piniella had played for American League Manager Earl Weaver of Baltimore when they were at Elmira, NY, in 1965. I do not believe I ever heard what triggered it, but Weaver was said to have gone over a picnic table in the clubhouse one day in an effort to get at Piniella, who also had a low boiling point.

That hatchet had been buried, to the best of my knowledge, by '72, but as luck would have it, Weaver and his Orioles were playing in Kansas City on the day when it was to be announced who the reserve players would be for the All-Star Game. "You have been selected for the All-Star Game," Weaver is said to have announced to Piniella, "but don't bother bringing your glove." Piniella had developed

129

into a decent leftfielder by that time, but Weaver either didn't believe it or merely wanted to get in a little jab at Sweet Lou.

Piniella grounded out as a pinch hitter in the 10th inning of the mid-summer classic, Scheinblum also went 0-for-1 while relieving Bobby Murcer in right, and Rojas was one of the game's heroes. He hit a pinch, two-run homer down the leftfield line for a 3-2 American League lead in the eighth, only to see the National League score single runs in the bottom of the ninth and 10th innings for a 4-3 victory.

Despite the final score, I will never forget the joy Scheinblum, wife Mary and 5-year-old son Monte had in Atlanta. Scheinblum would turn 30 before the year ended, and was enjoying what he probably realized was a "career year" in his only full season in KC. They collected every souvenir they could, starting with All-Star posters in the hotel.

The game ended in walk-off fashion when eventual Hall of Fame second baseman Joe Morgan singled to right-center to score Nate Colbert.

It was either later that night or at the airport the next morning when a grinning Scheinblum approached and said, "Do you know who got the game-winning ball?" He pointed, happily, to himself. He had picked up the ball from his right-field position, and when no one clamored for it, obviously decided he had a good home for it, even if he was on the losing team.

Piniella and Scheinblum were heavily involved in another national story when they were part of a six-man chase for the American League batting championship. Minnesota's Rod Carew eventually won it at .318, which was the lowest winning mark for this seven-time batting champion and eventual Hall of Famer, but it was a daily scramble coming down the stretch.

Piniella wound up second (.312), with Scheinblum (.300) sixth behind Dick Allen and Carlos May of Chicago, and

Oakland's Joe Rudi. First baseman John Mayberry (.298) and Otis (.293) gave the Royals four players in the top nine and led them to the best team average (.255) in the entire league.

What a tribute to Charley Lau, who moved up from organizational hitting instructor to major league hitting coach! Lau quickly became known as one of the sport's top hitting gurus, and the soft-spoken former catcher was a dear friend until his early death to cancer when he was only 50 in 1984.

It was widely known Piniella was compulsive about his hitting stance and swing, sometimes even mimicking it between pitches when he was standing in left field.

Buddy Blattner and Anita Piniella both told me stories that resonate all these years later.

Blattner was the Royals' radio and television anchor, and really the organization's best-known personality. He never went into a broadcast without his trusty binders loaded with stories, which he could call on when the situation dictated if he did not have sufficient personal vignettes to fill a lengthy broadcast.

By the time he came to the Royals, Blattner already had more than 30 years of high-level history, starting with playing the infield for the St. Louis Cardinals and New York Giants, and later writing and emceeing various TV shows in his native St. Louis, broadcasting for the St. Louis Browns and Cardinals, eight years as the serious side of the CBS-TV "Game of the Week" broadcast team alongside Hall of Fame pitcher and comedic storyteller Dizzy Dean, and seven seasons calling the action for the California Angels.

But on this day, Blattner and hand-picked partner Denny Matthews were in their radio booth at Municipal Stadium in mid-afternoon ahead of a Royals game. The press and broadcast boxes protruded from the bottom of the upper deck. They may have lacked for amenities, but they offered a wonderful view of the entire playing field.

Blattner was taping promotional spots for the Royals' sizable network of stations when he heard a ruckus below. Now, Piniella had been on one of his exceptional hot streaks with the bat in recent days, which had him at or near the top spot in the American League batting race.

Piniella was his own worst enemy at times, though, because of his intensity to excel. The commotion occurred because Piniella had worked himself into a slump during batting practice three hours or so ahead of the game, when he likely would collect another two or three hits.

"I can't handle this (blankety blank) game; it is too (x#4*?) tough," Blattner believed Piniella had said. As further witness to the hitter's frustration, he had heaved his bat high up on the sloped home-plate screen that protected fans from angry foul balls.

Anita Piniella was as lovely a woman as one would meet, with her Miss Tampa crown a few years earlier if any proof was needed. I had a nice relationship with the dark-haired beauty as with most of the wives in the Royals' family. One day, after that torrid batting race had ended, she confided that she was awakened in the middle of one night late in the season only to find her husband missing.

Those who knew him might have guessed by now what his wife shared with me. She went looking for Lou, and found him standing in front of a full length mirror in his batting stance. I will save some of the visual affect, but he was not in a full set of pajamas, she told me.

Anyone who knows Lou no doubt has their own stories of this lifetime .291 hitter's intense desire to succeed. He had a temper to match his hitting ability. Fortunately, it was aimed at himself a great deal of the time.

The Winter Meetings were held in Honolulu for the first time that December, much to the chagrin of Kauffman. He felt it was frivolous, and was reluctant to see the Royals pay to send more than a bare-bones contingent headed up by

Tallis and Gorman, the director of minor league operations and scouting.

John Schuerholz, the bright assistant Gorman had brought in from the Orioles, and I were determined we should be in Hawaii, both because our counterparts with other teams would be there and, well, because it was Honolulu.

I was able to make a deal with Kansas City businessman Bill Phillips, who was trying to build a baseball vendor business. Phillips was one of the most outgoing—and fun-loving—of the Royal Lancers, who sold season tickets at such a pace every year that the Royals were envied by most every other American League team. My role would be to get him introduced to some of the potential buyers from both the major and minor leagues.

I was fairly quiet about the relationship when I was with my fellow PR directors, trying to protect both my team and my own pride. I represented the Royals in the normal manner, preparing press releases as appropriate and attending meetings.

The usual gathering place in Honolulu when not working, or while awaiting developments on a possible trade, was the stunning setting of the Sheraton Waikiki's pool. I do not believe any Winter Meetings headquarters hotel since has been able to match up. It was just off the famed Waikiki Beach, where one could look in any direction and be amazed by one hotel after another, Diamond Head, or seeing Santa wading in the Pacific Ocean.

However, I had one very embarrassing day during the trip. Julie made the trip with me, and whenever I could get away for a few hours, we would take in some of the historic sites Honolulu had to offer.

On this particular day, we went to Pearl Harbor. It took several hours but was well worth it. How very sobering. I had an uncle who survived the horrific attacks, but talk about a surreal setting.

We had barely gotten back from Pearl Harbor, though, when writers and other club officials started asking, "What did you think of the trade?" What trade?

I had been assured by my boss nothing was about to happen in those few hours we were away from the hotel.

At least, I was not alone with my embarrassment of not being available when my team made an important deal. Cincinnati's Jim Ferguson, a friend then and now, and his wife Joanne also had been gone.

In one of the biggest swaps in the young Royals' history that December 1, 1972, Kansas City obtained hard-nosed Hal McRae and highly regarded pitcher Wayne Simpson while giving up to the Reds our top expansion draft choice, pitcher Roger Nelson, and Scheinblum, who had barely finished his best major league season.

Acquiring McRae, who played some third base and the outfield before becoming one of the game's regal designated hitters, was one of the major pieces in getting the Royals to the baseball pinnacle even if it did take a few more seasons to climb that mountain.

Schuerholz, whose career would eventually take off as a master leader of both the Royals and the Atlanta Braves, and I had one more memorable day in the sun during the Winter Meetings while touring the back side of Oahu, with my wife as a witness.

Surfers know waves do not get much better anywhere in the world than in the area known as the Bonzai Pipeline. The waves were good enough on this day for two naive baseball men to try some body surfing.

We got hammered by the waves which would flip us over and over. It was tremendous fun, but it was only when back on the mainland that this rookie body surfer from Nebraska learned how dangerous this activity could be.

Baseball would have missed out on at least one dynamic career (Schuerholz's) had any of the waves sent us to the hospital, as many amateur surfers know could have happened.

Royals Stadium Opens
And the All-Star Game Comes
To Kansas City

1973

It did not take any of fellow Nebraskan Johnny Carson's antics of looking into the future to know what an important year 1973 was going to be for the Royals. Beautiful Royals Stadium—it still is one of baseball's most attractive venues more than 40 years later—was opening and giving the franchise a reason to separate itself from the Charlie Finley-Municipal Stadium images which reeked of second class. It debuted on a frigid April 10 evening in which the Royals routed Texas 12-1 before a record Kansas City baseball crowd of 39,464. Only three months later, the team was hosting the All-Star Game. The 40th anniversary All-Star classic to boot.

Little could I have imagined how my life would change in the most dramatic of ways little over a year later, probably in large measure because of hosting that All-Star festival. First, spring training was abbreviated for me because of all the work needed to get ready for the stadium unveiling, as well as for hosting several hundred media members who would invade the new facility for the first time during the All-Star festivities. My family stayed in our Independence home that spring since my Fort Myers spring training stint was only about half of the normal six to seven weeks.

The team could easily be a secondary thought to the majestic baseball half of the Truman Sports Complex. This colossal center was unique in the entire country in that Royals Stadium and Arrowhead Stadium for the Kansas City Chiefs stood side by side with only a parking lot separating two brand-new and modern facilities.

136

Cedric Tallis had played an important role in developing Anaheim Stadium—the Big A, as many called it. This was only two years ahead of him becoming general manager of the Royals, so he brought a grand vision of amenities. That foresight helped set Royals Stadium apart from any other new facility of these times. Combined with Kauffman's vision and the planning of the Jackson County landlords, a picturesque plan took shape.

The centerpieces would be a 12-story, $2 million scoreboard in the shape of the Royals' crowned logo with captivating waterfalls covering much of the outfield landscape. The dazzling fountains, which were not ready until shortly before the All-Star Game, were used selectively, including for home-team home runs and immediately after each game. They were the likes of which had never been seen in a major league baseball stadium. The setting made for so much anticipation for both the locals and out-of-town visitors from Missouri, Kansas, Iowa, Nebraska or anywhere else in the Midwest.

My opinion was not sought much at all in the planning stages, but as the team's publicist, I had plenty of challenges as to ways of promoting the stadium and its amenities.

Where I had an opportunity for input was in the programming of the scoreboard. My pet belief as a baseball purist was that the progress of every major league game should be shown as much of the time as possible, but the vertical shape made it daunting. How could we fit in the uniform numbers of pitchers, a staple of those times, with the team name, the inning and which team was at bat—and do this for an entire league? Countless hours of working with the scoreboard staff of only five or six people were consumed as we messaged what I wanted to see and what was possible.

I also worked closely with a New York artist, Hilda Terry, who had been hired to create cartoon-like animations to be displayed for every stolen base, home run, pitching change and ... well, you name it.

Terry, complete with what I would describe as total artist eccentricities, did not know a great deal about baseball, so it became an interesting challenge to combine the cleverness of her work with the reality of baseball. Would the casual fan understand each animation? Would he or she be amused? The contrast was night and day from the only message board we had at Municipal Stadium, with room for eight letters across and eight rows; 64 characters in all.

At Municipal Stadium, we communicated with the single message board operator by intercom from the press box to his location beyond the right center field fence. That helps explain what happened with one message we planned, stating that someone—it probably was Reggie Jackson—was on pace with Babe Ruth's home run record. When the message was posted on the board, it read Roof instead of Ruth because journeyman catcher Phil Roof was playing in the game that day. He managed only 43 homers in a 15-year major league career.

It was an embarrassing few seconds for this perfectionist until the message could be taken down and corrected.

Even though our scoreboard at Royals Stadium was much the talk of baseball in '73, we did not even have the ability to play video on it at the time. That must seem impossible to comprehend for today's fans, who are used to being dazzled with every conceivable gimmick, from showing a play that just took place anywhere around the baseball world to using the Kiss Cam to replaying the home run that has just been struck.

Sports Illustrated did a piece that I recall was high in its praise of the Royals Stadium scoreboard, but that fact was challenged to me one day by *Chicago Tribune* baseball writer Richard (Dick) Dozer, one of the scribes I shared many a fond moment with later in my career. Dozer felt the Wrigley Field scoreboard, virtually unchanged for many a season, was more informative in that it detailed half inning-by-half inning scoring for every major league game played that day.

He had a point.

A frosty 39-degree evening greeted everyone the night Royals Stadium opened, but the stadium's very presence gave every sports fan in Greater Kansas City a bragging point.

The buildup to the All-Star Game was both fun and challenging. Since Chicagoan Arch Ward had introduced the All-Star concept 40 years earlier, it was fitting to not only honor those chosen for the 1973 classic but also every living member of the '33 game.

I loved this type of challenge, and felt I knew what we should do to be perfect hosts to this distinguished group, which included many Hall of Famers, as well as the hundreds of journalists who would be covering the game, which in those days usually produced the largest television audience of any event all summer long. NBC-TV, which brought in a crew of 80, said 50 million people would watch.

For highlights of the game, Willie Mays would be tying Stan Musial with his 24th

All-Star appearance (two games were played a few times). Future Hall of Famers in addition to Mays on the rosters included National Leaguers Hank Aaron, Johnny Bench, Joe Morgan, Ron Santo, Willie Stargell, Joe Torre, Billy Williams, Tom Seaver and Don Sutton, as well as American Leaguers Rod Carew, Carlton Fisk, Catfish Hunter, Reggie Jackson, Brooks Robinson, Bert Blyleven, Rollie Fingers and Nolan Ryan.

Ryan had gotten familiar with the Royals Stadium mound earlier in the season when he threw one of his no-hitters, a 12-strikeout, three-walk gem.

Nineteen of the 1933 All-Stars attended, including starting pitchers Lefty Gomez (American League) and

"Wild" Bill Hallahan, who shared ceremonial-first-ball honors with Royals Owner Kauffman.

The game itself left something to be forgotten fairly soon in that the National League continued its dominance of those years by blitzing the American League in the middle innings, taking a 7-1 waltz. We still like to think that the standing-room-only record crowd of 40,847 wasn't too disappointed because 27 people who had been elected to the Hall of Fame, including home plate umpire Nestor Chylak and nine of the 1933 stars, took part in the festivities. The eventual Hall of Fame turnout included Cooperstown-bound Managers Dick Williams (American League), recovering from an appendectomy, and Sparky Anderson (National League).

San Francisco Giants star Bobby Bonds, who Anderson called "the best player in the National League" at the time, won Most Valuable Player honors because of his two-run, fifth-inning blast over the left-centerfield fence that built a 5-1 National League advantage. He later had a hustle double to finish 2-for-2.

Baseball made certain the returnees from that very first 1933 All-Star Game shared the spotlight, with Commissioner Bowie Kuhn honoring them at a luncheon and presenting them Linde Star All-Star rings in Claret Red, compared with the Fern Green color that highlighted the rings for the '73 players.

From a PR perspective, I was proud of the event and what we were able to accomplish. We had special transportation from the moment each of the '33 and '73 All-Stars and the baseball dignitaries got to the airport. Our media kit, press conferences and hospitality at Kansas City's best hotels made for a comfortable setting in this pre-digital age.

As a result, involvement in the All-Star Game seemed to enhance my career, although you will have to read a little longer to learn more on that front.

While it would have been easy for the team to get lost in all of the hoopla over the opening of Royals Stadium and the All-Star Game, first-year Manager Jack McKeon (who succeeded Lemon) and the maturing group of players would not allow it.

McKeon, still a widely-respected baseball man in his 80s after years of leading various major league teams including the 2003 World Championship Florida Marlins, paid his dues as a minor league catcher and in an extensive minor league managerial career that started when he was only 24.

Always colorful and upbeat, the cigar-puffing McKeon proved he was ready by leading Kansas City to its best season, an 88-74 campaign that lifted the Royals well beyond the predicted fourth- or fifth-place finish in the American League West to a solid second, only six games behind Oakland. We had been in first place in the division as late as August 15. The Athletics went on to their second of three consecutive World Series titles.

It was fun to be the PR man as Steve Busby hurled the first no-hitter in franchise history (3-0 in Detroit on April 27) and as southpaw Paul Splittorff defied doubters by becoming the first 20-game winner in the city's major league history. Otis finished a city-best third in American League MVP voting, and the dazzling duo of second baseman Rojas and shortstop Patek led the team to 192 double plays, a total not seen in the American League in 17 years.

Attendance shot up by more than 90 per cent over the previous year to 1,345,341, a number that may not seem too impressive today, but only Detroit and Boston had higher totals in the entire league.

Looking back, 1973 also should be remembered because of the major league debuts of eventual Hall of Fame third baseman George Brett and Gold Glove second baseman Frank White.

White's ascendancy after less than three full minor league seasons was widely heralded by the Royals since he

141

was the first—and practically the only—graduate of the Baseball Academy to reach the major leagues. He had gone to school only about a block away from Municipal Stadium, but Lincoln High School did not field a baseball team, so he got some degree of experience in the sport in local amateur leagues. Frank had played both basketball and football, but his limited baseball experience made it easy to trumpet the Academy concept of turning athletes with exceptional eye-hand coordination into baseball players as viable.

While White hit a decent .223 in 139 at-bats in a rookie season in which he shuttled between Triple-A Omaha and Kansas City, Brett struggled at third base and managed only five hits in 40 at-bats (.125) in his two stints with the major league team without an RBI.

Brett was barely 20 when he broke in, and even though he was an American Association All-Star that season it was difficult for me to imagine the brilliant career that was ahead.

Thank goodness scouts knew what they could see in the young Californian.

From Early Optimism in KC
To a Major Move to NYC

1974

We had many a reason to feel upbeat as the Royals headed into their sixth season even though three of the players who had been so much a part of the organization up to this point had been traded. Steady starter Dick Drago had gone to Boston for another right-hander, Marty Pattin; versatile Ed Kirkpatrick had been part of a five-player swap with Pittsburgh that brought in St. Louis and Pirates World Series veteran Nellie Briles; and most significantly, Piniella had been shipped to the Yankees for aging bullpen star Lindy McDaniel, who was set to enter his 20th professional season.

It was especially painful to see Piniella go, but McKeon did not want him around after a .250 season, even though he was third on the '73 team with 144 games and tied for third behind the potent bats of young first baseman John Mayberry and centerfielder Otis in runs batted in. The personalities of Piniella and McKeon did not match.

Tallis, who had been so adept in making trades, did not seem to have much choice in order to keep his manager happy.

The face of the early-day Royals (Piniella) was gone, and it was not easy for any of us to watch for the next decade as Sweet Lou became a popular fixture at Yankee Stadium. He was there for those bruising playoff tussles between the two teams in '76-'77-'78, each won, sometimes dramatically, by New York.

Part of me was thrilled that McDaniel was coming to Kansas City since I had been an incredibly devoted St. Louis Cardinals fan when he and brother Von broke in in heroic fashion. But McDaniel's two years in Kansas City were mediocre, as pretty much could be predicted at the time since an aging Lindy was no longer a dominant pitcher.

The third player in the Piniella-McDaniel swap, righty Ken Wright, provided one of the most amusing stories of that or any other time. Wright had been in the Royals' bullpen much of the time since 1970, offering promise because of his sometimes overpowering fastball. His eating habits, supposedly including multiple McDonald's hamburgers at a time, were virtually as well known as the powerful pitches.

One offseason, Wright went off to play winter baseball but only after promising he would keep in touch with Tallis regarding the pounds he was to lose before spring training. Faithfully, postcards came in reporting progress. We listed him at 6-foot-2, 225 pounds, but he had blossomed by another 15 pounds or so by the previous season's end. One postcard might say: "I am down to 235." Then it would be something like 232, 230, 225, 220, 218. Tallis was pleased.

But when Ken got to spring training in Fort Myers, he refused to even get on the scales. The mere sight of him proved the postcards had lied ... by quite a bit. The 82 walks Wright gave up in 80.2 innings in 1973 pretty well sealed his fate, even though he allowed only 60 hits. He got into exactly three games after his trade to the Yankees, and his major league career was over.

My season included a couple of blunders, as well. I chalk both up to experiments that did not turn out as I had hoped.

I decided to have all of the inside pages of our Royals media guide, which featured a beautiful aerial shot of Royals Stadium on the cover, printed in light blue. I thought it would lead to other teams doing the same thing in future years. Instead, I received occasional criticism— thankfully, not from my boss—that the copy was difficult to read in outside light; sometimes there seemed to be a glare.

I would do it all over because of giving us a distinctive look, but make certain the paper would not glare and insist to the printer that the type face must be larger.

The other episode—somewhat embarrassing—came about because future Detroit Hall of Fame outfielder Al Kaline was retiring at season's end. We knew he did not want a fuss made over him, but I decided (and must have gotten approval, although I do not remember for sure) that we would make a special public address introduction the first time he came to bat in the last Tigers game of the season in Kansas City.

Kaline, a gentleman's gentleman whom I got to know a little bit in later years, struck out after the introduction. I was told later, although I never saw actual proof, that after getting back to the dugout, he went down into the tunnel leading to the clubhouse and used his bat on some of the light fixtures.

Sorry, Al.

Years later when I was handling publicity for the Hall of Fame golf tournaments in Cooperstown, our paths would cross on occasion since Gentleman Al was one of the most accomplished of the golf-playing baseball stars. I never had the nerve to talk about my decision from years earlier. What a coward I am.

I traveled with the Royals roughly half the time during my six seasons with the team. It was often my decision, much to the annoyance of my wife, but a publicity man who was on the road could provide so much help to both our media and that of the other team. And, after all, this was where the action was, which was my motivation for getting into the sports business in the first place.

I went on record with Kauffman and Joe Burke, who by now was running the daily operation, in mid-summer that I needed to be looking to the future. I had proposed a possible expanded role for myself that would include the promotional side of things if I was to stay in Kansas City.

145

Then, on a July trip, I made it a point to visit with Joe Reichler of the commissioner's office. Reichler had been one of the top writers for years, breaking story after story for The Associated Press. He and Milton Richman of United Press International often had stories before anyone else because they had developed great rapport with so many players, managers and executives.

Reichler had moved on a few years earlier to the commissioner's office, where he was invaluable for understanding what the media needed and became an even more important confidant to Commissioners William Eckert and Kuhn, the latter in office since 1969.

I knew I had achieved a certain amount of respect for my work in Kansas City, probably more than ever because of my preparation for both the '33 and '73 All-Stars the previous year. I could have stayed with the Royals forever and enjoyed most parts of my job because of my love of being involved in the daily games and my confidence that I was contributing as the franchise developed.

But I was making all of $18,000 a year, which kept the Wirz Family afloat, though it was far from building security Julie and I needed for ourselves as well as for Jeff and Brad. Besides, it was a tough existence because of the hours. I was often gone from 9 o'clock in the morning until nearly midnight when the team was home for a stretch of seven to 10 days, and if I took the next trip and bounced right back into another home stand ... well, it was not great for a family.

Sure, she and the boys could come to any game and be treated respectfully, but they would arrive by themselves and sit in nice seats behind home plate by themselves or with other wives, and, at best, I might leave the press box for an inning to join them in the stands.

I realize someone less devoted to his job might not have worked quite these hours. It was not a demand like Steinbrenner often made of his staff. But daily writing of

146

press releases and media notes were necessary, and the additional tasks were unpredictable. When would one of the TV stations need help lining up an interview, when would an out-of-town columnist need background for his story, or when would some national media member call? I tried to be not only reactive but also proactive in a market such as KC, where I could encourage someone from the media to do a piece he or she had not considered.

Anyway, Julie and I had started talking about whether this could be my long-term job, no matter how much I loved it.

A troubling development had taken place with the '74 season less than half complete and the team struggling. Kauffman dismissed Tallis, who had both developed the on-field product much quicker than anyone thought possible for an expansion franchise and been popular with most of the staff and players.

Tallis was easy to like, and occasional quirkiness in managerial style was not difficult for most of us working for him to overlook. The atmosphere he had maintained was such that I doubt anyone dreaded coming to work, even when tough losses put any type of damper on things.

Burke, another veteran baseball man who had come in from Texas late in the 1973 season to run business affairs, was elevated to handle general manager duties. While he was very gentlemanly and got considerable credit when the Royals rose to the top in the years down the road, those of us who had been brought in by Tallis were not thrilled with the move. There could be little argument that Tallis and Lou Gorman had given the baseball side of the operation its foundation.

So, there were multiple reasons I wanted to plant the seed of my dilemma with Reichler, although I approached it from the standpoint of what I saw as baseball's need for someone to specialize in preparing for the game's top events, the All-Star Game and World Series, instead of leaving it entirely to the host teams.

I had seen firsthand how one team would handle the giant media entourage in one manner at Site A and another team would handle the task totally differently at Site B. The needs of the media were growing, even though it was still some time before sports radio and 24/7 coverage of the game would be what it is today. This was not the way to run things. The National Football League could prepare for the Super Bowl because the site and date were determined far in advance. Baseball's All-Star Game was that way, but not its crowning event and team sports' No. 1 annual party, the World Series.

The sport needed to provide similar accommodations from city to city and season to season, and until now they had varied a great deal.

A combination of factors made our teams prepare differently for major events. Some top management was PR-savvy and understood the impact if we went the extra mile to be certain writers had the best opportunities to see the games and to write their stories, even if there was a chill in the air late on October evenings. Others had a difficult time giving up precious seating or arranging for something as meaningful to writers as a table inside, where it was a bit warmer.

Remember, a press box that seated 50 or even 100 people during the regular season could not begin to accommodate four or five times that many during the World Series, so temporary platforms had to be constructed that would allow for a typewriter or computer and perhaps have an electrical outlet.

No team was immune from misunderstanding what was needed in the changeover from the regular season to the postseason. The Yankees and Dodgers were prime examples. Every year, baseball had to coax the Yankees to give up some quality seats that were under cover and away from rain for the media, even though any revenue lost by diminishing the number of tickets sold to the public did not by any stretch all belong to the home team. And these were Steinbrenner years, so staff members were not certain how far they could go in making the necessary changes without possibly getting the wrath of The Boss.

The Dodgers were extremely good at providing for their local media, but they were not quick to concede how much upper deck space was needed and how many portable benches had to be constructed in what was commonly known as the auxiliary press box.

Reichler was very cordial, and may have known at that time he would soon move from serving as Director of Public Relations to become more important to the commissioner as a special assistant. Joe was not a typical PR person anyway. That was not his strength. He was far superior at being able to whisper in the commissioner's ears about solutions to troubling issues, or to pick up the telephone to a major media type like Dick Young or Jerome Holtzman or Jim Murray in an effort to promote some new baseball venture or quell a problem.

Weeks went by without any major developments, although at some point, the Royals offered that I take on the added responsibility of serving as both Public Relations and Promotions Director for $2,000 of additional compensation. It was still a few years before marketing departments sprang up and created a whole new way of looking at the money-making side of the business instead of relying so heavily on giveaway days, such as Bat Day, Ball Day or Old-Timers Day, for getting more people into the stadiums.

Then word came of Reichler moving into the Special Assistant to the Commissioner role and Max Nichols, a writer from Minneapolis, replacing him as Director of Public Relations. I was not encouraged a door in the New York City offices would open to me.

Nichols' tenure lasted exactly one day. Yes, a single day, as the story was often told to me. He called Kuhn on the second morning and asked if they could talk. When the commissioner told Nichols to come to his office, Nichols supposedly said, "I can't; I am back in Minneapolis."

It would not be fair for me to speculate on the details behind the Nichols Family's change of mind in moving to the East Coast, but the job of running the Information office in the commissioner's office at 51 West 51st Street in New York City was once again open.

Kuhn's office asked the Royals for permission to talk to me, and an offer and an acceptance took place very quickly.

I convinced my wife, without great difficulty, as I recall, that we should give this job a couple of years to see if our lives were improved. I did not need any convincing, of course, because it was the best package deal. It kept my great desire to continue in baseball alive and posed an incredible opportunity for growth because it would encompass nationwide exposure.

I could not think of any downside, although in retrospect, I doubt that I fully comprehended the difference from being aligned with a team where one could savor the joy of victories and the agony of defeats. Tallis had long talked of how only half the people with the teams were happy on any given day while the others felt some level of sadness or frustration. It is certainly not as much fun to cheer for attendance figures, umpires and a seven-game World Series, as I learned came with the territory when anyone worked in the commissioner's office or a league office.

At least, the pending move allowed me to get over a disappointing season in which Kansas City slipped from the hoped-for contender position to fifth place in our six-team division, eight wins short of even playing at a .500 pace.

I was to start officially in New York on November 1, but I actually accepted the offer in early October and flew directly

150

to Los Angeles to be an "observer" during the World Series between the Dodgers and Oakland Athletics.

I probably did not need an airplane to cover these 3,000 miles, as excited as I was. And as a bonus, I believe this was the cross-country flight where sex goddess Raquel Welch was seated across the first-class cabin and only a row or two behind me.

So much had to be done over the next few weeks, not the least of which was selling our home in Independence and deciding where to live in the East. Julie did not feel New Jersey was right and Westchester County's taxes scared us, so we decided Connecticut was where we should look to buy.

My salary nearly doubled with the new job, but the ranch house we settled on in Wilton, CT, cost twice as much as our sale in Missouri. We had a little more property and a tiny stream running through it, but we had to settle for less house. It was not as new or as well laid out.

We tried to analyze the commuter train options as best we could as we looked at homes in Westport and Weston along with Wilton, and the only thing clear was that I would spend a whole lot more time on Metro North trains than I did driving to and from Royals Stadium. It boiled down to virtually two hours door to door in the morning and slightly less time coming home, although the reality was that from Monday-Friday all winter, I would leave and arrive back home in darkness. I have often joked, mostly with myself, that I did not realize until years later when my commuting days ended that there was an active life during the day in Connecticut.

I had to start the job something like two weeks before my family would be able to move, and the office put me up in the staid, older Roosevelt Hotel. It was not easy as I rode the elevators to be certain what the No. 1 language was for people in New York. Talk about a change for a boy from Nebraska!

151

My first Major League Baseball office on West 51st Street in New York City

When Julie, 8-year-old Jeff and 5-year-old Brad finally arrived, it was a few more days of living in what then was the Holiday Inn in Norwalk, CT, where we had to sneak our beloved dog Ginger onto the elevator. Julie spent her days, as I recall, watching Interstate 95 out of the hotel window with hope our moving van would show up. That seemed to take forever.

What a Year, What a World Series

It did not take long—in fact, the first game was still three months away—for me to be tipped off to the overriding issue I would face in serving in the commissioner's office for the next decade, primarily working with Kuhn, a man for whom I would have everlasting affection and with whom I would have a wonderful relationship.

On December 31, 1974, exactly two months after I started as Director of Information for Major League Baseball, Jim "Catfish" Hunter was declared a free agent and signed a historic five-year, $3 million contract with the New York Yankees.

Hunter had been a major part of the Oakland A's winning three consecutive World Series, including a four-games-to-one thumping of the Los Angeles Dodgers when I was essentially eavesdropping before starting my new job.

Hunter had claimed a breach of contract against Athletics owner Finley, and he won. The first year of salary arbitration cases also were heard before the season started.

Now, this book is about the love of the game, so it is not my intention to dwell on free agency, but it is important to remind everyone we were about to see some dramatic changes. As alarming as this would be—distasteful, to many of us—it was becoming reality and will need to be discussed from time to time in the chapters which lie ahead.

What free agency did to my daily life in the commissioner's office is somewhat challenging to explain even to this day. One must understand that while Kuhn sat at the top of the game and thereby was the target of many an arrow from fans, media and even other baseball offices, he could not always say what was on his mind because of the complexities of the labor negotiations. I often wondered how he could maintain an even keel with everything swirling around him.

The commissioner's role in labor relations matters seemed to change often, sometimes like the daily tide coming and going. My duties in this area were not overly demanding much of the time because either the baseball owners' Player Relations office or the American and National League offices were on the direct firing line of issuing statements or conducting press conferences during the major negotiating sessions between Baseball and Marvin Miller and his powerful Player's Association.

What virtually never changed was that when the commissioner was hunted by the media to do an interview or make a statement about labor matters or some other topic, it invariably came through my office. Countless trains were missed at the end of the day because Kuhn, to his everlasting credit, would reach out to every involved office (teams, the two leagues, Player Relations, and even the Players Association) to let people know where he stood on issues at hand before he would communicate with the media or allow us to line up appearances on "The Today Show" or "Good Morning America" or any number of other credible outlets.

Kuhn routinely got smacked around because of this, but he was steadfast in feeling all involved parties should be notified before he made an announcement. This held true whether it was a labor deal or one of the countless disputes with the likes of owners such as Steinbrenner, Ted Turner or Finley.

So much of that first year was learning what I had gotten myself into by taking the job. Since a new department had been created to disseminate information on behalf of all of baseball and it was pretty much under my charge, there was not a blueprint to follow.

Although the magnitude of dealing with every aspect of news in New York could be so enlarged over what I was accustomed to in Kansas City, it became apparent pretty quickly that all we needed to do in getting a news story out was to get in touch with The Associated Press and United Press International. We—my staff largely started out with two secretaries and myself, along with Monte Irvin—could not possibly reach out to the various radio and television networks and the major newspapers one by one.

I worked at both understanding the wire services, and getting to know the baseball writers and desk staffs. It would take time to meet and get to know writers at *The New York Times, New York Daily News* and *New York Post.*

My nature always had been to be proactive. To reach the most important writers and columnists around the country, I had to see to it that we developed a thorough mailing list so we could distribute information that extended beyond the immediacy of a decision by the commissioner to perhaps fine or suspend someone or introduce some new undertaking, such as balloting for the All-Star Game.

Everyone needs allies, and mine started internally with Sandy Hadden, baseball's secretary-treasurer and general counsel and Kuhn's constant business companion, and from the outside with Bob Fishel, who handled PR matters for the American League.

Both league offices were housed a few blocks away from our headquarters at 15 West 51st Street in midtown, and while the commissioner was the kingpin in the game, the leagues ran their own affairs with their teams. They could—and frequently did—have autonomy.

Pete Rozelle ran professional football. He could make a decision, and everyone had to fall in line or stand isolated. Baseball was a different animal altogether with three distinct leaders: the commissioner, and the two league presidents, who for most of my time were Lee MacPhail in the American League and Chub Feeney in the National League.

No one in baseball at any level was more respected than Fishel. He had been with the maverick Bill Veeck with the St. Louis Browns and in Cleveland, then had moved on to handle public relations for the New York Yankees. A modest man, Fishel could pretty much call up any team president, PR director and media voice in New York or across the country.

Except for the media people from the American League teams and a scattering of writers around the league—and in KC, of course—no one knew Bob Wirz. I had to learn the reality that when the commissioner had to come down on an owner or a player from a specific franchise, the media was most likely going to side with the home team.

It was only common sense Atlanta media would have more timely access to Braves owner Turner or at least to his publicity staff and to hear their side of any argument than they would to the commissioner. Ditto with decisions involving Steinbrenner with the New York Yankees or the Galbreaths in Pittsburgh or the Busch Family in St. Louis. You get the idea.

I would not go to Fishel if our offices had varying attitudes on some issue, but I could go to him—and did—for general advice. Our personalities were similar, even though as time went on, I might want to take the lead on how a World Series or All-Star Game PR operation might be run so that the media could expect similar treatment when they were covering a major event in Los Angeles or Boston.

I had good fortune in dealing with my first All-Star Game in Milwaukee, as well as my first World Series, where I had much say that fall, between Cincinnati and Boston.

Baseball had not totally centralized All-Star and World Series activities under the commissioner's leadership as yet, leaving much of the planning and grunt work to the host team.

My education in dealing with a major political figure at one of our jewel events came quickly that July of 1975 in Milwaukee. Secretary of State Henry Kissinger was to attend, and as I recall, his staff was much more determined to challenge baseball. They wanted every tiny detail of his visit covered than was the case in several subsequent instances in which the president or vice president would be paying a visit.

Kuhn had grown up being interested in politics because of his law background, and he also understood—maybe to a fault—how important politicians could be when baseball needed a favor, such as protecting the reserve-clause exemption the sport enjoyed. This changed the PR games when a politician came to a game. It became commonplace for our staff meetings leading up to one of our major events to devote more time to planning out the care and feeding of someone like Kissinger than to all of the hospitality of the two-day All-Star party and ceremonial festivities combined.

Of course, one also had to remember that one mini embarrassing slip-up involving the secretary of state's visit could bring uncounted amounts of negative press to the game. Thankfully, that never happened on our watch.

I guess I felt particularly satisfied that I was entrusted to work out quite a few of the details with the Kissinger staff.

By the way, the All-Star Game was a good one, and although the National League won it 6-3 on the strength of three ninth-inning runs, the highlight to me, which I can still visualize all these years later, was Carl Yastrzemski's dramatic pinch-hit, game-tying three-run homer into the bullpen in right-center.

The day after the All-Star Game became tense, somewhat surprisingly so, because the commissioner was up for re-election. To show just how difficult re-election was in those days, the commissioner had to get a minimum of 75 per cent of the votes from owners in each league, a herculean task no president of the United States would ever get.

157

Mind you, the commissioner was expected to keep owners in line, fining or suspending them for major infractions, but they could turn around and vote him out even when a major portion of them might very much like the way he was handling the sport's affairs.

With constant thorns like Finley (Oakland) and Steinbrenner against Kuhn keeping his job, they needed only to find two more dissenters to force the commissioner out. To the surprise of many, while the National League was supporting my boss 12-0, the American League seemed to have four no votes. That would mean only a 67 per cent majority in that league.

Walter O'Malley of the Dodgers was widely reported to hate the potential of Kuhn being ousted, and his overnight work in a Milwaukee hotel—the Pfister, I believe—brought enough sanity to bear. When the commissioner was elected to a new seven-year term the next morning to solid applause from owners, the total vote was said to be 22-2. Wouldn't most anyone like that type of favorable vote, whether for dogcatcher or commissioner?

The most enjoyable weekend of the summer—then and now—for baseball and certainly for senior staffers in the commissioner's office came a few days later when the Hall of Fame enshrined its new members at picturesque Cooperstown, NY.

The Wirz Family, like others, got to feel like royalty as we stayed at the quaint Otesaga Hotel, which is now virtually unavailable to all but those with official credentials for this three-day retreat. We would ride the elevators with the Hall of Fame members, and eat lunch alongside their families in the guests-only dining room or the ground-level outdoor setting. Kids seemed to have the run of the resort from the ping pong tables to the grounds overlooking Lake Otsego to the inviting swimming pool that was nestled near the terrace.

The veranda of the hotel, complete with a bevy of rocking chairs and overlooking the golf course and lake, was magnificent. It was very common to find newly-elected Hall of Fame members such as Ralph Kiner and Billy Herman and veterans like Bob Feller and Brooks Robinson holding court with baseball executives or the media, all the while accommodating autograph seekers since security was not nearly as extensive as is needed today.

My job, such as it was for the next decade, was to prepare remarks for the commissioner's use as he saw fit during the Hall of Fame induction ceremonies and occasionally schedule an interview for him. They were not heavy-duty chores, so I could spend time with my family and friends.

I also got to attend the coveted Sunday night dinner that was a once-a-year opportunity for the Hall of Fame members to enjoy each other's company and tell a few stories. Only a very limited number of staff members from our office, the American and National League offices, and the Hall of Fame got to be elbow-to-elbow with big-name baseball heroes. On more than one occasion, I was blessed to sit next to Roy Campanella, already paralyzed from his brutal auto accident but sharp-minded.

The new inductees who received their Hall of Fame rings on this summer night were Kiner, Herman, Earl Averill, Judy Johnson and Bucky Harris.

I cannot say that it felt this way at the time, but I got a lucky break a couple of months later when it became World Series time. Not only did it turn out to be a seven-game classic between the mighty Cincinnati Reds and the Boston Red Sox, but it stretched out three extra days due to rain in Boston.

Everyone knows that the Bosox eventually tied the Series at three wins apiece on Carlton Fisk's dramatic foul-line-leaning, 12th-inning home run in Game 6 and that Cincinnati won the championship with a ninth-inning run the next night, but only those of us intimately involved remember what happened during those three soggy days in between.

How do you keep several hundred media members involved without games at the end of an already lengthy season, as well as keep the nation from moving on to the football season?

I knew what had to be done, even if all of my colleagues, including the PR men from a number of the teams who had volunteered to help out, were weary.

It was essential—yes, ESSENTIAL—that we had a meaningful press conference every day to give the hordes of writers some fresh access to the newsmakers. While the teams could go to a nearby college to get in some exercise and perhaps indoor batting practice, there was not an opportunity for most of the media to get a fresh, exciting story.

One time (it may have even been more often), we arranged for Kuhn to update the media from a makeshift platform under the stands behind home plate at Fenway Park (one of the many concessions areas today). The more important step we had to make happen was to use a sizable hotel ballroom downtown, where the media members were staying for a daily media conference. Today's social media tidbits and teasers would have come in handy.

It was easier to get Reds Manager Sparky Anderson and some of his players to take part each day because they also were downtown; they did not have much reason not to cooperate. And if you knew Anderson, well, he was one of baseball's best ambassadors throughout his career.

The Red Sox were more difficult, as any home team would be, because their homes were scattered all around the area so they were not sequestered in one hotel. Most of them also had friends or family members in town for the World Series.

Darrell Johnson managed Boston, so we wanted him to attend every day, if possible. I will forever remember that Dwight Evans made himself available, I believe more than once. The right fielder could do no wrong in my mind because of his ultimate cooperation. It seemed fitting later on because it was his wonderful catch of a Joe Morgan drive in the top of the 11th inning of Game 6 that kept the Reds from ending the World Series, in which case the 12th-inning Fisk miracle home run never would have happened.

I believe it is fair to say the '75 World Series played an important role in re-energizing the game in the mind of the everyday sports fan. There was a fairly common thought in the late '60s and early '70s that baseball was "slow" and "boring," especially to many of the casual fans. That feeling pretty much disappeared after this spectacular World Series, which got an extra boost from Fisk's homer that ended Game 6. Noted NBC Director Harry Coyle captured Fisk's hand-waving gesture as he headed toward first base, trying to keep the ball from going foul. How many times have we all seen that replay in the last few decades?

And, in my mind, those press conferences which helped keep the Series from being forgotten during the five days between Games 5 and 6 may have added a tiny bit to the media telling us all for many years since that 1975 produced one of the best World Series ever. It engaged a new generation of baseball fans who were previously pretty passive about the sport's fun potential.

Most everyone who remembers Fisk's leadoff blast in the bottom of the 12th well past midnight knows exactly where they were, just as we remember what we were doing when we learned President John F. Kennedy had been shot.

In my case, I was just re-entering the press box after going into the press dining room a few steps behind it. That part of Fenway's overcrowded rooftop also was serving as a makeshift work room for the writers, many of whom were missing their East Coast morning deadlines.

I would like to say I saw the ball carom off the foul pole, but I could not say so with total confidence. Next came a hectic scene. Within an instant, the end of the four-hour,

161

one-minute dramatics sent everyone scrambling to write the new and astounding lead for their story and to start thinking about Game 7.

A Sad Night in Philly, Fun In Cooperstown and Free Agency

1976

Most any year for at least the next quarter-century in baseball could be summarized by whatever the labor issues of the day were, but as I promised earlier, these stories will largely be left to others who spend their life with a typewriter. That is pre-computer talk to the younger generations.

In my later years of working with Kuhn, Sandy Hadden, Johnny Johnson and other leaders in the commissioner's office, I learned to do my best at being ahead of the game—anticipating what challenges I might face and questions that would be asked by the media. However, there also were times when it was better to get caught without a hint that some major story was about to break.

It was less likely I would put my foot in my mouth and say something that would make the back page of the New York tabloids if I truly did not have the answer the media wanted when my telephone would start ringing. But it also was more awkward that way; it showed if I was out of the loop.

One major story that broke that summer came in the evening of June 15, the trade deadline in those days. The maverick Finley had sold three of Oakland's stars, Vida Blue, Joe Rudi and Rollie Fingers, for $3.5 million. It was the biggest sale in baseball history. Blue was to join the Yankees for $1.5 million, while the other two were going to Boston for a million apiece.

I shouldn't have felt too bad about being caught off guard on this one. As far as I know, the commissioner was as well.

I learned with each passing year that major stories involving the commissioner were almost predictably made at deadline time, at the end of the work day or late on Friday afternoon. Finley, Steinbrenner and other thorns to the league presidents and/or the commissioner knew all of these offices were more vulnerable at these times. They might just get away with some trickery or at least get the media involved and leave the executives holding the bag.

At any rate, the Blue, Rudi and Fingers deals signaled to Kuhn that Finley was decimating the Oakland A's. The commissioner held up approval of the sales, and scheduled a hearing for two days later.

It was a wild circus. Kuhn had supporters among some club owners and some in the media, but there were a whole lot more detractors.

By June 18, before a packed media conference, the commissioner turned the sales down "in the best interests of the game." It was one of the strongest decisions of his 15½ years in office, and there was little doubt I was working for a man loaded with integrity for the sport, which he, too, had loved since his youth.

A great amount of sadness crept into the lives of those of us in the New York baseball offices about a month later in this year in which the bicentennial of the country was being celebrated.

A tragic event occurred on the very night of the All-Star Game in Philadelphia, where Bill Giles and his Phillies staff outdid themselves with lavish entertainment of the baseball crowd, part of it within a long fungo bat drive of the Liberty Bell itself.

Baseball labor peace—at least the closest the game came to such hope in those years—was achieved the day before the All-Star Game. A four-year agreement was reached, ending months of strife which had included nearly three weeks of an ownership lockout at the start of spring training until the commissioner ordered camps to open.

164

The labor agreement resulted in one scene your humble writer had difficulty watching when Kuhn; labor boss (and arch enemy) Marvin Miller; Kuhn's No. 1 sidekick, secretary-treasurer and general counsel Hadden; and one or two others had their picture taken literally arm in arm around a table stacked with hors d'oeuvres.

Then came a terrible telephone call right after the game ended. Hadden's daughter, Betsy, had been the victim of a train accident back home in New Canaan, CT. It seemed to be known from the start that her injuries were critical. I do not believe she lasted the night.

As baseball's chief in-house counsel, Hadden was largely unknown to the public but was widely respected throughout the upper ranks in baseball. He most certainly was Bowie Kuhn's most trusted and most loyal associate. Seldom were they apart when major matters were under study.

Hadden also had been important to me in settling into this new life, someone I could go to when I needed to sort out how to handle a thorny task. He also was in charge in our little office of 25 or 30 people in those days, especially since the commissioner had to travel so much.

From a personal standpoint, it was no small matter to the Wirzes when we first came to Connecticut that Hadden was able to help clear the way for a loan so we could buy our first home in Wilton, given that the cost was so much higher than it had been in Missouri.

It is next to impossible to think back to 1976 without more labor-related stories, but once again, Hall of Fame weekend in Cooperstown brought some welcome relief from that issue.

The friendship Julie and I had with Bob Lemon never diminished no matter where he or I was working. He had been elected to the Hall of Fame in January along with another of the game's workhorse right-handers, Robin Roberts, so this was their time to be inducted.

A rainy day in upstate New York forced the ceremonies to be moved from the steps of the Hall of Fame Library to a room in the Otesaga Hotel, which could handle only 200-300 people. Others watched from the hotel's charming balcony, and many more were shut out altogether.

What made that weekend extra-special in my lasting memory was the night we closed the downstairs bar. I am not certain if it was the night before the induction or, more likely, the one following. Regardless, it was a fun setting with various baseball luminaries coming by to congratulate or share a story with Lem and Robin.

It finally boiled down to just five of us holding court with Bill Madden of the *New York Daily News* and my oldest son, Jeff, rounding out the group.

My boys got a healthy taste of baseball in their early years, such as a surprise clubhouse visit or private meetings with managers and coaches in our home. I always hoped that those special times would make up for the events we all missed out on, occasions when fathers should be on hand but could not be because of doubleheaders or road trips or spur-of-the-moment press conferences.

On this night in Cooperstown, Jeff got to stay up late, listen in as two wily pitchers told stories and probably had one too many, things not normally part of a 10-year-old's life. I had enough sense to realize this was a once-in-a-lifetime memory for Jeff and me to share. I did not usher him off to our room, and both of us treasure that evening to this day. He will one day share the details with my three grandsons—or perhaps he already has.

Cincinnati won another World Series, sweeping the Yankees, with catchers Johnny Bench of the Reds and Thurman Munson of the Yankees putting on an incredible offensive show. Bench, already acknowledged as the best the game had to offer, hit .533 (8-for-15) with two homers and six runs batted in, and Munson was at .529 (9-for-17) although all of his hits were singles and he only drove in two runs.

I point this out because of an awkward moment I witnessed in the cramped Yankee Stadium space created for post-game media conferences. Reds Manager Anderson was at the microphone and had been asked to compare the catchers. While I do not believe anyone could interpret his comments as intending to discredit Munson, Anderson made it clear he did not feel the Yankee backstop came close to matching up with the skills of his future Hall of Fame player in this World Series.

What made it awkward was that Munson had just entered the room, and was out of Anderson's view as he awaited a turn at the podium. I was not alone in just wanting the moment to pass quickly.

More baseball history was only two weeks away in the form of the very first free agent draft of those players who had gone through the season playing with a contract automatically renewed by their team.

Management dreaded a day like this, but, like it or not, it was our job in the Information Department to be prepared to distribute the results. Baseball had chosen the Plaza Hotel in New York City as the site —a move that backfired when some writers chose to point out the oddity of using the opulent Plaza, with its sparkling chandeliers and other suggestions of wealth, at a time when many owners were still dragging their feet to accept this free agency system that was certain to make payrolls escalate.

There was a part of me that relished a day like this, not because of what it represented for the sport but because it was an opportunity to excel at PR ambition and ingenuity. Baseball did not have a great reputation at exceeding the media's expectations in either the basic physical setup provided for anyone covering an event or the background information that was provided.

167

This was like a serving of red meat, as far as I was concerned.

I might falter or fail on occasion, but it would likely be from trying to over-deliver. I have steadily believed in my own intuition. In some ways, I even feel some of my confidence that we could deliver beyond the media's expectations could almost be traced back to my pre- and early-teen days in my upstairs bedroom, where I would amuse and satisfy myself by constructing rudimentary scoreboards that would provide more information than a friend might consider possible from the bits and pieces I could pick up from various radio broadcasts.

These were pre-computer days for us when the free agent draft started, so we had some of the secretaries from the office on hand to type the results as each team made selections, in reverse order of their 1976 regular season finish, of those they wanted to negotiate with for the future. There were only 24 players in the pool, but each could be selected up to 13 times.

We provided the basic information, such as Round 1, Montreal selected Reggie Jackson, and before the day was out, we supplemented that by listing the 13 teams that obtained rights to negotiate with Jackson, the round when each selection was made, a list of all of Montreal's choices, etc., etc.

We kept the Plaza's copy machines humming for several hours with these lists on the free agents, who included such major names as Jackson, Fingers, Willie McCovey, Don Baylor, and Sal Bando.

Dealing With the Yankees
And Searching for Lindbergh's
Grave

1977

Baseball enjoyed a pretty decent ride this year, with record attendance (nearly 39 million); mostly victories in the courts against the likes of Finley; and Jackson's record Game 6 of the World Series, when he swatted three home runs.

Somehow, details of some of these events have been overtaken in my mind in favor of three events that hit closer to home for me.

The All-Star Game was played at Yankee Stadium, and even though the mid-summer classic truly pitted American and National League stars against one another for league supremacy, much more than happens these days, there was a side issue for this July event.

It was the hottest day of the entire year in New York, the thermometer hitting an official 95, but sticky enough that it seemed several degrees higher. My family had taken the train in from our Wilton, CT, home since I was staying at a midtown hotel and they could enjoy the All-Star Game, even though they would be in the stands and I would be at my usual post in the press box. It was pretty standard that I would work next to the host club publicity director, in this case, the Yankees' Mickey Morabito, and near my counterparts, Fishel of the American League and Blake Cullen of the National League.

We always had to have multiple telephones available to handle any sudden developments, and a phone or intercom to the public address announcer. We also tried to have our seats close to the three official scorers and the wire services.

169

Everything was going pretty well, as I recall, until I received an urgent call in about the seventh or eighth inning from my wife. Some lout in the row behind them in their nice seats above the walkway and behind home plate, no doubt more interested in drinking beer than seeing the best players in the game, had left his lunch all over people around him.

Julie decided she would get 11-year-old Jeff and 8-year-old Brad out of there. They had ridden one of the official buses from midtown, and were told exactly where to meet the bus for the return trip shortly after the game ended.

The game was not yet over, of course, so the buses were not at their appointed locations, not too distant from one of the main Yankee Stadium exits. But plenty of people were milling around outside of the stadium. The biggest problem for Julie and the boys was that they could not get back into the stadium.

After many anxious minutes that probably seemed much longer, they were able to get someone to allow them back into the ground-level office entrance and to help her reach the press box, where I could be summoned. Remember, cell phones were still years away.

She was neither relaxed nor calm by the time I got on the line, and, frankly, it was not the best of times for me, either, because we always were busier as the game was drawing to its conclusion and there were matters to be handled immediately. There was the collecting of Most Valuable Player ballots, assigning club PR representatives to postgame interviews on the field and in the interview room, and being timely in coordinating notes and statistics from the game as well as from the interview room and both clubhouses.

I seek no sympathy, but each of these details was crucial for those of us coordinating activities if we were to keep baseball from any follow-up black eyes from the nation's media because of tardy or shoddy performances on our part.

Everyone in the Wirz Family survived, but it did not leave a great taste for the last

All-Star Game that I believe my family attended together.

The biggest challenge in preparing for an All-Star Game or World Series at Yankee Stadium in those days—we had both this particular year—was working with stadium management. The regular press box almost never was able to accommodate the media regardless of where these events were being played.

But at Yankee Stadium, whether by design since Steinbrenner and the commissioner often were at odds, or by the nature of the people assigned to oversee seating, it was often a hassle we would handle well in advance.

I did not have a great deal of direct authority, and official instructions given to the teams were more general than specific. I always tried to approach the task of reviewing plans with each team's PR department on a professional basis. But we needed to be consistent from venue to venue.

We needed sufficient seating for 400 or so working media members, and it was not ideal to put them in the upper deck in right field. We also needed a work table, plus outlets for power and telephone installation. The tables were not always easy because not only was construction needed, but it also often was the case that the table overlapped the row in front, which meant losing more seats that could be sold. Television monitors visible to most of the writers also were preferable.

We usually would end up with the auxiliary press seating at Yankee Stadium being in the lower deck to the right of home plate, although it took a considerable amount of debate, multiple meetings and the gnashing of teeth to get this accomplished.

The challenges were greater in some of the older ballparks like Tiger Stadium and Comiskey Park, although as a norm, the people we worked with there were more cordial.

No one can ever say the media does not know how to pick a fight. It was during the sixth—and final—game of the '77 World Series between the rival Dodgers and Yankees and in the Media Capital of the World (New York) when I was approached in the Yankee Stadium press box by none other than *Sports Illustrated,* which wanted reporter Melissa Ludtke to be allowed into the clubhouses at the end of the game.

SI wasn't about to make this request during a spring training game in March with only a few reporters on hand. There would have been no headline in that, so like a sleeping cat awaiting the mouse, the magazine released its claws.

While female reporters in the clubhouse has become pretty commonplace in baseball and other sports for years now, this was 1977 and those areas had always been considered the dressing quarters for players and coaches. Baseball was not opposed to female members of the media, although there were very few of them around with any regularity, but felt privacy for players to shower and dress was necessary. We were willing to bring the players outside of the clubhouse to be interviewed.

As I recall, the Baseball Writers' Association of America, a strong organization in our sport with considerable clout, let us twist in the wind.

This threw a cloud over the day for the commissioner and for me on the immediate firing line, in some ways taking away from the Yankees' right to celebrate another World Series title.

We denied access on this night, although *SI's* parent, Time, Inc., filed suit against baseball a couple of months later. It took several more years before this issue went away completely, and accredited female reporters became regular clubhouse visitors.

That fall, it was back to Honolulu for the Winter Meetings, with the Sheraton Waikiki our base for a second time. Everyone who had been there knew we could look forward to that refreshing breeze billowing through the hallway leading outside and to all that Hawaii has to offer.

I will never forget one day when the meetings were over, and Julie and I headed to a few days at a remote resort in Maui, where my travel agent brother-in-law Harry Jefferies and my sister Bev had both recommended we stay and set up some ocean-view amenities we likely would not have gotten on our own.

Julie had read some of Anne Morrow Lindbergh's books about the oasis she and husband Charles had found and the gravesite overlooking the Pacific that was to be his final resting place. We headed out in our rental car, not knowing what was ahead except that it was next to impossible to drive all the way around the island in those days.

We were alone in that most of the baseball people who had migrated to Maui after the Winter Meetings were in the more heavily populated beach towns. We were advised we should leave quite early in the morning, and probably have the resort pack a lunch for us. We did not try to leave at 4 a.m. or whatever it would have required for sunrise at the volcano, but the ocean views on the road to Hana were breathtaking, to be sure. We looked and looked, sometimes asking natives for guidance, to find the little old church and nearby cemetery where Lindbergh's understated grave was located.

Finally, after parking and walking along what passed for a driveway, we found what is known as Palapala Church, which was founded in 1864. The tropical vegetation was all but gone and the landscape barren and dry, but the view of the ocean well below was exceptionally picturesque. Despite its beauty and serenity, it is difficult for this writer to comprehend why one of our heroes would not be in a resting place where the pathway could have been attended to a whole lot better.

Once we had found the Lindbergh site, the Sacred Seven Falls, one of Maui's treasures, was beyond our reach, but we headed in that direction a little longer, only to have a car coming back stop and the driver jump out and head our way.

It was our friend Jim Ferguson of the Cincinnati Reds and his wife Joanne, so many miles from where each of us had started out that morning, let alone from our respective homes in Ohio and Connecticut. Instead of an emergency, Jim had some wisecrack, almost certainly about the trade he and I had missed being on hand for five years earlier between the Big Red Machine and the Royals.

I have no idea how many of the 617 curves in the highway and the 54 one-lane bridges on the road to Hana and beyond we covered, but it was one special day putting the All-Star fiasco and dealing with *SI* in the rearview mirror.

174

From a Catchy Slogan to a Free Ride With the Yankees

1978

Baseball never has a quiet year, and this one was typical, with umpires staging a one-day, in-season strike; the commissioner warning of economic disaster as player salaries continued to jump; more headlines because Finley was once again trying to sell the Oakland A's to people the sport did not exactly embrace; more than the normal number of managerial firings; and constant Yankees headlines, including a major spat between Manager Billy Martin and star outfielder Reggie Jackson.

One has to admire ingenuity, and I witnessed it twice up close and personal during the year.

Tom Villante, a recognized advertising executive who also had important experience putting baseball broadcasting packages together, especially for the Dodgers, had been hired by the commissioner as our new Executive Director of Marketing and Broadcasting.

Villante popped into my office one morning with the proud announcement that he was creating a new slogan for our sport. I believe his term was "Ball Fever—Catch It". I liked the concept immediately, but just as quickly, I told him it needed editing to "Baseball Fever—Catch It".

He went with my altered suggestion, and the phrase became widely used in short order. Our television promo spots utilized it, and teams started adapting their own versions such as "Phillies Fever—Catch It" or "Cardinals Fever—Catch It". The media often used it in some manner; youth baseball teams adopted it for their leagues; and to this day, I have to believe it played a significant role in the revitalization of the sport, along with the ricochet benefits from that magnificent 1975 World Series.

Regular season major league attendance topped 40 million for the first time with the third consecutive record count, which I would work into as many of our normal press releases as possible.

The other show of unusual ingenuity took place at this year's All-Star festivities in San Diego.

Up until now, the day before the All-Star Game was always known simply as workout day, when the two teams, usually for only an hour apiece, would get familiar with the speed of grounders coming off the grass and the deep spots in the outfield so as to make great catches without plowing into the fence and getting hurt. Many players would just as soon skip their team's workout, which meant they also avoided the media during these most accessible hours of the day.

The Padres came up with a wrinkle, which had to have many thinking "That was so simple; why didn't we think of it?" They got permission to open up the stadium so fans, especially those who could not get tickets to the game the next night, could see the all-stars. I've always heard the idea as being credited to Elton Schiller, the team's vice president and business manager and an acquaintance going back many years when he worked for the Dodgers and I was with Denver.

What an instant success, with about 33,000 fans taking advantage of the opportunity! The All-Star break has never been the same, with "workout day" eventually turning into the annual Home Run Derby, staged on the night before the game with expensive tickets, a sellout crowd and a nationally televised event. That innovative undertaking in San Diego also eventually led to All-Star Fanfest, which draws thousands of people for a five-day run in the host city, and the Futures Game on Sunday, when baseball parades the best young players in the game and often also includes a third capacity crowd.

I believe my major contribution to that '78 All-Star Game, aside from my usual coordination of media activities with the host team, was getting the game's most valuable player, Steve Garvey, and his stunning wife Cyndy together for the trophy presentation before television coverage ended.

The Garveys were widely recognized as an all-American couple in those days, at least a poor man's Elizabeth Taylor and Richard Burton. Steve was a classy man starring at first base for the Los Angeles Dodgers, who were to play in three World Series in a five-year span ('77-'81), and Cyndy was his photogenic wife. They typified Hollywood glamour.

I had noticed that Cyndy had been in a broadcast booth next to the main press box during the late innings. She could not be missed, with her blond hair and striking white outfit.

The postgame interview and photos of the MVP usually amounted to the player receiving the trophy from the commissioner and possibly being interviewed by one of the talking heads doing the telecast, then being photographed by himself.

Why not do something a little different since the opportunity was there for the taking by getting Cyndy down to field level so she could be in those postgame photos? I don't remember precisely how we alerted Cyndy and got her to the right location, but it could not have worked out any better.

The photo of Steve and Cyndy—and the commissioner's trophy—was everywhere in the next day's newspapers. I was pleased.

The postscript to this story is that the Garveys divorced five years later. Steve considered a run for national political office from California after his playing days, before settling into a fine business career. Cyndy went into television, including co-hosting shows in Los Angeles and New York with the likes of Bryant Gumbel and Regis Philbin.

Baseball's most celebrated moment of the entire year was the one-game playoff between the Yankees and Red Sox at Fenway Park to determine which of these fabled franchises would win the American League's Eastern Division title and move on little more than 24 hours later to take on Western Division champion Kansas City in the League Championship Series.

I had to get to Kansas City to be ready in the event the Royals advanced to the World Series for the first time so that all of the advance planning for the media would be in place. But first, I was on call to accompany the commissioner to Boston for the afternoon playoff game. It was not exactly an unpleasant experience, especially since our office was not facing any major issues at that precise time.

I watched most of the game with Kuhn from one of the press-level boxes high atop Fenway, which allowed a very nice view of such memorable plays as when old friend Piniella battled the early-autumn sun for a staggering catch in right field to save the day for the Yankees and set the stage for Bucky Dent's dramatic, three-run, division-clinching home run — still one of the most unforgettable round-trippers in the game's storied history.

I faced a dilemma on how to get from Boston to Kansas City in a reasonable manner, a problem solved when the Yankees offered me a seat on their charter flight. While reluctant to accept since they would be in such a celebratory state, it was easily the best of my options.

I told Bill Kane, the traveling secretary, and publicist Mickey Morabito to put me in a back-row seat where I could be virtually anonymous. Not too many of the players knew me anyway, but I did not want anyone noticing this thankful passenger.

Everything was going according to plan for what I estimate to be the first half of the flight. Then I was summoned up front because Lem had learned I was aboard.

It was a strange setting because Tallis, who had given me my opportunity in Kansas City, was by this time the Yankees' general manager. Lem, fired only weeks earlier by Chicago White Sox Owner Veeck, had become manager in late July when a tearful Billy Martin resigned, with New York still barely in the divisional race after once trailing Boston by an unreal 14½ games.

With his low-key approach, Lem had guided the Yankees back into the race, including an early-September four-game sweep at Fenway, when the New Yorkers annihilated the Bosox by a 42-9 total score.

Anyway, I got to Lem's first-class seat and he insisted I join him. I do not believe I ever knew who I displaced. If ever there was what I would call an awkward thrill, this was it. Here I was on this historic night sitting with the manager of the New York Yankees. Those who did not know me—and probably others who were not exactly fond of Kuhn—must have watched in more disbelief than my own.

How totally ironic. The Royals' former PR director sitting with the former Kansas City manager as the Yankees headed out to give the Royals their third in back-to-back spankings to advance to one more World Series and prevent the KC hopefuls from reaching their first.

Lem, who by the time I slithered down into the aisle seat next to him had taken in more than a little iced tea (wink, wink), insisted I stay for the remainder of the flight. How could I ever forget that trip?

179

President Carter's Visit Changed World Series Plans...at the Last Minute

1979

I sometimes find that events blend together, especially when trying to recall them from more than 30 years ago. When was the commissioner at odds with this owner or how did a certain pennant race unfold? The All-Star Game and World Series are much easier to look back on when you are working in the commissioner's office.

I remember the spring of 1979 for a separate reason. Except for a little work with 8-year-olds, it was the first time I stepped up to attempt managing my boys' baseball teams. Jeff had turned 13 in April, so he was now advancing to full-sized baseball diamonds. I had to give it a try, even though every weeknight game was going to be a challenge because of the need of getting out of our midtown office and onto a Metro North train at Grand Central Station no later than 4 o'clock. Business decisions often came down late in the afternoon.

But with an understanding boss, the devoted father of four himself, and capable assistants, I wanted to try. I did not know many of the other 13-, 14- and 15-year-olds, but Jack Matera, who has been a dear friend ever since, generously helped me when Wilton Little League held its draft of players.

I felt a little like superman in that I would put a change of clothes in my little Saab (train) station car, and often had to change from a suit into something more baseball-like while trying to make every light between Norwalk and Wilton in order to arrive before the first pitch. As long as I had another father or two as backups in case I was late, I could give it a go.

I had not been active on a baseball diamond other than in various media roles since shortly after high school, so this was very enjoyable duty. I never viewed myself as much of an instructor on such things as pitching grips and batting stances, but I also knew I would have a leg up on most of the other father-managers because of the thousands of lineups and game-day situations I had put myself in for all these years since I started following the game.

Jeff—and later Brad—knew this was something their dad could do when he was a dismal failure at helping build the fastest go kart in Boy Scouts, constructing the best tent for weekend campouts, or erecting a sturdy hideaway in the trees on the hill behind our home. I swallow any pride when I say this, but their mother was so much better with many of these endeavors.

The point is coaching little league teams was something I could do, and I would like to think the boys have memories of these days that come close to matching mine, even without the championships we managed at a rate better than what anyone probably deserved.

Back in the majors, Dave Parker's bat and brilliant arm from right field dominated that summer's All-Star Game in Seattle, although two other events seem to have stuck with me more.

One of the major worries for our office for both the All-Star Game and World Series was the weather because of the way it could turn joy into anxiety since rescheduling impacted not only the fans but also several hundred players, management and media members. With Seattle playing in the Kingdome, we anticipated no such concerns. But think again.

Seattle was hit with a heat wave the likes of which the Northwest seldom sees, and all of a sudden, we were holding the all-too-familiar contingency meetings in case of a blackout. It never happened, although we had been put on notice and tried to stay ready.

All-Star hosts in those days tried to outdo one another with a unique party for a couple of thousand people or more on the night prior to the game. The gala had been at the San Diego Zoo the previous year, and this time it was to take place on an island a ferry boat away from downtown Seattle.

One of the joys of any baseball gathering for those not directly involved in the games or high-level meetings is the opportunity to see friends. After all, the baseball industry— football and basketball professionals and even travel agents would feel the same way—is comparatively small. The few hundred established media members know one another, and in PR, we knew all of our counterparts because of meetings and games.

I had been busy with something and had to settle for one of the later ferries taking everyone to a lavish salmon fest and a beverage or two, followed by a great fireworks spectacular, that would have everyone looking back toward the beautiful city of Seattle.

And who did I find on the same boat? The Brett Brothers, known for having a good time. I did not run into George Brett very often after I left Kansas City, so seeing him in a relaxed state was fun. I believe that may have been the first time I met Bobby Brett, who turned out to be the business leader when the brothers started buying minor league teams in baseball and other sports, and as friendly as George. Ken Brett, a quality major league pitcher for many years, may have been on the junket, too, but I cannot remember for certain.

It was only a couple of weeks after this joyful break in the season when tragedy struck in baseball. Thurman Munson had perished in a small-plane crash.

He was one of the game's most identifiable personalities, and stood out among catchers because of his all-around ability, which included solid defense, a .292 career batting average that was still climbing, and leadership skills. This was only heightened by the fact he was captain of the Yankees, who were riding high after back-to-back World Series titles in '77 and '78 following a 15-year drought. The Steinbrenner steamroller was getting into full gear.

I had just walked into the commissioner's outer office late that afternoon of August 2 when his longtime secretary, Mary Sotos, handed me the telephone to talk to Steinbrenner. Kuhn and the Yankees owner often were at odds, but on this occasion, Steinbrenner was calling to inform the commissioner of the shocking news about Munson's death. The commissioner had departed for some event at Shea Stadium.

So, I heard about the airplane crash direct from Steinbrenner, and promised to get the news to the commissioner right away. We were able to track him down.

Steinbrenner definitely had a softer side to him that did not always surface. The next few days with Munson's funeral and the Yankees' next home game were going to be very challenging.

The World Series that October was a good one for the game, with Pittsburgh outlasting hometown Baltimore in Game 7 at old Memorial Stadium as future Hall of Famer Willie Stargell provided the biggest blows for the Pirates.

My recollections center around the first and last games for very different reasons. Game 1 was postponed for a day when moisture, some of it white flakes not expected until much later in the fall, hit. It was the first time a Game 1 had ever been postponed.

Anyone who knows the game realizes how much we can get caught up in statistics and details. There is such a thing as overkill, but at the same time people—often the media—want to know such things as: Has snow ever delayed a World Series? What is the lowest temperature when a World Series game has been called off? You name it, someone would be certain to ask, and I wanted to be able to give an accurate answer. I was as interested in details as anyone else would be.

I am almost certain, even though more than 30 years have passed now, that postponement was the trigger to jump in and start developing a World Series Fact Book. Why should we have to dig for information instead of already knowing it?

I got my staff involved shortly after the World Series ended to create both World Series and All-Star Game Fact Books, which, in those days, were put into three-ring binders. Not very sophisticated today, but they worked until computers made it so much easier. We culled facts from everywhere we could find them.

Want to know the total gate receipts for the 1912 World Series? What about the top 10 batting averages by individuals? (Babe Ruth was tops at the time by going 10-for-16, .625 in 1928.) Did a commissioner ever miss games? Why? What were the most controversial plays or the most significant injuries, or who threw out the ceremonial pitch to start a game? We had the answers in those thick, three-ring binders, along with an index that was almost as detailed.

I felt we had made another decent contribution to the game when this project was finished.

The World Series Fact Book would have been of major assistance for Game 7, as well, when President Jimmy Carter decided it was a good time, almost spur of the moment, to helicopter from Washington to Baltimore.

We knew once the fact book was done that it was the 11th time the president of the United States had been to a World Series and that he was the sixth president to do so, but I doubt we knew it when Carter's visit became known. Baseball officials may not have scrambled for information like we did back when Calvin Coolidge was the only other president to attend a Game 7, in Washington, no less, in 1924.

But scramble we did. Ever since the World Series started playing night games (in 1971), there has been more need to help the baseball writers since the newspaper deadlines can come and go before a game ends.

And when a president or even a vice president is attending an event, the security issues become more pronounced. The dignitary often likes to visit one or both clubhouses, which means they are on virtual lockdown to anyone else. A media pool of three or four people might be possible; then the pool shares quotes with everyone else.

We were given assurances via White House channels that with this being the final game of the World Series, the president would forgo visiting the teams. Guess what? That decision held up until the eighth inning when we got word Carter would indeed like to go see the players. Chaos would certainly follow from the media ranks, which would not exactly put either the president or baseball on a pedestal.

I worked the phones feverishly with the commissioner and our security department while trying to prepare for a media pool if it had to come to this. Baltimore's highly respected PR man, Bob Brown, did the same from his end. We were assured the decision had been reversed, but in the top of the ninth inning, we were confronted with the same circumstance all over again.

Who knows for sure what was happening? Who was actually calling the shots, and was Carter actually made aware of the extra challenges created if he went to the clubhouses? All the while, Pittsburgh was clinging to a 2-1 lead. The top of the ninth was lengthy because of pitching changes and a rally by the Pirates which resulted in two more runs. The mood was not improving for the Orioles.

Baltimore went quietly in 1-2-3 fashion in the bottom of the ninth, so at least we were not dealing with a deliriously happy stadium full of home fans.

The president did go to the clubhouses—both of them, if memory serves me correctly. We had a pool of reporters to cover the scene on behalf of the entire press corps. While deadlines were no doubt missed, at least, with quotes from the winning and losing teams and details of Carter's chats with those in uniform, everything was not lost.

Such is life behind the scenes with the ABC-TV audience most likely unaware of any of our anxiety. In fact, the game drew the third-best television rating of all time for a Game 7, a whopping 36.9, trailing only the wrap-up of that magnificent '75 World Series between the Reds and Red Sox and the '82 skirmish in which St. Louis outlasted Milwaukee. Yes, I cheated. The World Series Fact Book gave me these details. Baseball would love to get a decent fraction of that television rating today.

Philly-KC World Series
Overshadowed Howard Cosell

1980

As is true in other sports and in the entertainment world, personalities are so much of what makes baseball attractive to fans. We love the personalities who fit into society in common ways, the people we like so much that we would be happy to have them as a son or daughter or as the next-door neighbor.

Every segment of the sports and entertainment world also has its jerks. We usually know who they are, and we do whatever it takes to try getting along with them, often using so much more energy than we would like to use if only to avoid ugly situations.

Thankfully, most of those with whom I had regular contact fit into the decent—or better—category.

When the first African-American umpire to work in the major leagues gave up calling balls and strikes, he became associated with the commissioner's office and he was essentially assigned to me.

This was a delight because it meant I got to know and enjoy being around Emmett Ashford. The only awkward part was that Ashford lived in California and he did not really have specific duties. He was available when we needed someone to stand in for the commissioner at a banquet or a funeral or a minor league event. Ashford would have liked to have done more than what we were asking.

In today's world, where Major League Baseball seems to have a surplus of funds, we could have had Ashford appearing at every significant youth event across the country because he was an entertainer by nature. I think field managers of the '60s and '70s would have been in favor of this personable man telling stories and doing some light baseball clinics instead of working behind home plate or on the bases because many of them did not look at Ashford as the most skilled of umpires.

He could put on a show with the best of them from the time he made his debut in the American League in 1966, and his 5-foot-7 height and stocky frame made him a perfect foil.

I had had a few years of involvement with Ashford when on March 1, 1980, we got the sad news his life ended because of a heart attack. He was only 65.

One other decision was made regarding Ashford, with the complete agreement of his wife, Evelyn. His final resting place would be in a cemetery overlooking Lake Otsego in Cooperstown, NY. I doubt it was a mile from the Hall of Fame.

The thought was that Ashford's grave could be the first in this location, with other baseball personalities eventually being laid to rest in the same area. We had known of Hall of Fame members, as difficult to imagine as it might seem, who did not have an ideal burial site.

It was an excellent idea, although I do not believe others have been buried there more than 30 years later.

The two League Championship Series this October were events for the ages. They were best-of-five series in those days, and Philadelphia and Houston needed at least one extra inning in the last four of their five games before the Phillies advanced to their first World Series in 30 years.

I was in Houston where the last three games were played because the Astros had never been in a World Series, and a great deal of preparation was needed to be certain the Astrodome was ready for the influx of media. I had never heard a crowd so loud, and perhaps never did again although the Metrodome in Minnesota gave it a run.

Game 3 on a Friday afternoon was masterful. Neither team was able to score, as Philadelphia's Larry Christenson and Joe Niekro of Houston played the primary mound architects, until the Astros pushed across a run in the bottom of the 11th inning when future Hall of Fame second baseman Joe Morgan got things started with a triple. One can only imagine the volume level because this got Houston within one victory of its first World Series, which would not happen for another quarter-century.

Little could I have imagined that my day was just getting started.

Kuhn said, "When you are finished with your work, come by the (hotel) suite." He had invited Don Drysdale and Howard Cosell, who were working the Phillies-Astros series for ABC-TV, to join he and Luisa to watch Game 3 at Yankee Stadium, where Kansas City had taken a 2-0 series lead on the Yankees, to whom the Royals had lost in playoffs in three of the four previous American League Championship Series. "We will order some dinner in the room," the commissioner said.

If Ashford was a celebrity—and he was—he was dwarfed, both literally and figuratively, by Drysdale, Cosell and Kuhn. Cosell was the "midget" at perhaps 6-2 or 6-3.

Sandy Koufax and Drysdale were among the best 1-2 starters baseball had ever known during their heyday with the Los Angeles Dodgers. Koufax's curve could buckle any hitter's knees, and Drysdale had the power and the willingness to be mean on the mound.

Cosell and Kuhn were in the process of becoming good personal friends after a frightful honeymoon when the bombastic announcer was forced on baseball by ABC Sports boss Roone Arledge. Cosell was loud and opinionated and initially left little doubt he thought baseball was eons behind football. He also was the loudest of a mouthy crowd that covered boxing, which still had a grip on a nice chunk of the nation's sports fans.

Cosell, Drysdale and Kuhn also liked vodka, and with their big frames seemingly could handle it. I knew Bowie for more than three decades and knew him well for much of that time, and I never once felt he was even remotely under the influence of a martini.

It must have been the fourth or fifth inning by the time I got to the suite, and the Royals and Yankees were far from deciding that game, let alone the series if New York won, as it almost always had done against my former team.

If only the country could have seen what I walked into that evening in Houston. Cosell was as big a sports personality as anyone in those days. But he had already enjoyed too much of his favorite nighttime beverage. Words were not coming out as smoothly as we were used to hearing from this giant of a man.

Not too much time had elapsed after my arrival when Drysdale said something approximating this to Cosell: "Come on, coach, I think it is time to get you to your room."

That ended their evening with us, and Kuhn, Luisa and I sat back down to watch George Brett hit a Goose Gossage delivery into the third deck in right field at Yankee Stadium for the last three runs of the Royals' 4-2 triumph, which gave them a sweep of the series.

What a historic day for this still starry eyed Midwesterner—a wonderful pitching duel in the afternoon; a one-evening demise of Howard Cosell; and my former employers, the Royals, headed to their first World Series, with so many of those I worked with like Frank White, Amos Otis, Hal McRae, Paul Splittorff and Dennis Leonard in prominent roles.

While I had to remain as neutral as possible, the World Series between the Phillies and Royals was still ahead. Philadelphia was making history itself because this was only the third time in nearly a century after the Phillies joined the National League (in 1883) that they had gotten this far, and their other two World Series had ended in defeat.

I'm confident that was overshadowed to me since the Royals, born in '69, were in their first World Series.

Mom and dad were able to come to Kansas City for Games 3, 4 and 5, and we arranged for Jeff, now 14, to be there because he had his grandparents to sit with during games when I was at my busiest.

My biggest memory, other than that Philadelphia won in six games, was George Brett's totally unexpected battle with hemorrhoids. He made it through most of the second game, even going 2-for-2 with a walk, before he had to come out. It was far from certain whether the Royals' star would be able to play two days later when Royals Stadium hosted its first World Series game.

Hemorrhoids could not be overlooked by the media when it was a star player who was suffering on baseball's greatest stage. Brett being Brett, one of the game's greatest clutch hitters, not only was in the lineup for Game 3, but he homered in his first time at bat.

What I remember most, however, came later when Brett had to slide into third base. There was a collective "ugh" in the press box. None of us could imagine how it must have felt. Somehow, Brett hit .375 (9-for-24) in the six games, but two wins from another future Hall of Fame member, Steve Carlton, and unbelievable bullpen work by Tug McGraw carried the Phillies to their first World Championship.

From the White House
To a Precedent-Setting Strike
To South Korea

1981

The ups and downs of a year often leave my head spinning if I stop long enough to dwell on the events going on around me. This was to be a classic few months, in and out of baseball, to drive the point home.

How could it be any better than to be at the White House with the President of the United States and the largest gathering of Hall of Fame members ever up to this time?

President Ronald Reagan, the old baseball announcer-turned-actor-turned politician, invited all 49 living members of the Hall of Fame to dine and talk baseball on a late March day. Thirty-two of the baseball elite showed up, including Roy Campanella and Red Ruffing in their wheelchairs, plus Stan Musial, Joe DiMaggio, Willie Mays and Duke Snider.

I was blessed to be one of the few baseball people without a bust hanging in Cooperstown to be included, and to get my picture taken with the President. I hate the way I look in the photo of the two of us because Reagan was tall and handsome and I was in a three-piece brown suit, had ugly sideburns and looked like I needed a haircut. At least, it was proof I had hair at one time and actually met the President, which was reason enough to keep that photo on my website for a long time to come.

Reagan took great delight in talking about his years as a Chicago Cubs broadcaster, including the re-creation of games, and his role of portraying pitcher Grover Cleveland Alexander in the movie of his life.

"I've always been proud I played Old Alex," Tom Boswell's story in *The Washington Post* said. "Bob Lemon, who's here, can tell you about that. He was my double."

I was very familiar with Lem's involvement in Reagan's training, which also included trying to teach him how to look like a pitcher. Doris Day, a big baseball fan, also was in the movie. Lem had told me earlier, "She threw much more like a pitcher than Reagan."

My assigned seat that day had me at a side table, but there could not have been 100 people in the State Dining Room. Seated to my immediate right was James Brady.

The opportunity to swap some dialogue with the press secretary seemed priceless, especially since I always felt we lived in a fish bowl at the commissioner's office, even if it was a fish bowl a fraction of the size the leader of the free world lived in.

This event took place on March 27. Imagine my shock three days later when the President was shot as he left the Washington Hilton Hotel in downtown Washington, DC, and while Reagan was not believed at the time to be seriously wounded, Brady became a major casualty. The world knows Brady never was close to being the same vibrant person he had been prior to John Hinckley Jr.'s attempted assassination. The severe head wound left the 40-year-old Brady with slurred speech and partial paralysis, although he recovered enough that he and his wife, Sarah, became major campaigners against gun violence. The White House Press Briefing Room was renamed years later for Brady.

While the event I attended at the White House could not have been better for baseball, which was still enjoying what seemed like an all-time high in fan interest, the continued labor strife wore everyone down.

The first midseason player strike in the history of professional sports hit June 12 and lasted until August 10.

Baseball had to accept a split season, which meant a team with the best overall record could be left out of the playoffs.

That actually happened to both Cincinnati, which had the best overall record (66-42), and St. Louis, tops in the National League East, on the sidelines when postseason play started.

Many a relationship was strained. I will never forget late that year running into St. Louis Manager Whitey Herzog. Julie and I had been guests on multiple occasions at parties in his home in Independence, MO, where he and wife Mary Lou were terrific hosts. But Herzog brushed past me one day after the '81 season with a scowl, which seemed to indicate anyone working for the commissioner of baseball was not his friend.

Baseball had many memorable moments that season, both before and after the strike, and one effort at starting to heal the deep wounds of so many was to reschedule the All-Star Game in Cleveland for the day before the season resumed.

Comedian Bob Hope, who once owned a piece of the Indians, delivered some of his best lines at an All-Star luncheon. During the game itself, Mike Schmidt struck a game-winning two-run home run for the National League, Gary Carter blasted two round-trippers for the winners, and a record 72,086 fans turned out at Municipal Stadium.

I got an extra treat that year by accompanying Bowie and Luisa Kuhn on a trip to South Korea. Technically, I was a guest of the Korean Amateur Baseball Federation, which was hosting the International Association of Amateur Baseball Congress and the 10-team World Baseball Championship Series. My participation was intended to get a better understanding of the workings of amateur baseball worldwide, so that I might advise the United States Baseball Federation (it goes by USA Baseball these days) on certain PR undertakings as our sport bid to become a full-fledged member of the Olympic Games.

I had not traveled outside of the country except for a few baseball events in Canada, so I had so very much to learn about protocol and the handling of multiple languages.

What a whirlwind of learning for about a week, including how to enjoy first-class recliner travel overnight from New York to South Korea, with a brief stop in Alaska, where I saw very little outside of the giant polar bear in the Anchorage airport because of the lack of daylight. I also learned how to like garlic at most every meal, how to dress and act when we took a day trip to the demilitarized zone separating the two Koreas (Luisa was warned to dress extremely conservatively), and how Seoul had both upscale and poverty-stricken areas.

It is satisfying to remember all these years later that the professional Korean Baseball Organization (KBO), which was in its first year, and all of the amateur people were extraordinarily gracious to be around. I also well remember how excited the Italian baseball people were when they pulled an upset on the first day of the World Championships. Flag-waving and dancing on the dugout roof are visions I still have.

In some regards, it seemed like this year would never end. It was difficult not to enjoy the Winter Meetings, when we could spend time with our counterparts in a reasonably relaxed setting and the host hotel in Fort Lauderdale, FL, overlooked the Atlantic Ocean. I can still see the view in my mind from the commissioner's suite far above the lobby, where I would normally spend some time helping him prepare for what was considered his State of the Game address.

But the telephone started getting unusually busy one day because Milton Richman, the sports editor and lead columnist for the wire service *United Press International*, came to us with a story about the possible ouster of the commissioner. I cannot remember if he had actually released the story, but Milton had great sources.

195

Murray Chass of *The New York Times*, widely known for siding with the Players Association and increasingly difficult to work with as each year passed, had details indicating as many as nine owners had signed a letter wanting my boss to either resign or at least not seek re-election when his term expired in another 20 months.

Nothing major happened on this subject during those meetings in Fort Lauderdale, but it did not put any of us working for the commissioner and believing in his leadership at ease.

Kuhn's Tear-Inducing Speech In Hawaii

1982

Baseball recovered beautifully from the lengthy strike, breaking the all-time attendance record (more than 44 million fans) for the ninth time in 14 years, thanks in major part to four good divisional races and a nail-biting World Series won in seven games by St. Louis despite fabulous offense from the Milwaukee duo of Robin Yount and Paul Molitor.

But the entire year was an uneasy one for the commissioner, and, to a considerable degree, for his staff. A minority of owners continued to blame Kuhn's lack of business leadership for keeping the game from reeling in more revenue while they continued to hand out major paydays to the players.

Nothing had been officially settled by December when everyone gathered in Honolulu for the third and final time for a Winter Meetings convention. Kuhn had seen enough negative handwriting that he devoted most of his annual State of Baseball speech not to the highs I always prepared for him but rather to what meant the most to the game: the people.

There were numerous wet eyes in the audience as the commissioner gave many an example of the dedicated people who gave so many long hours despite compensation well below what they might have earned in other endeavors.

He genuinely enjoyed baseball people, perhaps especially those in the minor leagues, where it was easy to single out the dedicated staff members who had been in their jobs for 20 or 30 years or even longer with not a lot to show for their countless hours except for their memories and friendships.

One steady understanding between the commissioner and myself year in and year out was that I should be looking for events for him to attend in the cities of all sizes where his presence meant something extra to the team and most likely to its owners, general managers and so on down the staff food chain.

Many in baseball understood that holding the Winter Meetings in Hawaii was a special treat to these same people because it served as a bonus for the long, hot home stands and 70-hour work weeks. The expense was not much greater than if these same meetings were in Florida or Louisiana because of pre-arranged charter flights and negotiated hotel rates, although a limited number of owners could not see it that way and nixed continuing the five-year rotation to Honolulu.

While I am giving a backhand to others, I know that I was not always the best boss to my staff. I believe I was fair when it came to understanding family obligations and not asking them to take on some task I would not do myself, but they often labored in the background while I was out front in my utter devotion to helping the commissioner any way that I could, as well as being in the PR spotlight for our major events.

I had any number of assistants and secretaries in more than a decade of total time in the commissioner's office, but never more than two PR-trained aides and two secretaries at any given time.

I hired a youthful Art Berke out of Hoosier-land; Ohio State alum Chuck Adams after he had served such as *The Associated Press*; Rick Cerrone, who had bravely taken a glossy baseball magazine from idea stage to publication when that was one major task; and Marty Appel, previously a Yankees publicist.

My No. 1 secretary in the early years was a loyal Swiss woman, Wally Weibel, who had already been in the commissioner's office before I arrived, and later it was another dedicated worker, Helen Stone. Susan Aglietti moved over from broadcasting, and this free spirit was an asset because she loved sports much more than Weibel or Stone. Aglietti went on to work for the National Hockey League and NBC Sports, the latter largely for Olympic planning.

I know that Berke could have throttled me on many an occasion, especially at All-Star and World Series time, because he was largely confined to making certain every media handout—it might be 15 or so on any given night—got distributed to each media area and was available to all of the several hundred journalists who relied on the quotes, notes and statistics our group produced. This was no easy task, especially since we usually depended on runners for the actual distribution. I was comfortable Berke was the best person to take charge, but it was a thankless task and it kept him from taking on a job that would have allowed him to be on the field or in the clubhouse.

Not surprisingly, he went on to have a great career at *Sports Illustrated,* where he headed up many a promotion department project, including the someone's-got-to-do-it job of escorting each year's *SI* Swimsuit Issue cover girl as she scurried around New York to make all of her media interviews.

Cerrone became the New York Yankees' No. 1 PR guy, probably setting a record for lasting more years in the Steinbrenner compound than anyone else.

My staff benefited from the visibility a job in the Information Department gave them, and their talent took over.

The St. Louis-Milwaukee World Series was very satisfying for me because it was the only time I had a major role when the Cardinals, my boyhood heroes, were playing. I love the history of that franchise to this day, and still can feel my heart skipping a beat when I see the wonderful bird-on-the-bat logo, even if it is merely on television or at a spring training game.

I did get a bonus when we went to Honolulu in December because my Nebraska Cornhuskers were playing the University of Hawaii in the final regular-season football game. I did not get to see the Huskers often because it just wasn't practical—mostly financially—to get to Lincoln once I was living in Connecticut.

For nearly three quarters in 1982, it looked like Nebraska might be in for an embarrassing repeat of the 6-0 loss to the undersized Rainbows in Lincoln on the Saturday before classes started for my freshman year at the university, but the Huskers finally got in gear to make the fourth quarter a time to relax and enjoy my alma mater's gridiron prowess.

Some Highs, And One
Very Low Blow

1983

This would turn out to be the most troubling year of my life, as you will soon learn, but it also was not without tons of memories for other reasons. Many of them were wonderful.

My son Jeff provided some of the proudest moments. He was a sophomore at Wilton High School, where he became the No. 1 pitcher on the junior-varsity baseball team.

When someone was as wrapped up in baseball as I had been for nearly 40 years already, I did some of my living—as most parents should—through my children. My playing days, as I have already explained, were limited to high school and our Halsey Town Team, so I wanted the very best for my boys. It turned out the sophomore season probably was the highlight for Jeff since his varsity coach the next season pranced like a peacock in his uniform, but knew little about developing a team and even less in those days about mentoring young people. Jeff did reasonably well in Babe Ruth play over the next couple of summers, but that sophomore year gave me special joy.

I would do my best to take an early train if I knew Jeff was going to pitch. I lived every pitch with him, and probably would not have been more proud of his success had it ended up coming on a professional diamond. I never considered myself a very good instructor, but I knew the game enough that in our many games of catch or hours of hitting and fielding grounders on local diamonds, much had stuck with him. Even if he couldn't overpower a hitter, he usually got an out because of his ability to change speeds and move the ball around.

I mentioned earlier how the slogan "Baseball Fever: Catch It" came about. It was a very popular phrase by now, being used not only by Major League Baseball but also by many a college, high school or youth program. It was a perfect fit for most anyone promoting a team or any other facet of our great sport.

We even did some outreach to ask star athletes, writers and politicians how they caught Baseball Fever.

My research files for this book turned up two especially intriguing examples.

James Wechsler, a noted journalist who entered Columbia University before his 16th birthday and was in charge of both the news and editorial pages of *The New York Post* by the time he was 33, wrote a charming piece, from which I draw some excerpts.

"Whether it be called fever, opiate or aberration, I know I have had it (Baseball Fever) most of my conscious life. I was eight when I was taken to my first big-league game. It was in 1923 at Yankee Stadium. The Yankees were playing the Philadelphia Athletics and, for some reason or other, my only clear recollections are that Bing Miller hit a home run for the Athletics and that the sky was blue."

Fast forward in the column to two years later.

"In that year there was other evidence that, at the age of 10, I was irretrievably hooked. That was my first summer at a boy's camp known as Chicopee, near a town called Gilillee, PA. It is where I first played in organized games.

"I must have been already pretty far gone. I was studying the sports pages and cherished my reputation as a precocious baseball scholar."

Wechsler, far more scholarly than this humble writer, was born in New York City rather than Nebraska, but his early memories reverberated with me when he added this paragraph:

"Long ago I learned to play baseball in my head, constructing imaginary games as a form of reverie. I began doing that in boring elementary school classes and still do it during tedious lectures."

Columbia established an award in Wechsler's name. Sadly, he died of lung cancer when he was only 67, only months after writing the lovely column about "Baseball Fever."

The Baseball Fever phrase also had its fans in high political circles. How often would the president of the United States reply to such a query as ours, adding anecdotes of his own ... and even a handwritten P.S.? This letter, ironically dated on the day of my son Jeff's 17th birthday, found its way to my desk:

The White House

Washington

April 6, 1983

Dear Bob:

Many thanks for your letter of March 1, 1983 asking how I caught "Baseball Fever." As a kid, sandlot baseball was the game we played. My boy-hood friends and I had never seen a professional game. My first experience with professional baseball was a unique form of total immersion; I'll never forget it.

After college I landed a job as a sportscaster with radio station WHO in Des Moines. Baseball was the mainstay of our sports programming, and I was told I'd be broadcasting the home games of the Chicago Cubs and the Chicago White Sox. The catch was that I wouldn't be in the press box watching the games. I'd be 400 miles away in our studios reading cryptic descriptions of the action being telegraphed from the stadium.

I did have one trip to Chicago to imprint the view from the press box on my mind, and Pat Flanagan gave me lots of good tips on how to describe the action. Then it was back to Des Moines.

I developed a knack for filling in a little color. But I'll never forget the time when the telegraph went dead for a few minutes. I had to conjure up a series of foul balls for the hitter until the line went live again and I learned that the hitter had popped out on the first pitch. WHO listeners got a little more for their money than the fans in the stands that day. In fact, I think we may have created a record for foul balls – but you won't find it in any record book!

Having to describe games I wasn't actually watching turned me into an especially avid fan once I started seeing the games. Now television brings the big leagues into our millions of homes. So, I guess it's easier to become a big league fan than it was when I was young. And maybe even more fun.

With best wishes,
Sincerely,

Ronald Reagan

P.S. I should have mentioned I also enjoyed the experience of spring training with the Cubs each year when they trained on Catalina Island.

The All-Star Game was equally important and challenging this year. It was the 50th anniversary of the event, and since it came out of the fertile brain of *Chicago Tribune* Sports Editor Arch Ward, it was planned for the South Side of the Windy City at aging Comiskey Park.

Like so many older stadiums, Comiskey did not have room or amenities for expanded press seating or press briefings. We had to come up with something. We looked at the noted Bard's Room, where many a story was embellished over a beverage after games for decades, and we even trekked through something I recall as nothing more than an antiquated paint room with the hope inspiration would hit.

Regardless of the taxing and final solution for media activities at the stadium, Fred Lynn, once the magical centerfielder for the Boston Red Sox, who had moved on to Anaheim, made it a memorable event. He struck the only grand slam in All-Star history as the American League ended an 11-game losing streak in this mid-summer classic with a 13-3 pasting of the National League.

Julie and I celebrated our 20th anniversary in August, although it would be a stretch to call it a celebration. We separated only weeks later despite the fact Brad was just starting high school and Jeff was entering his junior year.

It does not require genius skills to realize this was the "low" point in my life. Neither of us had been really happy for some time, but I was not ready to call it a day with the marriage. The long hours and my devotion to the job were a burden on family life, to be sure, but we had experienced so many wonderful times and had two terrific sons. It would not be too much longer until they would be on their own, our financial outlook would be stronger, and we could look forward to the benefits of the so-called golden years.

I always felt—I believe she did as well—that our happiest times were when we could have some time alone and together. Our approach had always been that when we had free time, it would be for the four of us. We needed an occasional weekend or a few days to ourselves, and with our parents halfway across the country and baseball not being the highest-paying profession, it seldom worked out that way.

All of a sudden, I found myself living in a middle-of-the-road motel for a time while still handling four hours of daily commuting and doing all that I could to be certain the boys had whatever they needed, short of two parents living under the same roof. Jeff was in better shape because he had a driver's license, a part-time job and a good circle of high school friends.

As time went on and we could talk about it, the boys had so many friends in similar circumstances because of divorces. We lived in an area those from the outside looked at as a wealthy Fairfield County, a major bedroom area for New York City commuters.

Brad was the biggest concern. He was extremely bright, but merely entering adolescence and in need of parents who could be certain he had all the love and inspiration he needed, as well as someone reliable to get him to his school and church activities. I could not be there at many of the hours when he needed assistance.

Money also was a sizable issue. I had gotten steady raises and Julie had gone to work for a newspaper, but we were not making Fairfield County-type money.

We eventually tried divorce mediation, an agonizing and probably necessary process if both parties wanted a marriage to continue. I still believe only one of us truly wanted to move forward.

I soon had to leave to get ready for the World Series, which turned out to be between Philadelphia and Baltimore, and I joke that there must have been some additional message in that I had several days of diarrhea right in the middle of the Fall Classic.

The Orioles' veteran trainer, Ralph Salvon, tried to help, and when his normal remedy did not solve the problem, he sent me off to the team physician's office. I even stayed behind for an extra day when the Series moved to Philadelphia. I was not one who wanted to miss out on handling my normal duties, but I had little choice.

In time, my tummy settled down, the divorce became final, and my life took another turn. It certainly was a few months to forget.

I am at the podium in Gallaghers Steak House's upstairs dining room in New York City, where we held many a media conference, this one including Commissioner Peter Ueberroth, left, and American League President Bobby Brown

The author, with, from left, John Schuerholz, Haywood Sullivan and Bowie Kuhn

Look at that smile from George Brett

Lou Gorman obviously had a funny line during this baseball dinner in
Los Angeles in 1980

Charley Lau's Death
Plus a New Boss

1984

Perhaps it was a prelude to the rest of this year when one of the people I had grown to respect the most in baseball lost his life to colon cancer. His loss meant a great deal to some of the game's great hitters—to George Brett, to Hal McRae, to Reggie Jackson. You get the idea.

But I felt the loss of hitting guru Charley Lau, too.

This quiet, perhaps even introverted man, had become the Royals' organizational hitting instructor in 1971, then joined the major league team in the same role the next year. The players mentioned above—and many others—would not have had the success they enjoyed without Lau, a catcher or pinch hitter with a career .255 batting average and a mere 16 home runs in his 11 major league seasons.

Before his life ended all too prematurely at the age of 50 in March of this year, he had written a couple of books on hitting and become the game's most celebrated hitting instructor, moving to the New York Yankees in '79, then three years later to the Chicago White Sox, where he was drawing what for the time for coaches was an amazing $90,000 a year on a long-term contract.

Somehow, Lau and I connected during our mutual time with the Royals. We had a comfort with each other, whether at the ball park or in our private time. I was still learning what made major leaguers tick, and Charley was a great help.

Two things stand out to this day, apart from watching him develop Brett and McRae. One was listening to Lau and the Minnesota Twins' Rod Carew, who was still in the early years of his Hall of Fame career and was on the quiet side, break down the complex subject of hitting so laymen would not get lost in the technicalities. This came during one of our Dugout Club luncheons in Kansas City. If only we had a tape of that 15-to-20-minute master class.

The other was sharing a telephone conversation with Lau's widow, Evelyn, some time after his passing, when she and I discussed our losses, hers to death and mine to divorce. "Yours is even worse," was Evelyn's message, because my former partner lived on and hers had died.

My files are full of columns written at the time of Lau's death, chronicled by the likes of Jim Murray of *The Los Angeles Times,* Dave Anderson of *The New York Times,* Phil Pepe of *The New York Daily News* and Jerome Holtzman of *The Chicago Tribune.* Not every coach—or even manager—gets that type of recognition.

As I said, Lau's death in some strange way set the tone for me for the year of 1984.

Everyone knows what it is like to wait for what seems like a very long time. It may be to learn whether you will land that terrific new job or wait until you can afford an upgraded home or learn whether the new baby will be a boy or a girl.

All of us in the baseball commissioner's office had an interminably long year because it was known early on that Kuhn would not be our boss much longer. First, it was a question of who the next commissioner might be. By early March, it was announced at a Saturday meeting in Tampa that the position would be taken by 47-year-old Peter Ueberroth, a self-made millionaire out of the travel industry who was heading up the Summer Olympics in Los Angeles.

But—and this was important to us—he would not start until October 1, several weeks after the Olympics. We would not see or talk to or get to know what Ueberroth expected until that time.

It is pretty much a given at this level that department heads can be sitting ducks. As much as a new leader,

211

especially someone coming from outside the industry, would need experienced hands in such key areas as security, broadcasting, marketing, legal, and my area, PR, he might also want to bring in his own people.

By this time, I was very comfortable in my ability to serve as Director of Information—Chief Spokesman, in reality—but that would not mean anything if Ueberroth wanted someone else that he already knew.

The burden of handling my personal family issues only added to my anxiety.

The Olympics were a huge success, especially financially, because Ueberroth had found the magic touch with the corporate world, which propelled the Los Angeles games to unparalleled levels. He was riding an unbelievable high. Everyone wanted a piece of Ueberroth—to have him speak, to give him an award, anything to have the man with the supposed Midas touch come to their event.

To this day, more than 30 years later, I cannot believe how little guidance we were given. While Kuhn was still on hand and in charge until September 30, the final day of the regular baseball season, he had to map out his own future, and he could not tell us a great deal of what his replacement would want.

Suddenly, it was October 1, Ueberroth became commissioner, and the two League Championship Series, Kansas City and Detroit in the American League and San Diego and the Chicago Cubs in the National League, were set to begin the next day. Oh, yes, the umpires also decided to strike. The initial games were actually worked by stand-ins, including what *The Sporting News'* Official Baseball Guide said were, among others, airplane and food salesmen, a postman, and some college umpires.

What a baptism for the new commissioner! It was a great opportunity for the umpires to pressure him, and for the media to see the new-guy-on-the-block put to a test.

212

Ueberroth had the umpire fiasco settled in less than a week, doing so by agreeing to a boost of more than 100 per cent in postseason compensation, which supposedly angered some of the owners.

What I remember most about those whirlwind first few days when Ueberroth and his wife, Ginny, made the rounds of all four playoff cities were incidents in Chicago and Detroit.

In Chicago, *Hartford (CT) Courant* writer Claire Smith, a really decent person and wonderful writer who later spent years as a columnist for *The New York Times*, was denied postgame admission to the clubhouse after it had been agreed qualified female reporters would be allowed in.

I was in the middle of this one. I was caught short, just as Smith was, because the Cubs had agreed beforehand but did not follow through. It was not the first go-around for this issue, nor the first time one of the teams failed to live up to a promise, whether by accident or as a way of embarrassing baseball's New York offices. After a series of meetings, she was allowed in for future games.

The second incident occurred when we were in Detroit for Game 3 of the best-of-five series, with the Tigers firmly in charge because they had won the first two games against Kansas City. The City of Detroit was volatile in those days, so there was anxiety over what damage might be caused if Sparky Anderson's crew won once more to advance Detroit to its first World Series since 1968.

Our little delegation from the commissioner's office included only Peter and Ginny Ueberroth; our security director, Harry Gibbs; and myself. The Tigers scored the game's only run in the second inning, but for some reason, Peter decided we would leave before the game ended. It must have been about the seventh inning. I was not feeling secure enough in only Day 5 with the new boss to suggest it might be a bad decision.

213

Thankfully, we were not traveling by limousine. It may have even been a taxi. We got outside of Tiger Stadium, and the street was packed with people. Being generous, you could call them fans or revelers or whatever, but many of them were in what one would loosely call a celebratory mood. Our car was rocked from side to side for some time. While we managed a safe getaway, I shudder to this day to think what might have happened had anyone recognized the man made famous by the Olympic Games only weeks earlier.

The tone of those days in Detroit probably best is explained in what took place about 10 days later when the Tigers polished off San Diego four games to one in the World Series. There had been so many fires and ugly scenes in the area that we were advised to caution the media not to leave Tiger Stadium until well after the immediate excitement had worn down and then to take only the buses baseball always provided to assure a safe environment getting back to the downtown hotels. Tigers management provided a helicopter which landed in the middle of the diamond and delivered a couple hundred pizzas for the media during the postgame writing and waiting period. The pizza was easy to provide since Owner Tom Monaghan founded Domino's Pizza.

It probably was about the time the World Series ended when one of the other executives in our office let me know that Ueberroth was pleased with the way I had handled my work during this transition period. That felt good, of course, although it was only one step.

I could tell my days ahead would continue to be a challenge.

The most difficult task day in and day out for my staff and me was handling all of the requests that came in for Ueberroth.

The Sporting News named Ueberroth its Man of the Year; *USA Today* called him Achiever of the Year; and in

December, *Time Magazine* topped everything with its honor of *Time* Man of the Year. Requests to speak or accept an award from prestigious people and institutions were never-ending, and everyone made it seem like the invitations were coming from an old buddy.

We could understand the relative importance of each event, but we had no idea who was or was not important to Ueberroth. We could have resolved each day's invitations with a three-minute conversation, but Ueberroth was of practically no help. The people he brought with him, primarily secretarial level at that stage, or his Olympic PR people couldn't do much either.

We were on our own, with me often making the final decision. It was the first real tip to me that he liked to keep everyone on edge. Pressure, baby, pressure!

I also saw this side of him on occasion in a staff meeting or some other session where 30 or 40 talented people might be gathered around a U-shaped table while Ueberroth talked about the issue of the moment. He could embarrass the dickens out of someone, a role Kuhn would have handled in a more dignified manner.

Ueberroth was sharp. He was clever. He was cunning. No doubt about it. And I learned a great deal from him in a short span of time. I remember one occasion when we were walking the few blocks from our Park Avenue office to a luncheon meeting with some of the editors and writers of *Sports Illustrated*, located just across Sixth Avenue.

I always had a laundry list of topics I would like to discuss with the commissioner in those precious few minutes. He halted me, and said we needed to concentrate on what might take place over the next 90 minutes or so at *SI*. "Don't divert your attention," in other words. I have thought of that lesson countless times in the years since.

I believe it may have been at that same luncheon when someone commented about the daily frustrating clog of traffic in Midtown Manhattan. I doubt that it was even put

215

in question form because that would have nothing to do with a get-acquainted session between baseball's new leader and the best brains at one of the sports industry's leading voices.

No, problem, that traffic issue. Ueberroth had a resolution. I seem to remember he would have outlawed delivery trucks except during overnight hours and refused all traffic coming into the city with fewer than two or three people.

Too bad he never became mayor because it would have been worth a try.

In my file on Ueberroth which I pulled out in preparation for this chapter of the book, Peter Gammons, the noted baseball writer now equally adept in television work, summed up my boss in one paragraph of a story he wrote that winter for *Sports Illustrated* after the major league general managers meeting: "He (the commissioner) made it very clear from the outset that he is an independent man, a *very* independent man," Gammons quoted an unnamed general manager: "He's not like a lot of people in this game. He doesn't *need* baseball, yet he also made it clear that he's going to try to go about this job the way he went about running the Olympics. Unlike Kuhn, Ueberroth plans to take charge by doing what he thinks is right, and if any— and I mean anyone—steps out of line, Ueberroth will put him right in his place. In fact, he gave the impression that he's likely to knock someone down right away, for the sake of an example."

Ending One Major Life
And Starting Another

1985

Some weeks of getting to know and understand the new commissioner passed during the winter of '84-'85 until one day when I wanted to talk to Ueberroth about the one-day meetings I conducted every March in Florida and Arizona with the team PR directors.

When our discussion was over, he said I should stay home and have my assistants, Chuck Adams and Rick Cerrone, each handle one of the meetings. It was not like he said, "I need you here." I do not believe he gave much of any reason.

Adams and Cerrone both had ability, but they weren't experienced in running these meetings. I had been handling these sessions along with two- or three-day meetings at each year's Winter Meetings for about a decade. My absence would be shocking, even if some of the people might, at least jokingly, have been relieved to see someone else at the podium. I felt it would be obvious I had been knocked down a peg.

I had long felt that if the time ever came when I needed— or wanted—to make a career change, I would like to try running my own sports PR house. I had even started a list, way back in my Kansas City days, of potential clients I could pursue. I had idea after idea I would like to try to introduce. The platform of 10 years of running the Information Department for Major League Baseball had made the list longer, and no doubt more impressive.

I know I was tired, too, from what often was a seven-day-a-week grind. I might only be in the office for five days, but even if I had the luxury of being at home for the weekend, the telephone might ring at any hour because of some new

217

issue in the game where the media would seek me out in order to get a statement from or an interview with the commissioner. The marital separation added a great deal more pressure.

I went home that night—almost assuredly a Friday—with the thought I might resign the next week. My love for the game was never stronger, and my confidence that I meant something to baseball was high. I knew that my determination to provide consistent quality to the PR operation at the All-Star Game, World Series and Winter Meetings had elevated the way the media looked at baseball.

I also knew my leadership in bringing statistical uniformity into every publication out of any baseball office had been helpful instead of the hodgepodge ways of the past, just as my work on the Official Baseball Records Committee had brought a semblance of order instead of chasing down the endless hints that a hit or stolen base had been incorrectly reported back in the early 1900s when there was far less sophistication to recordkeeping.

Most of all, I had proven my capability of seeing that the Commissioner of Baseball was made aware of the needs of so many in the media, even if it was not always possible for him to grant every interview the media world would have wanted. I knew the big names—and many of those with lesser publications—throughout the industry, even though it was a tenuous assignment, especially in working with the few who had blinders on that the Players Association was always right and Baseball Management was always wrong.

I huddled with my two sons that weekend at the condo we shared in Norwalk, CT, explaining to them that I was thinking of leaving my baseball job to work for myself. Jeff would soon turn 19 and head off to college. I do not believe that my pending decision rocked his foundation since he had gained a ton of confidence through his part-time job at the Village Market in Wilton, as well as his role as vice president of his high school class, which added to his popularity with peers and gave him semi-independence.

Brad, on the other hand, had not yet turned 16, so he was much more dependent on his parents. His recognition of possible changes in our lives seemed to stand out. He was somewhat ashen.

Still, when Monday came around, my mind was made up. As much as I loved working in my dream field of Major League Baseball for the past 16 years, I felt it was necessary to move on.

I let Ueberroth know, but at the same time, I told him I would stay as long as he wanted me there—within reason, of course—because he still could use knowledge of the people who would be writing and talking about him, and of the industry standards for most any element that involved PR. He was respectful, regardless of how he may have felt down deep. It certainly helped clear a path if he wanted one or more of his Olympic people sitting in my chair.

We continued business as usual for a number of weeks, including the day in March when we called a media conference where Ueberroth made a big play by "reinstating" Willie Mays and Mickey Mantle to the good graces of the game.

"Welcome Home" splashed the headline on the cover of *Sports Illustrated*, which also featured the broad smiles of the two Hall of Fame greats and the commissioner.

My opinion on this decision was not sought, of course, but it was strange to be there helping Ueberroth because I had felt—and still do—that Kuhn had made the correct decision when he told the two men they could not work in baseball and for a casino at the same time.

The media, of course, loved to say Kuhn "banned" first Mays and later Mantle. He did no such thing. These brilliant centerfielders and game-changers made their own decisions all along, which was to accept gambling-supported money while also trying to work in baseball.

Mays largely played golf with some of the high rollers from Bally's Park Place Casino Hotel in Atlantic City, but he also worked for the New York Mets, where he had every reason to know which players had sore arms or legs, seemingly innocent pieces of information unless the gamblers chose to use it to their advantage while wagering on that night's game.

Mantle could let similar pieces of news innocently slip as he shared time with the patrons of Del Webb's Claridge Casino Hotel.

I used what free time I could muster between work and the boys to develop my business plan and even make some contacts for that eventual day when I would walk out of the commissioner's office for good. It was awkward for me, and when we reached about the three-month mark from my original notification to Ueberroth, I went back to him to explain.

We set a departure time in that meeting, and by May I moved on to my brave new world.

While it was far from what I needed to survive, pay alimony and help educate my two boys, I was assured of one $25,000 consulting deal for the first year of Wirz & Associates. It was with what then was known as the United States Baseball Federation (merely USA Baseball these days).

With the help of my friend John deCesare's graphic design business, we developed what I thought was a workable brochure describing my experience and expertise, and I set about contacting everyone I knew who had a business linked to baseball or other sports and mailing the brochure to many others.

I felt positive about the opportunity because I was an idea generator and a hard worker, and I had built up so many contacts across the country, although those in the media stretching from coast to coast could only help if I had projects worthy of being publicized. I realized the challenges were enormous as I would be working on my own out of my condo in Norwalk, CT, and I did not have the type of financial reserves where I could afford much of a lag period. I needed clients, and I pretty much needed them now.

Major League Baseball became my second client with another $25,000 deal for one year. While I felt there was quite a lot I could offer, I soon decided this probably was more of a going-away present than a legitimate consulting opportunity that might continue for years into the future.

I made some contacts for consulting jobs with major league teams, especially those nearby like the New York Mets, but nothing ever came of those efforts even if I had what seemed to be good relationships with the decision-makers. I don't believe I ever tried to land a full-time position with a team, as much as I loved the game, because I truly felt building a business through PR and consulting work was what I wanted.

One element that no doubt hampered my ability to develop consulting deals with the teams was that while I had plenty of meaningful associations with everyone from owners through general managers, I was more comfortable working with people at my level, which basically was the PR director or the promotions director. I was not a social climber, as I saw many a time with associates who turned to consulting when their jobs dried up. This is a worthwhile lesson for future generations, although playing up to the boss is not easy for everyone; it certainly was a challenge for me.

Meanwhile, I was very thankful I had developed a nice relationship with the United States Baseball Federation's executive director, Dick Case, who I would describe as another hardworking commoner. He wanted me to help publicize this national governing body for amateur baseball, which would help grow it since the USBF was still somewhat embryonic even though our sport had gotten very

221

important roots planted as a so-called demonstration sport in the '84 Olympics in Los Angeles.

Case was a go-getter, total energy all the time and very upbeat. The USBF was located in an understated two-floor building in Hamilton Square, NJ, not too far from Philadelphia. Case's wife, Barbara, kept the office running, especially when he traveled, which often was with ambitious assistant Wanda Rutledge. Case reported to Dr. Robert Smith, who I had gone to South Korea for about three years earlier on behalf of the International Baseball Association (IBA). However, Case had a lot of autonomy since Bob Smith was located in the Midwest and spent much more of his energy on IBA business.

As the relationship developed, the USBF had me devote considerable attention to its top annual honor, the Golden Spikes Award, which went to the country's top amateur baseball player.

Recent honorees had included future major leaguers, such as Bob Horner, Tim Wallach, Terry Francona and Dave Magadan. I got lucky in 1985 in that the award went to first baseman Will Clark of Mississippi State, who went on to lead the National League in runs batted in a mere three years later and had a 15-year major league career in which he hit .303 with more than 1,200 RBI and nearly 300 home runs.

I have never known any ballplayer who seemed to have more self-confidence, which was easy to understand after I got acquainted with his parents, who spoke admiringly of his all-around talent, whether with a baseball bat or a rifle used for hunting as he grew up in the South.

I got even luckier two years later when we had more resources for publicizing the Golden Spikes Award because the Oscar Mayer people became sponsors and the honoree was pitching phenom Jim Abbott.

Words truly cannot do justice to Abbott, the University of Michigan left-hander born with only part of his right hand.

222

I had known some about his courage to pitch—even hit—with this handicap, but one had to see his adept exchange of his glove in order to field after throwing a pitch to get a truer understanding of his talent and determination.

And one had to meet the tall, quiet and articulate young man to get a full measure of what he was all about.

We put on a media luncheon in New York City, which was the type of showcase the USBF needed to grow and the type of arena where I could fully utilize my media contacts and, I would hope, some expertise to give Wirz & Associates credibility with other potential clients.

The media loved Abbott because of both his story and his nature. It was not difficult to get him covered by *ABC-TV's World News Tonight, "Good Morning America", The Boston Globe, Sports Illustrated* or *The Associated Press.*

One of the places I traveled with Abbott to publicize the Golden Spikes was to St. Louis, where the Cardinals and Minnesota Twins were battling it out in what was to turn into a seven-game World Series that went the Minnesotans' way.

I will never forget the chilly St. Louis evening we shared, sitting among the fans at the World Series. Abbott was much in style as he journeyed to Busch Stadium without socks. He proved his human side by shivering throughout the night.

You can imagine my personal joy six years later (September 4, 1993) when my then-wife Maybeth, another couple, and I happened to be sitting in the mezzanine at Yankee Stadium as the now-established major league pitcher threw a no-hit game at Cleveland, winning 4-0. Abbott won 87 regular-season major league games, mostly with the California Angels, as they were known at the time, and the Yankees, and this was the best of all of them.

I had to excuse myself for a few minutes when the game ended to slip into the back of the room while Abbott was in the middle of his postgame media conference. I had not

223

seen him in some time, perhaps since our frigid trip to St. Louis, and I wanted to congratulate him in person. It was fun to see his smile of recognition when he noticed me eavesdropping as he explained his no-hit performance. We had a short but warm chat when he finished with the media. He is one of the nicest of the entire fraternity I have known.

How neat to be on the scene when Jim Abbott threw his no-hitter

Working for the USBF was not the only real active client relationship I was fortunate enough to have in the early startup months of my new business.

Relief pitchers were finally getting respect for the increased role they were playing in major league baseball, and I was about to win a major opportunity to help build their pedestal.

While I was at the commissioner's office in 1976, the Major League Baseball Promotion Corporation, which was an early-day sales arm to today's powerful money-printing

224

machine known as MLB Advanced Media, and the New Jersey-based pharmaceutical company Warner-Lambert had gotten together to creatively introduce the Rolaids Relief Man program.

Warner-Lambert produced Rolaids, and there was a perfect fit to promote the often gut-wrenching parallel between what a relief pitcher did to stymie ninth-inning rallies in tight games and the fast-acting relief of the chewy tablet.

I have never known for certain, but I presume Joe Reichler, the man I ultimately replaced as spokesman to Kuhn, played a sizable role in coming up with the Rolaids Relief Man and perhaps the fast-developing slogan "How Do You Spell Relief—R-O-L-A-I-D-S".

Peter Ueberroth unknowingly helped me out this time. When he became commissioner, one of his early acts before the 1985 season was to tell established MLB sponsors, such as Gillette and Warner-Lambert, that if they wanted to continue, the price tag was going up. I understood that price was to jump from about $1 million a year to $5 million, with specified portions of the money to be spent on local and national advertising in baseball events, in tickets and as a rights fee.

Gillette, which had been associated with baseball for many a year, said "no." So did Warner-Lambert.

The Rolaids brand people—the entire company, for that matter—liked what they had going with the Rolaids Relief Man because the media and fans had caught on to "How Do You Spell Relief". A reliever who finished games was awarded points for "saving" the game or for being the winning pitcher.

I was in an airport check-in line—it might have been at Newark—when Joe Conlan, the promotional boss for Rolaids, approached me and said, "We need to talk." I presume that conversation would have taken place eventually even if we hadn't bumped into each other that day.

We had known each other for some time because I had helped introduce some of the publicity for the awards program, and Rolaids put on some fancy receptions at places like the annual Winter Meetings, which both team officials and the media loved. One might even walk away with a full case—no exaggeration—of Warner-Lambert products.

Conlan could use my services to publicize the season-long buildup to crowning a Rolaids Relief Man champion in each of the major leagues since Warner-Lambert no longer was an official MLB sponsor, and there was no doubt I could benefit from another prestigious client.

Unheard of in the promotional world, the Rolaids-Wirz relationship lasted for 21 years. I must have done a few things right.

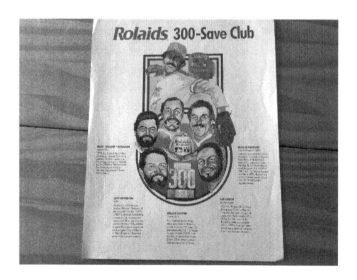

What a proud opportunity to promote the 300-Save Club in a myriad of ways

A frequent occurrence was presenting the Rolaids Relief Man trophy

1,588 CAREER SAVES -- All five major league pitchers with 300 career saves will gather at baseball's Winter Meetings in Miami Beach December 10 for induction into the "Rolaids 300-Save Club." From left to right are Bruce Sutter, Jeff Reardon, Rich "Goose" Gossage, Rollie Fingers and Lee Smith. The group has combined for 1,588 career saves, 11 Rolaids Relief Man titles, six World Series championships and 25 All-Star Game selections. (Photo by Tom _____)

Banners were paramount for our promotional events because the media often ignored mentioning sponsors

Hall of Fame pitcher Rollie Fingers was very active for two Wirz & Associates clients, Rolaids and Just For Men. His 'stache was his trademark

A Year of Adding Key Clients

1986

I was truly in my new world by now. I could not waste a day while my name and reputation were still fresh to my myriad of contacts. I had plenty of work to do in establishing the relationship with Rolaids, to say nothing of keeping up with obligations to the United States Baseball Federation and Major League Baseball, but these three clients would not be enough to make Wirz & Associates successful.

So, I had to juggle the often tedious task of being certain the clients knew they were important and I would do what was expected of me, while simultaneously trolling for new accounts.

One of my traits which is to be admired on one hand but dangerous on the other is that I am always thinking of what I can do for the client that they did not expect—that new idea, new outreach—while not trapping myself to a point where I could not deliver with the basics.

I have long felt one of the problems in the publicity world is that the job is never truly complete. Case in point: When a relief pitcher had accomplished some rare feat, say breaking his team record for the most saves in a month, I could tell that story in a press release, but the greatest impact on behalf of my client was to get on the telephone with individual media people to be certain they had seen the details. I did not want that release to sit on their desk without being noticed while the writer or broadcaster was off chasing some other story. Then, when I reached, say, the beat reporter for *The New York Times*, I needed to make the same effort with the *New York Daily News* and *New York Post*.

Remember, there was no such thing as a tweet or a text message or an email in those days. The telephone was our

229

major tool; sometimes a fax would work, although that was not a rapid way of reaching a number of people.

Contacts and persistence were the best tools, along with neat ideas for the would-be client.

It eventually became a very good first full year for Wirz & Associates—something to build on because the Rolaids relationship was blossoming, and I also started representing Little League Baseball out of its Williamsport, PA, base, and IBM on some of its baseball projects, and added two cornerstones of the aptly-named baseball family. *Baseball America* was—and is—a neat arm for the game in that it covered the minor leagues and college baseball in a depth no one else did. And Howe News Bureau out of Boston handled minor league statistics, a vital job yet perhaps under-appreciated by the game, at least from the standpoint of a willingness to pay a great deal for the service.

I also did some work for the Denver Baseball Commission, which was still trying to lure a major league team. My days with the Denver Bears helped, as did my major league time, although I would like to think my public relations skills and creative mind were the best tools.

More than anything—and pretty much aligned with the level of my compensation—I really dug in on the Rolaids and Little League tasks. I knew that all things being equal, my talent was a very good fit for each although for separate reasons.

Major League Baseball's Promotion Corporation and Rolaids had taken some very nice steps with the Rolaids Relief Man awards, developing an easily identifiable Fireman's Hat trophy (the relief pitcher would come into the game with the intention of putting a fire out, right?); starting an annual media guide; and selecting monthly winners in each league, a season-long champion with each team and even minor league awards.

What was missing was a publicity specialist, someone who had fresh ideas on how to get the results to the media on a regular basis, as well as being adept at staging events to celebrate each year's winners ... and getting Rolaids' name mentioned.

I would like to think I could present a master's class today using nothing but these relief awards as the so-called bible on how to make a sponsor proud of its involvement.

This is not to say every idea going forward for the next two decades was mine, but Wirz & Associates—largely me at this early stage—was involved in every step. That might involve staging an event in spring training, whereby some fan who had entered a Rolaids sweepstakes would get to bat against a major league pitcher, or bringing the American and National League winners to the prestigious New York Chapter Baseball Writers' Association of America banquet every frigid January. We started hosting a media reception prior to the evening's major event so the writers could do an interview and the broadcasters and photographers could do their job with the trophy and Rolaids banners properly positioned as a backdrop to be seen across the country.

We actually would often present the trophy three times— at the New York dinner, in the home city of the winners during a time when there was a void of baseball news in the winter, and again at an early-season home game.

I believe to this day my greatest success was in getting The Associated Press and United Press International, the two biggest wire services, to run the top 10 standings in each league three times a week under a heading reading: "Rolaids Relief Man Leaders". It might take only two or three inches of space in a newspaper, but that "filler" on a baseball page or an agate page gave my client so many millions of impressions.

The Rolaids awards were a staple for teams, media and fans, ranked virtually alongside the MVP, Cy Young and Rookie of the Year honors.

Warner-Lambert allowed me to be at each year's All-Star Game, World Series and Winter Meeting, and I would always have some type of media release in the media work room. If anything, I did this so long many a media person felt I worked for Rolaids rather than running my own company.

I doubt this identity ever hampered my ability to represent another client. The national media knew me from my days in the Commissioner's Office, so it was not difficult to get a journalist, no matter how big, to hear me out even if what I was pitching might be the Little League World Series or *Baseball America's* newest ranking of prospects.

The annual media guide on the Rolaids Relief Man program had 30 pages before Wirz & Associates got involved, grew to 44 in our first year (1986), and was 114 for the last one we produced (2005). What a great tool it was when I would visit major league spring training camps because the entire world had yet to go fully to looking for everything online, and the book had become a virtual bible on the history of relief pitching.

Baseball writers and columnists could rely on finding background for most any story they were doing on relievers. Mostly, what we wanted was some use of our unofficial slogan: How do you spell relief? R-O-L-A-I-D-S.

My work on behalf of Little League Baseball was vastly different from publicizing relief pitching.

Dr. Creighton Hale, the longtime CEO, and I had one thing in common: It did not hurt one bit that he was from another tiny Nebraska town. His was Hardy. No jokes, please, about being Hale and Hardy.

As I recall, Dr. Hale came to visit me at the Commissioner's Office on Park Avenue in New York City. This was an honor because he was "Mr. Little League", a well-deserved description not only for his administrative guidance of the organization, but also through his lead role in developing such safety measures as improved batting helmets, chest protectors and rubber cleats on baseball shoes.

We had met previously, but only briefly. We seemed to hit it off right away. This relationship eventually grew in directions neither of us could have imagined at the start, but the original intent was for me to utilize some of my major league experience to help Little League reach for some higher plateaus.

The organization dwarfed all other youth baseball (and softball) organizations, boasting of about 500,000 volunteers and 2½ million participants around the globe. It also had the backing of Major League Baseball, and it benefitted from having some major personalities whom Dr. Hale had nurtured. He could rely on the likes of Los Angeles Dodgers President Peter O'Malley, New York mogul Bill Shea (yes, Shea Stadium was named for him), comedian Bob Hope and my longtime boss, Commissioner Bowie Kuhn.

I sensed early on that what Little League did not have was a staff with the experience—and perhaps the freedom—to take its existing programs to higher levels.

Williamsport, three hours or so west of New York City and just beyond the beautiful Pocono Mountains, always had been—and probably always will be—headquarters. That is the way it should be, too, because there would be something fundamentally wrong with Little League being run out of a Chicago or Los Angeles office. That would fit the same way that moving the baseball Hall of Fame out of sleepy Cooperstown, NY, to some major city would feel. It would just be wrong.

Thinking outside of the box to create more modern-day appeal and developing a more influential staff to carry out the ideas was possible, however, and, at least in my mind, that was a role I could play. I had come from a village much sleepier than Williamsport, although I had benefited by this time from 16 years of working in Major League Baseball.

Little League had some real blue chip staff potential—people like Tim Hughes, still a board member and local businessman long since on his own after serving in a key staff position when we first met, and current President Steve Keener, who was the publicity director. All they needed, and perhaps I will bruise some feelings when I say this nearly three decades later, was to be introduced to bigger ideas and to be given freedom from a one-man leadership, which was pretty much the way Dr. Hale operated.

I do not want to even think about how many times I was told "we don't do it that way" to one of my ideas. "This is not the big leagues."

Well, no, but if one keeps everything in context, the idea can work for Little League in much the same manner as it would in the majors.

Cases in point:

The Little League World Series was dominated for years by the youngsters from Japan or Taiwan. I have no idea if they followed the territorial or age rules for determining their representatives who came to the United States and played against lads considerably less mature looking who represented a small community in Pennsylvania or Texas or California. ABC-TV, which carried the World Series finale on its popular *Wide World of Sports,* had made it known to Little League well ahead of my arrival on the scene that two brackets were essential for the World Series so that the United States would have a team in the championship game.

But as Little League worked its way toward that Saturday afternoon championship game, it had two "semifinal" round games. One semifinal had two U.S. teams, and the other had two teams from around the world.

I knew it would be better if those "semifinals" were turned into a U.S. Championship game and an International Championship game. The pairings were the same, but each game would now crown a champion, which also meant that every year Little League could proudly honor a United States Champion even if the team with the

234

taller, harder-throwing young men from outside our country happened to dominate the final game.

Little League also was against "exposing" its participants to night games in those days, which seemed more than a little odd since many teams already were playing night games in their home region before advancing to the World Series.

At the risk of sounding too much like a know-it-all, I was confident I could help in many ways if I could bite my lip at times and wait for the right opportunity to suggest changes or, better yet, if I could plant a seed and stand back while Little League thought it through and introduced changes.

A Year of World Series Memories Plus Jack Nicholson

1987

I know full well how much I have been blessed to attend and often to play a significant role in literally hundreds of the greatest events baseball has to offer. I counted up one time recently that I have been at more than 150 World Series games even though I do not often go these days, and I wonder how high the total would be if I added in All-Star Games, Hall of Fame inductions and Winter Meetings.

This year was somewhat typical of my opportunities in the '70s, '80s and '90s. How is this for living the good life, even if some long days and nights were included when I had a significant role:

June: College World Series, Omaha
July: Major League All-Star Game, Oakland
August: 40th Anniversary of the Little League World Series, Williamsport
October: World Series games in Minnesota and St. Louis

My work for *Baseball America* was centered around publicity, including the development of releases highlighting the major stories in each issue, and founder Allan Simpson and publisher Dave Chase had me handle significant announcements in person. This usually meant working with each year's Minor League Player of the Year in either a media conference or media tour of some type, as well as going to Omaha to host a media conference on the day before the College World Series started to reveal the all-America team and the College Player of the Year.

I did these events for the better part of a decade, which meant working with the likes of minor league heroes Derek

Jeter, Andruw Jones, Frank Thomas, Sandy Alomar, Jr. and Tom Gordon, and collegiate honorees Robin Ventura (Oklahoma State), John Olerud (Washington State), Ben McDonald (LSU), Mike Kelly (Arizona State) and Jason Varitek (Georgia Tech).

I would imagine the perception of setting up an event to honor the College Player of the Year would be one of a horde of writers and television cameras, much like we see every December these days when the Heisman Trophy is awarded to college football's outstanding player in New York City. That event follows weeks of anticipation of who the candidates might be, with most every game story each Saturday extolling the passing yards or touchdown receptions of the prime hopefuls, and several days of intense hype immediately ahead of the actual announcement.

However, college baseball attracted very little national coverage leading up to the College World Series in those days. Television did not carry many games locally, let alone nationally, and the greatest buzz came early each week when *Baseball America* and *Collegiate Baseball* revealed their rankings. This was long before the Super Regionals started, too, so when a team qualified for the CWS, it was fortunate if the score of the regional finals ran in major newspapers, let alone any stories ballyhooing the fact a certain pitcher might be 15-1 or a home-run hitter had erased his school record.

We had to be prepared to be certain the player we were going to honor would be available to travel to Omaha if his team was not in the eight-team field for the CWS. And, if his team was playing, would our pre-announced press conference start time conflict with the NCAA-arranged practice schedule for his team?

It was a given that *The Omaha World-Herald* would publicize—perhaps even feature—the Player of the Year and the all-America team, and that The Associated Press and United Press International would run something on the top player and agate listings of the all-America squad.

But I would be on pins and needles wondering whether we would draw even a handful of media to the conference, given that most of the media members who were coming to the CWS were there to cover a specific team and they were much more interested in covering a practice to do a pre-game story. Many times, the teams were only arriving in Omaha on the day of our event, but we had no other windows because of autograph sessions, other media conferences, and the opening night banquet set up by the NCAA. They all took precedence.

The College Baseball Coaches Association and *Collegiate Baseball* also had similar awards to those of *Baseball America,* so this awkwardness of revealing our No. 1 player in all of college baseball and having maybe five or 10 media people on hand along with a trickle of school representatives and parents was terribly difficult. I wanted the events to be special for those being given these really important awards so they could brag about them for life and not fear that they would have to tell friends they were honored in a virtually empty room.

Some years, our conference coincided with the start of Major League Baseball holding its Free Agent Draft, which meant we would arrange to pipe in the conference call from New York City with the first few selections. This added more spontaneous excitement, but it also meant the *Baseball America* announcement might be upstaged if the same person was one of the top two or three draft choices.

It was a whirlwind 24 hours or so for me because of arriving, making certain our conference room was ready, and contacting the eight CWS teams in an effort to get any players on our all-America team to attend along with the head coach and any media traveling with them. I also had to set up a schedule to FAX out our handouts in as timely a fashion as possible because the media can be terribly sensitive if one outlet gets even a five-minute head start in revealing results.

The email blasts today make it so much easier, but we had no such luxuries.

I would hustle out to Rosenblatt Stadium after our conference to hand-deliver releases to the ESPN production crew and announcers with the hope they would mention or show a list of the *Baseball America* honorees when the World Series opened the next day.

Despite this one-man marathon to promote my client, I always eagerly anticipated the trip to Omaha because, after all, this was a blue-ribbon event which meant a chance to see old friends and perhaps even prospect for additional clients from somewhere within the baseball world. One never knew when a uniform supplier or another media company would take notice of the talent I had to offer.

I would typically stay for the opening doubleheader the next day, a Friday in those instances, and then jump in my rental car and drive four or five hours to spend the weekend with my parents in Halsey before getting back to business and the boys in Connecticut early the next week.

While I must admit many of the events I conducted on behalf of *Baseball America* blend together all these many years later, two stick out because of the people involved and the circumstances.

Robin Ventura, whose accomplishments included a 58-game hitting streak while playing third base for Oklahoma State, was honored various times, including as College Player of the Year in 1987 and Player of the Decade for the '80s. I once was asked to introduce the gentle Ventura to the media in New York City, and then accompany him the same day to Chicago, where media awaited in the Bard's Room, a noted postgame watering hole at Comiskey Park.

The Chicago portion of the trip was especially ironic in that Ventura was to become a great player for the White Sox and, much later, their manager.

It is impossible to know how players are going to develop over a career, but I got to meet Derek Jeter and escort the eventual New York Yankees all-time great for a chuck of a day in 1994 when he was the magazine's Minor League Player of the Year. He started that season by hitting .329 in 69 games in Class A (Tampa, FL); then .377 in 34 games in Class AA (Albany, NY); and finally .349 in 35 contests in Triple-A (Columbus, OH).

I met Jeter and his dad in the lobby of the Grand Hyatt Hotel in New York City at a time when he could walk through Grand Central Station next door and never be recognized. Quiet and, I would believe, privately confident would be good descriptions of young Jeter, I could have told anyone after that meeting. He had only left his teenage years on June 26 of that year. Late the next season, he started his record-shattering career as the Yankees' shortstop and later their captain.

I went to the All-Star Game in Oakland in July, making my rounds of the social and media events to give my clients some visibility, and then settled into my seat two-thirds of the way up in the lower deck and behind home plate.

It might have been a quiet day for me in what turned out to be a scoreless tie into the top of the 12th inning except for a developing sideshow. My client from Warner-Lambert (Rolaids), who did not know a great deal about the personalities in the game, and I were enjoying normal conversation when early in the game, who should show up but actor Jack Nicholson, along with either Cheech (Marin) or (Tommy) Chong, one half of the irreverent comedy duo?

This says a lot about me—and possibly a good deal about baseball people in general since they often seem to live in oblivion to the rest of the world from February to November—but I had virtually no knowledge of Cheech and Chong, even though they had been big on the comedy circuit and in movies for some time prior to 1987.

240

I believe they had one ticket between the two of them—they certainly had no more than one—but the fans were all too delighted to make room for them. After some seat juggling for a time, one friendly couple took their child on their lap, so who was on my immediate left for the remainder of the game but Nicholson? I believe Cheech (or Chong) was one row in front.

Fans quickly took notice and started hovering in the aisles left and right to take pictures or make small talk. Then they wanted autographs. Nicholson set the rules, as anyone who knows his movies would expect. If you were seated in our section, autographs were fine. If you came from anywhere else in the stadium, you were out of luck.

Nicholson was very friendly to everyone. I clearly remember putting my foot in my mouth when I said, "Jack, I knew you were a big basketball fan, but I did not know you liked baseball." "It just shows you what you know," he replied.

The pair stayed for virtually the entire game, although I could not say for certain whether they saw Montreal's Tim Raines break up the scoreless tie with a two-run double for the National League in the top of the 12th.

As with Major League Baseball's major events, planning could not possibly have started soon enough to do everything Little League wanted to accomplish for its celebration this August of the 40th Anniversary of the Little League World Series.

I was getting pretty well entrenched with Little League by this time. Dr. Hale and the staff were looking to me for considerable guidance, and I cherished having another client along with Rolaids that could afford to pay a fair rate for my work, ideas and contacts.

ABC-TV was already set up to televise the championship game for the 25th consecutive year on *Wide World of Sports*, an achievement exceeded on the show only by the Indianapolis 500 time trials.

I helped get ESPN to agree to televise the semifinal games. This did not garner any direct revenue for Little League, but it was a meaningful accomplishment nevertheless in that the network had not covered any games from Williamsport since 1982. I deflect the credit to others, although I do not believe this powerhouse network has missed out on at least some of the World Series every year since, and it currently devotes many an hour to coverage throughout the 10-day event. The network also covers some of Little League's other championships.

Another significant event was the Little League Golf Classic, which Warner-Lambert sponsored because of its relationship through the Bubblicious brand. What a banner field, too, with no less than 33 former major leaguers scheduled to play beautiful Williamsport Country Club, including major names like Bill Mazeroski, Jim Kaat, Tug McGraw, Nelson Briles, Bob Friend, Early Wynn, Lou Burdette and Sam McDowell.

The added television coverage and major names in the one-day golf event were just the type of additions needed to bring more "buzz" from the nation's media.

As I had learned in the major leagues, side issues demand a ton of time in the months leading up to a major event. We had to think about the appropriate ceremonial first-ball pitchers in the majors, being certain we were politically correct for whatever cities the World Series ended up in, and which politicians to invite, then where to seat them. We sometimes joked that the games would take care of themselves if only we could get everything else correct without stubbing our toes in any manner where the media could take us to task.

For the Little League World Series—indeed for certain other Little League activities as well—the question was, "How do we handle the Carl Stotz issue"? Stotz was the virtually unquestioned founder of Little League back in 1947.

As the organization grew, Little League outgrew his capabilities, as could have been the case in many similar instances where someone had an idea and introduced it but could not keep up with the growth.

Stotz lived locally, and he was considered to be very bitter. It was only two summers earlier at World Series time when a series of stories threatened to scar the event. *The Los Angeles Times* headlined a major story "Founder of Little League Still Shunned" and *New York Newsday* called its feature "The Lost Legend of Little League". The Associated Press weighed in and quoted the 75-year-old Stotz as calling himself a "bull-headed Dutchman."

It was a painful situation for Little League, doubly so because some locals and some in the area media sided with Stotz.

Most in the organization wanted to go out of their way to embrace Stotz, make certain he was and always would be recognized as the founder, and invite him to throw out the ceremonial first pitch at the start of the 40th anniversary event. The Little League Board of Directors approved dedicating the Founders Room at the Peter J. McGovern Little League Museum next to headquarters in South Williamsport in the name of Carl E. Stotz.

Great lessons for anyone in PR. Be prepared and take the high road, if possible.

I was pretty much relieved to be mostly an onlooker by the time St. Louis and Minnesota got together for the major league World Series that fall.

Making Connections, Personally
And Professionally

1988

Little did I know when the snow was still falling, but this was going to be an amazing year, both personally and professionally.

I had done a fair amount of dating for the last three of the five years since my marriage had broken up, with much of the time with one terrific woman. For the most part, though, I did not like the singles world at all. It was awkward and often humbling. I might find someone whom I felt I would like to get to know only to be turned away, perhaps even for a simple dance at one of those singles events my minister/guidance counselor friend, Doug Abbott, and I would attend.

I had turned 50 the previous fall, had two boys in college, and hated the thought of starting over. Even more repugnant was the thought of living the rest of my life alone. I knew there was someone out in this vast world, if only I could find her. I thought I had something to offer, too, even if it was not Cary Grant looks or some wealthy businessman's money.

Abbott and I had become friends largely through baseball. Surprise, surprise! While he was a full-time counselor at New Canaan High School, his side job was much more meaningful to me. He was the associate pastor at the Wilton Congregational Church, a lovely New England house of worship which Julie and I joined when we first moved East and where the boys had been church school members for half of their young lives.

Abbott and I got acquainted during the social hour after church, where we usually would spend most of the time talking about the Red Sox, one of his passions since his youth in Beverly, MA. The assistant minister knew that Abbott, a devoted father of three, and his wife, Judy, had recently separated. This gave us more in common than merely our love of baseball, and our conversations eventually led to a friendship that continues all these many years later.

As difficult as it was for me to get out into the singles world, it was doubly tough for Doug. His religious roots often pulled him back, especially when I would come up with some singles event that was to take place in a Catholic church recreation room.

"Come on, Doug, what have we got to lose?" I might say this, about dropping in to some event on an otherwise lonely Saturday night. "We can play a game of cards, and leave when we want, but single women are not going to come knocking on our doors."

Abbott was aware of one new group, sponsored by another church, I believe, that was going to have a get-acquainted reception in a beautiful Wilton home, then wind up at the tiny Wilton Playhouse to see a production. People parked in the Wilton Congregational Church lot, then walked down Lover's Lane (no, I did not make this up) to the theater, which might hold close to 100 people.

He asked me if I would like to go, knowing full well I did not have a ton of other exciting options. A woman he knew had the same plan to venture out for this evening.

Guess what? Both Abbott and this woman, whom I later got to know, backed out of attending, for reasons I have long since forgotten.

It sounded so harmless that I decided I would go anyway, leaving my condo in Norwalk on this May 14 and driving 15 to 20 minutes to the appointed address, which was one of those larger-than-life New England homes so many people in this area owned.

The reception was on a wrap-around porch, and I suppose I was stumbling through the awkwardness of introducing

245

myself to various people and munching on cheese and crackers when one of the people I came across said her name was Maybeth Matton.

We struck up a conversation, I suppose exchanging such information as "Where do you live?" and "How many children do you have?" I am quite certain it was not a rocket-science conversation. Maybeth certainly fit the mold of someone I would enjoy getting to know, 5-4 to 5-5, short brown hair, a beige wrap and easy on the eyes.

It came time to drive the mile or so to Lover's Lane for the play, and when we arrived at the Wilton Playhouse, I somehow managed to find her and sit in the same row, along with others I have long since forgotten, so that our conversation could continue. She did not seem to mind.

I even walked Maybeth to her car in that church parking lot after the play and managed to ask if I might call her another time. This was hurdle No. 1, I suppose.

When I called her the next week, I asked if she might like to accompany me to Yankee Stadium, explaining that I was to be part of a presentation to Dave Righetti. I doubt I went into detail, but he was at the peak of his Yankees career in that he had won the Rolaids Relief Man award for the American League in back-to-back years. He was a big deal, too, having already thrown a no-hitter before he moved to the bullpen.

I remember explaining that this presentation would only take a few minutes, then we could enjoy the game together. Maybeth said yes to my invitation, then explained later that while her aunt had taken her to Brooklyn Dodgers games in her younger days, she had drifted from major league sports.

She insists to this day that when she got off the phone, she asked her son, Peter, the same age as my boys, and some of his cronies if "you have ever heard of someone named Dave Righetti." I understand they laughed themselves silly at her question.

246

In no time at all, Maybeth and I became a regular twosome. She was involved with her two teenagers, Peter and professional-dancer wannabe Amy, who was at the University of Massachusetts, the same way I was with Jeff and Brad. Maybeth was a landscape designer at that phase of her life, and we had similar easygoing personalities. I was one happy guy.

The longest we have been apart in the more than a quarter-century since was for a week that summer when I had committed to taking the boys to Honolulu for three days and for a four-day cruise to the other Hawaiian islands.

While it was a great satisfaction to be able to introduce the guys to Hawaii and satisfaction mixed with a bit of angst to watch them meet some of the fairer sex, I could feel good that when I got back to Connecticut, I'd have someone waiting who was happy to have my company.

Wirz & Associates took another giant step forward that summer, once more via Little League. Dr. Hale had considerable optimism that he had found a marketing company in New York City to launch Little League Baseball into the corporate sponsorship world. I believe that company did exactly $25,000 in business in a year's time, perhaps because it had treated the client in a little league manner while concentrating on its already-established Olympic sponsorship world.

So Dr. Hale came to me with the idea "you and I together can do better." I was no longer only a public relations man and consultant but also a marketing man, which certainly was new.

I felt the first task was to identify what we had to sell; what would Little League allow us to do when it needed more funding in order to grow its giant organization, but at the same time not join hands with any company or product that did not espouse the same all-American virtues?

In order to make this opportunity work while not diminishing any of the obligations Wirz & Associates had to

247

its other clients, I needed help. I had some full-time staff by this time, people who could do much of the day-to-day execution of publicity for Rolaids or Baseball America or Howe News Bureau.

I found right down the road in Westport a man by the name of Jack Klinge, who had helped market Topps Chewing Gum's hugely-successful baseball cards programs. Wirz & Associates would get what for us would be major commissions if we could successfully tread into the previously untested sponsorship waters for Little League. My deal with Klinge was mostly for him to share these commissions, also on a liberal basis.

We could not dawdle, though, because 1989 was going to mark the 50th anniversary of Little League's founding. What a major opportunity for all parties, but the marketing budgets often were committed well in advance.

The White House, Earthquake And Much in Between

1989

My work with Little League Baseball could have consumed every waking moment, so I certainly had to constantly work at time management.

The easy part of taking on sponsorship duties with Little League was that so many companies had a natural inclination to want to be involved because of the wholesome aura of working with youngsters and families. This fact made it much easier to get doors opened for a conversation or a meeting.

Realities never are that easy, though, because companies know what their objectives are. Could we offer opportunities that matched without compromising Little League values? And then there were the timing issue and the cost structure.

These were some of the opportunities we developed for potential sponsors to consider, along with some of the possible roadblocks:

- Title sponsorship of the Road to Williamsport with 12,000 games if all 30 countries were involved. One language was not sufficient.
- Tying in with the 6,000 local leagues sounded easy. The reality was we were always dependent on the volunteers who run those leagues to put up banners or hand out sponsor materials.
- Sponsoring a quarterly or annual newsletter with similar distribution issues
- Introducing instructional videotapes

- Becoming title sponsor of one or more of the regional headquarters, where training was year-round and games were seasonal
- Taking on a major role at the Little League Museum
- In broadcasting, taking on some role with ABC or ESPN, or one of Little League's lesser-known divisions in softball or baseball
- Developing drug-education, fitness or nutritional programs
- Paying to have a Diamond Vision-type major scoreboard erected for the World Series
- Managing instructional handbooks
- Planning nationwide photo or essay contests
- Underwriting a television special celebrating the 50 years of Little League
- Handling a U.S.-wide trip to deliver the first ball to the World Series

Remember, we were virtually shooting from the hip with many of these ideas, without a proven road map and uncertain of final costs.

Klinge and I, as well as Little League, were ecstatic with our results, which usually generated anywhere from a $100,000 to a $300,000 fee for Little League as we landed agreements (sometimes for multiple years) with companies such as Pizza Hut, American Express and Best Western combined, and Smucker's and Skippy, and, to a lesser extent, with sticker producers Panini USA, Redbook Magazine and Nabisco.

The national sports marketing magazine of the time, *Sports inc.,* said Little League was seeking sponsorships for its anniversary year that would total $2 million. I do not recall that any dollar amount was ever specified by my client as a goal, although we were certainly on target for such a figure, at least a couple of years into the undertaking.

These deals went a long way toward allowing me to pay every cent of the college costs for my boys and building my confidence Wirz & Associates could replicate marketing successes for other clients.

One fun aspect of the Best Western/American Express deal was that if Nolan Ryan threw a no-hitter, Little League would get a $250,000 bonus. It may seem like the odds were something like getting a hole in one to win a new car, but Ryan already had five no-nos.

He produced some seat-squirmers for us, pitching two one-hitters and carrying a no-hitter into the eighth inning or later an amazing five times. Twice, the great one got into the ninth before allowing a hit.

Little League had amazing pull, partly because every youngster playing baseball in the spring and summer and every one of the parents considered the kids were on a little league team even if many of them, as was the case, were participating in another youth program. Little League had a head start on most of the programs, too, and Dr. Hale and some of his strongest allies had nurtured relationships with a great many powerful people.

So it was that a day exclusively for Little League was set up on the South Lawn of the White House. No other youth program of the day could have arranged for this powerful setting. President George Herbert Walker Bush and his wife, Barbara, did not have to be sold on the idea. Their sons had played the game, and history says Mrs. Bush was a typical Little League Mom, carpooling the boys to each game.

The 50th anniversary lure almost cried out for an event because how can a U.S. President go wrong to have Little Leaguers and major baseball personalities like Stan Musial and Jim Palmer as part of the sun-kissed program?

Maybeth and I got to soak up this event, as did Jack Klinge and his wife, Jeanne. We could "brag" about it for months as we pitched our sponsorship ideas for the 1989 World Series and beyond.

A banner day at the White House, President Ronald Reagan with Orioles Jim Palmer (22) and Rick Dempsey

A sturdy handshake from President Reagan... wish I had gotten a haircut

252

My Little League boss, Dr. Creighton Hale, with President and Mrs. George H. W. Bush. Little League Chairman Luke LaPorta, my friend, is second from left

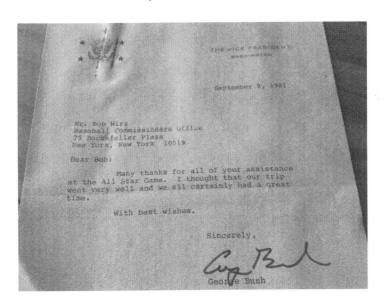

President George Herbert Walker Bush took time to write

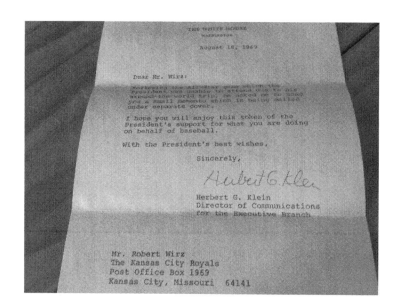

THE WHITE HOUSE
WASHINGTON

August 18, 1969

Dear Mr. Wirz:

Reviewing the all-star game with the
President who is unable to attend this in his
around-the-world trip, he asked me to send
you a small memento which is being mailed
under separate cover.

I hope you will enjoy this token of the
President's support for what you are doing
on behalf of baseball.

With the President's best wishes,

Sincerely,

Herbert G. Klein

Herbert G. Klein
Director of Communications
for the Executive Branch

Mr. Robert Wirz
The Kansas City Royals
Post Office Box 1969
Kansas City, Missouri   64141

Presidential recognition is always welcome

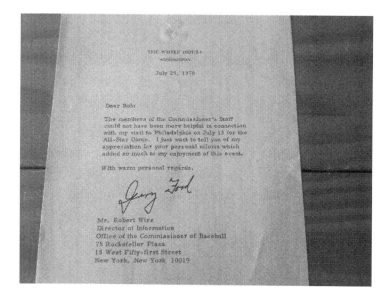

THE WHITE HOUSE
WASHINGTON

July 29, 1976

Dear Bob:

The members of the Commissioner's Staff
could not have been more helpful in connection
with my visit to Philadelphia on July 13 for the
All-Star Game. I just want to tell you of my
appreciation for your personal efforts which
added so much to my enjoyment of this event.

With warm personal regards,

Jerry Ford

Mr. Robert Wirz
Director of Information
Office of the Commissioner of Baseball
75 Rockefeller Plaza
15 West Fifty-first Street
New York, New York 10019

This one from then-Vice President Gerald Ford

Steve Keener runs Little League these days

President Bush even had *The Baseball Encyclopedia* on the lectern so he could recite statistics about the Hall of Famers present that day. I am not exaggerating. It was amazing to this baseball guy from Halsey, NE, to see the President of the United States joyfully reading from the *Encyclopedia.*

I chatted with one of the President's speech writers, Curt Smith, some days later, and I could not resist revisiting the presence of the *Encyclopedia.* Smith, an Upstate New York guy I call a friend to this day, is no innocent baseball historian, either, as his resume of books on the game, largely about the history of baseball broadcasting, continues to grow. "Bob, he (President Bush) keeps *The Baseball Encyclopedia* right in the Oval Office," where it is handy, Curt told me.

Both Little League and the Hall of Fame were celebrating their 50th year of existence in '89. Little League scheduled its Congress, which brought officials from virtually every corner of the globe, to Williamsport so those devoting so many hours to the program could see what home base looked like. Many had seen the kids sliding down the hill toward Lamade Stadium and the grove and museum only on television or in publications.

Wouldn't you know that both the Little League and the Hall of Fame scheduled 50-year events on the same day in June? Comedian Bob Hope, long a Little League supporter, agreed to highlight the Congress event in downtown Williamsport in the evening, and Baseball Commissioner Bart Giamatti, the former Yale president, was to take part in a celebration in Cooperstown in the middle of the day, then fly to Williamsport.

With my background in the major leagues, Dr. Hale wanted me to fly from Williamsport to Oneonta, NY, about 25 miles from picturesque Cooperstown, to accompany Giamatti on what probably was less than an hour's flight.

Even though I had spent 10½ years in the Commissioner's Office, Giamatti did not come on the scene until well after I had started my own business. We had never met.

There were only three of us in the plane except for the pilots. It probably could have seated eight. The third person was Major League Baseball's security rep, and he sat in the rear while Giamatti and I were face-to-face in the front. I don't think Giamatti knew—or cared much—about my background in baseball although he was cordial enough. As usual, I tried to be prepared with topical conversation, as it was needed.

I believe Giamatti dozed a little, and my biggest take-away from this adventure was that his suit pants had been patched. It may have been a one-inch square patch below the knee, but it strikes me a bit unusual to this day that the commissioner would wear a patched-up suit. I suppose that speaks to his humble nature.

This took place two months before Giamatti got all-time hits king Pete Rose to agree to the permanent ban on him from the game for betting, including while he was manager of the Cincinnati Reds.

The evening program was a major one because of the magnitude of Hope and the presence of the seventh commissioner of baseball. As I understood it, Hope had made two requests to Little League: He wanted a rubdown, and he wanted someone to care for his little dog. Dr. Hale and the two star attractions left once Hope and Giamatti had made their appearances, largely because of Giamatti's need to be able to smoke.

Little could any of us have known that less than three months later, on September 1, Giamatti would be dead at the age of 51, struck down by a massive heart attack while on Martha's Vineyard off the coast of Massachusetts.

We got one important break in late August (1989) when Trumbull, CT, marched to the championship in the Little League World Series. This drew huge attention. Led by future National Hockey League great Chris Drury, Trumbull's triumph gave us a winner from the United States; that the new champion was from the corporate stronghold of the Northeast was an added benefit.

While Little League certainly consumed much of my attention throughout this year, it did not prevent me from two other noteworthy trips.

Maybeth's daughter, Amy, was spending a semester in London, racking up more credits from the University of Massachusetts and continuing her passion and looming career—it was her major, after all—of dance. To show how my relationship with Maybeth was continuing to blossom, we spent a week in London. That was a special milestone for me since, aside from trips to Canada and Hawaii, I had not traveled beyond the U.S. Mainland.

We went mostly to see Amy, but as anyone in similar circumstance knows, our offspring did not want us hanging around 24/7. So Maybeth and I did as many touristy things as we could squeeze in from a trip on the M-4, as I believe it is called, with me behind the wheel from the right side of the car and trying to keep up at about 80 miles per hour.

We picked up a car near Heathrow Airport and promptly made an incorrect turn which took us right into the heart of the airport traffic before we could right ourselves and head to the lovely city of Bath. The queen's summer residence, Windsor Castle, scarred from a recent fire and located only a right turn and some steps from a large shopping center; Buckingham Palace; the somewhat dreadful London Zoo; the Tower of London; the Tower Bridge; and those magnificent churches all were part of our trip.

Amy, quickly developing into as lovely a future stepdaughter as one might ever like to see, did not take part in any dance programs while we were there, but she and her friends took us to an evening program that turned out to be so avant-garde in pushing the boundaries that if we want to tease Amy about anything now more than 25 years later, this is the way to do it. And this uneducated dance student from Nebraska was not the only one with a quizzical expression. I can still see the raincoats being waved back and forth with precision because one little slip-up in the choreography would have erased any sense of what was intended to pique our imagination.

I made my normal trip to the World Series that fall— well, normal except for what was about to happen to delay Oakland's sweep of the San Francisco Giants.

Maybeth was with me, and we were able to spend a day at the Senior PGA tournament in the heart of wine country, so I could scout it out as a possible site for a Just For Men booth. This hair-coloring industry leader was to be a major client for W&A, and the 50-and-over crowd watching the golfers of a similar age was truly ideal when it came to men thinking about coloring their hair.

We took in Games 1 and 2 of the World Series in Oakland before Maybeth headed home and I traveled across the Bay Bridge for the next three contests in Candlestick Park.

I was sharing a room in downtown San Francisco with John Montague, my client at Howe News Bureau. This becomes important shortly.

Montague and I made had journeyed south for nearly an hour to San Mateo on the day of Game 3 to see the vast baseball archives of Bill Weiss, who was known throughout sport but more than ever on the West Coast because he had been the official statistician, had written a newsletter, and was the all-around historian for the Pacific Coast League and the California League for decades. This is no exaggeration.

I had only heard about Weiss' collection of records, which was unreal in its size. While I have been accused of saving every game program and parcel of information from my various baseball jobs, Bill was the true master. We are talking pre-computer days; pre-calculator days; pre-FAX machine days. The Pony Express was gone, but Weiss had to be one of the U.S. Postal Service's best clients or worst nightmares because box scores were the lifeblood for maintaining accurate records even if they were received by Bill Weiss and officially recorded days after the fact, as opposed to our up-to-the-second thinking of these days.

The garage at Weiss's home had long since been turned into the most important building the Pacific Coast League or California League could imagine. If someone had a question, the answer was here, neatly filed into one of the hundreds of standard file drawers or an equally impressive array of full-sized cabinets. At least, they seemed to me to be neatly filed.

We absorbed as much of Weiss's priceless lore as one afternoon could produce, then Montague and I headed back toward Candlestick in a two-car caravan trailing Weiss and a friend of his.

This was a World Series, mind you, San Francisco's first since 1962 when second baseman Bobby Richardson hauled in Willie McCovey's liner in the ninth inning of Game 7 to preserve a narrow New York Yankees championship. We did not have parking passes, so we left our cars in a lot in what seemed like a few hundred feet above wind-swept Candlestick, and a several-minute walk from the smell of fresh grass.

Being baseball people instead of normal-thinking fans, we decided to brave it down a steep incline rather than a slightly longer and much safer path. Weiss was no youngster, having already attended more than 30 Winter Meetings while he was gathering paper for those precious files back in San Mateo.

Let me tell you, it was so steep it was all I could do to slide through the rocks and weeds toward level ground, and I somehow ended up helping Weiss. And that was the easy part of the evening.

Montague and I had seats high above third base, about halfway between home plate and the auxiliary (football) press box further into leftfield. We actually went through a portal a few rows above our seats, then walked down. It was at this exact moment when NBC's baseball anchor, Al Michaels, was trying to figure out why the lights were flickering in the broadcast booth and moments later how to tell the worldwide audience that the Bay Area had been hit by an earthquake.

I can honestly tell you I did not feel any shaking of the grandstand, which I can only explain perhaps because I was holding onto a railing and trying to find my way down to our seats. Montague felt it.

My first inkling of what had happened was the scurrying that started down below us on the Candlestick Park grass. There was instant milling around, followed by an emergency vehicle appearing on the infield with a bullhorn that was pretty much out of our range. Someone in the crowd had a portable radio, and began relaying that the Bay Bridge, which Maybeth and I had crossed at least a couple of times in the previous two or three days, was heavily damaged by this sizeable earthquake.

I remember my friend Montague saying to me, "You actually think they are going to play baseball, don't you?" How would I know, being an eternal optimist, and not able to see any damage? I had seen stadium lights go out at other times and come back on in time to play.

When we finally got word of the postponement and had watched Jose Canseco and his wife in the skin-tight red dress and the other players walk slowly toward the right-field corner, Montague and I started making our way out of the stadium, not knowing whether or how we would find transportation to our hotel downtown. The buses scheduled to take baseball people back to their hotels after the game and a postgame party in a tent beyond leftfield were not scheduled for hours.

As luck would have it, we ran into NBC's PR man, whom I had known, but his name, sorry to say, escapes me all these years later. He asked if I would like to step into the NBC trailer and use a telephone to let my family know I was OK since they had much better earthquake news than we did and probably were a heck of a lot more worried than we were.

I waited while (NBC analyst) Tim McCarver's wife made her call, then gave Maybeth a ring and asked her to let the boys and my parents know I was fine.

Montague and I found a city bus without too much trouble, and learned it would take us to within a few blocks of our hotel. I remember that former Kansas City Royals catcher John Wathan was one of those I knew on the bus. What a nice guy, but that is only a sidebar to our story for this day.

By the time we got out of the bus, it was dark, and about all we knew was the direction of our hotel, which we estimated was some eight blocks away. Not bad, if you could see. The only lights were in San Francisco bars.

Wouldn't you know, they were prepared with generators since most of the city was a strange black. We were not alone, of course, having been joined by other World Series visitors along the way.

When we finally got to the hotel, the lobby was filled with people wondering what their next move should be. I asked a hotel employee if we could go to our room, which was on about the 17th or 18th floor. "We wish you would," he replied, explaining that the stairwells had some light, as did the hallways on each floor.

Up we went. Not much problem at 52, especially since my days of lugging a heavy briefcase during the World Series were behind me. Montague and I propped a chair into the door to give us some hallway light. We also had use of the portable radio I took on trips; our first real connection to news. I managed to dial Maybeth once more, basically by Braille. I actually got through.

My plan had been to stay in San Francisco for the third and fourth games, then fly to Phoenix since Mom and Dad were already in Mesa, AZ, for the winter. Now, I was uncertain, as were countless others.

My next move after we caught up with some sense of the severity of the earthquake, which I know pretty much stunned Montague, was to say, "I'm going to bed". What else was there to do? I even slept pretty well, and when I woke up after daylight, the radio informed us that the San Francisco airport was open, and, as I recall, maybe half of the flights were going.

Both of us headed to the airport, and joining with three or four others, we found the driver of a white limo who was more than happy to take us. We found the skeleton of a newspaper that either the *Chronicle* or the *Examiner* had managed to publish, but still did not see any earthquake damage between downtown and the airport.

In 45 minutes, I bid Montague goodbye and was on a flight to Phoenix. It was only when I reached Mom and

Dad's condo and watched CNN that I got a real sense of the massive damage to much of the Bay Area. How lucky were we! The World Series resumed about a week later, and it probably was the first Game 3 I had missed in 15 years.

Wrigley Field
Plus
"The Cabin at the Lake"

1990

Since sports command so much time and attention, it is really nice to be able to get away from the grind whenever the opportunity allows.

This was one of those periods, especially in the span of May-July. I am not certain which one of us breathed the biggest sigh of relief when Jeff, now 24, graduated from Ithaca College. He loved the school, but just as with my own academic struggles three decades earlier, it was not easy for Jeff to collect the old sheepskin.

He has never been afraid of work, as his disc jockey business and his many hours at JCPenney in Ithaca proved. I have always suspected concentration was one of his big challenges, just as it had been for me.

Aside from seeing him with the signed diploma in hand, the two biggest memories I have of that day outside at the football stadium were the fact Mother Nature decided not to give us an ideal break, and the need—at least as we saw it—for Jeff's mom to have her private time with the new graduate and for us—Maybeth and me—to have a turn.

Both boys had taken a liking to Maybeth, but their mother had nourished them with her own strokes of love from birth. Even if the parents had been willing, I believe it would have been more uncomfortable for Jeff and Brad to see us sharing a graduation lunch than the way we handled it, with both Julie and me having our separate private time with the two people we jointly loved more than anyone else.

Brad and I got to share another event in July when he went with me to the All-Star Game at Chicago's Wrigley

Field. All too often through the years, we had been mostly separated at baseball's major events by my work and the devotion I gave it.

We had arranged so that once the All-Star Game was over, we would be met at O'Hare Airport by Maybeth and Brad's high school girlfriend, Ali, and the four of us would travel on to Nebraska for several days.

The first event on our calendar with Mom and Dad was to attend a rodeo in Broken Bow, the town where I was born. It probably was the first rodeo for Maybeth and Ali. Now all the locals know that mid-July in Nebraska is expected to be warm and humid. Not this time. We felt like we might freeze to death.

Our ultimate goals were to visit Halsey and take the Wirz Family's traditional steps, which meant some of Mom's basic, but comfortable cooking, then visit the forest, the Rodocker Ranch a few miles north of town, and the cemetery in Purdum, a "metropolis" of about 25 people which included Uncle Dana Harsh's store and the Purdum State Bank (owned and operated by more relatives).

Dad had only recently retired from 40 years of six-day-a-week delivery on his rural mail route, but both of us felt we could have driven the 12 miles from Halsey to Purdum blindfolded since we had done it so many hundreds of times.

Visiting the Nebraska National Forest, which I first mentioned in the introduction of this book, was considered a must for every visit, first because it was so familiar and comfortable. We liked showing off the nursery, from which millions of little evergreen trees were shipped out throughout the Midwest every year. I especially enjoyed talking of my summers from age 14 to 19 when I would count the tiny seedlings, water and weed them, or care for the Nurseryman's yard. Every young person from Halsey and some nearby communities would work at the nursery unless their parents were blessed with owning a ranch, in which case they would work at home to mow the pastures, stack the hay and repair the barbed-wire fences.

The highlight, though, was the drive of about three miles to the lookout tower. Whenever it was manned, you could climb the 60 or so steps and have a wonderful 360-degree panorama, mostly of the various pines, along with some of the pasture land ranchers lease for summering their cattle. On occasion, a beautiful deer or two will bounce through the landscape.

We had an extra trip planned to show off Nebraska's largest lake (McConaughy), where we could possibly do a little fishing. My aunt and uncle, Dana and Mern Harsh, had a cabin which would provide our lodging and allow Brad and I to show "our ladies" that there was more to Nebraska than what we natives think of as the "beautiful Sandhills."

I was seldom in Nebraska in the summertime because of baseball, but I had been hearing about "the cabin at the lake" for years. We traveled the 100 or so miles in two cars, with me behind the wheel of one along with Mom. Maybeth had been a little under the weather and was resting in the back seat, although she remembers the story I am about to relate, which we have laughed about for more than 25 years.

When we were approaching Lake McConaughy, we came to a turn. I knew the lake was to the left. Mom told me to turn right. "But Mom..." Turn right, she repeated.

Well, when we got to "the cabin at the lake" it was a very plain, rectangular wooden structure, and the grassy field next to it had been burned dry by the summer heat (despite our one chilly night at the rodeo).

Thank goodness Maybeth and Brad's friend had a wonderful sense of humor along with an equal sense of adventure! We tucked the women away in a tiny bedroom just off the not-so-modern bathroom so they would have some semblance of privacy at night.

We were able to drive the mile or so to the actual lake, and although the water level was well below normal, we

266

rented a pontoon boat, let it drift for much of our visit, and caught a few small fish—probably perch or bass. When the trip was over, we had had a lovely time, along with a story about "the cabin at the lake."

The year in business was just fine, thank you. Wirz & Associates was continuing to grow on its way to as many as seven full-time employees. We even branched out beyond baseball by looking into the growth of minor league hockey and by starting nearly a decade-long relationship with Combe, Incorporated, a largely Mom and Pop-run and hugely successful business located in New York's wealthy Westchester County, because of its dominance in the market with its Just For Men hair-color brand.

Sports was a desirable entity for promoting Just For Men, a do-it-yourself, five-minute process when properly administered, as well as Great Looking Gray, a brand just being introduced for those who were happy to stick with their new look but to clean the gray and white up a bit.

We did a great many things with these two brands, often working the Senior PGA golf circuit, where both the players and the audience were prime targets.

One of our first initiatives was to make a deal with Bob Murphy, a longtime touring pro who had moved on to play the Senior Tour, as well as the lead commentator for ESPN's coverage of events for the 50-and-over players. We sometimes set up a demonstration point outside our Great Looking Gray booth where we would give many hundreds of samples a day, so Murphy would offer putting tips to amateurs of all skill levels. The biggest thing we were able to accomplish was to arrange to have a telestrator available for the telecasts so Murphy could point out the contour of the greens or the slope of a fairway to aid viewers.

The telestrator is commonly used on television today to draw most anything, but it was hardly known in those days except for use by professional football analyst John Madden, who would show how a play developed. As I recall, it cost several hundred dollars to have the telestrator available, but we somehow managed the fee within our modest budget.

Because Just For Men advertised heavily on the Senior events carried on ESPN, with some added creativity, we were able to make a deal with the network so that once or twice each telecast they would say "now let us go to our Just For Men Telestrator." The JFM logo would pop up on screen at the same time.

It was truly groundbreaking to have the telestrator commercially sponsored, so Wirz & Associates drew nice kudos from our client.

Our creativity for Just For Men was a major achievement, and I personally got great satisfaction from coming up with unique ideas to prove sports was a perfect vehicle. Combe uses sports stars to this day to prove hair coloring keeps men young and desirable.

Since Wirz & Associates was largely known for its ability to land some type of mention for clients on the sports pages, we also developed questionnaires for fans to fill out at our booths at golf tournaments from New York's Long Island to wine country in California which we could turn into stories for the media. It might be something as basic as voting for your favorite Senior PGA player. We could turn the results into something perfect for creating a chart for the front sports page of *USA TODAY* or *Golf Digest,* or a short story in the local paper where the tournament was played. These placements were golden for getting additional mentions of Just For Men.

I had worked with Hall of Fame relief pitcher Rollie Fingers with Rolaids, and we hired him because his fabulous handlebar mustache was beginning to show gray, as were his temples. He was perfect for Just For Men in so many ways, and clients always cherished having a celebrity to walk around with at most any event.

We did a hair-coloring event in Chicago featuring Bears linebacker Dick Butkus. Not only did he have his flattop turned back into its original color, but he also persuaded former teammates to get a new look, and we could attract the media because of the star power. We would either land a story on the evening news or an invitation for a demonstration during a local morning show.

We chose a number of baseball venues, largely in the minor leagues because of lower costs, to set up demonstrations for Just For Men. It was amazing how many people from various walks of life would volunteer to try coloring their hair for the first time. Sometimes, we could do a before-and-after parade on the field so fans could see the transformation. We would have Combe specialists to supervise because it was key to choose the right color and not to leave it on for more than a few minutes. Very few people left the ballpark without knowing Just For Men had been there.

The 1969 New York Mets never lost their luster—pun intended—and when we set up a reunion on Long Island, we got a wonderful turnout with the bonus of several of these miracle World Series champions, now in their 50s and 60s, taking a liking to getting a more youthful look.

One other event we created—and duplicated in subsequent years—was to search for the greatest facial hair for Great Looking Gray. We sometimes promoted these contests in the local baseball venues, where the local winner would advance to our national competition. One time we held the finals just outside Mickey Mantle's restaurant, which bordered Central Park in New York City. Talk about attracting attention from the passersby! We could have several coloring stations going at one time, then wind up with celebrity judges, such as ESPN's Linda Cohn or WNBC-TV's Len Berman. If the plan worked out perfectly, the judge might use some footage on television.

The facial hair ranged from the immaculately groomed to Rollie Fingers-like handlebars to the wildest looks one could imagine.

269

We duplicated this event in Cooperstown, NY, just down the street from the National Baseball Hall of Fame. It was quite a perk for men judged to have the best facial hair to get a free trip to this historic village, and perhaps wind up with their photo in diverse newspapers or on television.

We arranged to have hundreds of photos taken because of the countless opportunities that developed after the events were over.

One of our facial-hair competitions for Just For Men, including spokesman (and Hall of Famer) Rollie Fingers

Clever camera angles always worked for our clients

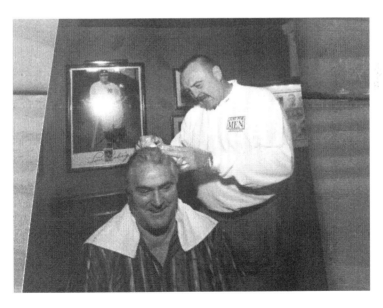

Chicago Bears great Dick Butkus gives teammate Ed O'Bradovich a new look

271

Gentleman Willie McCovey served as IBM Tale of the Tape
spokesman

I did not really sign, although it was a joy to see my name in this
mock-up during an IBM promotion at Wrigley Field

A Wedding and New Clients

1991

I am continually reminding myself that this book is supposed to be about my passion for baseball, but I must divert from the diamond long enough to talk about two life-altering events that took place during the first few months of this year. I will discuss them in reverse order.

I celebrated the second college graduation in as many years when Brad picked up his diploma from Syracuse University in the Carrier Dome and started gearing up for what has turned out to be a very rewarding career in marketing. I hope my pride in both Jeff and Brad has come through in this book because their success and their happiness mean everything to me. I only played a small part in seeing that they had the opportunity to get degrees at good institutions, then gave them a chance at Wirz & Associates until a meaningful job came around. I could finally cut myself a little breathing room for my own life once this had taken place.

The key ingredient to their success—I really believe this—has been their work ethic. I know that mine was handed down through my parents, and perhaps they saw what was necessary through some of the years when their dad may not have been at home as much as any of us would have liked for one basic reason: I was doing my darndest to make an honest life for our family by outworking most everyone around me. I realized there may have been smarter people, but no one was going to get ahead of me because I had taken my foot off the pedal.

I said that I would deal with the two life-altering topics of this year in reverse order. February 23, 1991 was the red-letter day I had hoped for for such a long time.

Maybeth and I exchanged our wedding vows in the beautiful Wilton Congregation Church, where my boys had gotten their childhood religious training. This stately hilltop-high white sanctuary has served New Englanders and all of us transplants for literally hundreds of years. While I am not an overly religious man, this church means a great deal to me to this day.

We were married at 11:05 in the morning, the same way baseball games often start five minutes after the hour so one can easily guess the person who established the time of the ceremony.

I believe there were 11 of us present, including Doug Abbott, my dear friend of most of my 40 years in Connecticut, with whom I would chat about the state of the Red Sox during coffee hours after church in the early years, then tiptoe through single life after our first marriages ended at the same time. He remains a cherished pal, along with his wife, Pam, to this day.

After the wedding, we had a simple family brunch at the Three Bears restaurant, where Jeff, Brad, and Maybeth's equally lovable pair, Peter and Amy Matton (she is now Amy Edwards), gave us a huge surprise. Amy was at the University of Massachusetts and Brad was finishing up at Syracuse, but they had deviously made excuses to come home one weekend so they could join Jeff and Peter in a handsome photo that hangs proudly in our den to this day, along with a replica of them in the same positions taken 20 years later.

The importance of those pictures cannot be overstated since the four kids (well, kids now at or nearing 50) mean the world to Maybeth and me. I feel, as I believe she does, they are "our four" even though they do not share the same last name or identical genes.

Maybeth and I were nestled into our "honeymoon" condo in our very favorite vacation destination in this world, Sanibel Island, FL, by nightfall to begin what has been such a blissful union. I knew there was someone out there who would understand and accept whatever I had to offer and to make my life feel whole, and it was this lovely lady who I now proudly identify to one and all as Mary Elizabeth "Maybeth" Wirz.

Since the honeymoon could not last forever, two weeks later I was back at my Wirz & Associates office, now located in nearby Norwalk, CT, ready to keep grinding out press releases and meaningful events for my existing clients, as well as to take on new undertakings.

These endeavors included a bevy of baseball headline-making events for IBM and a rapidly-growing Chicago statistical empire known as STATS Inc. I felt equipped for the challenges.

In some ways, working for IBM was not a natural. I did not fully understand its business, but give me a way to work with what baseball had to offer, including its meaningful numbers and its big-name people, and I knew I could find a way.

IBM and Major League Baseball were in collaboration with every team with what was known as its Student Pennant Race. The computer giant was co-host of the annual Hall of Fame Golf Tournament, and IBM was undertaking to use its technology to fairly estimate the distance of every major league home run.

For the Student Pennant Race, I helped reach out to the media to tell the story of how IBM's technological attributes were being utilized in baseball, with the nation's seventh graders as the primary target audience. The Hall of Fame golf event at the lush Leatherstocking Golf Club in Cooperstown primarily provided hospitality events for key IBMers and clients, and my task was straightforward in publicizing the one-day competition held exclusively for those inductees who excelled on the golf course. Who would not cherish watching standout golfers such as Juan Marichal, Jim Palmer, Al Kaline, Johnny Bench, Rollie

275

Fingers, *et al.,* try to stay close to par, or realize that others, such as Yogi Berra and Lou Brock, might excel in baseball but were not miles ahead of average Saturday-afternoon foursomes at the local public course.

About all I did was listen in to a Ted Williams-Stan Musial conversation, tell Ernie Banks where the beverage cart was, or guide a photographer to the hole where Joe DiMaggio could be found as I awaited the results and could send out my wrap-up story to the wire services.

STATS Inc., based in Chicago, was an interesting enterprise with early *Moneyball*-type findings through never-before-studied statistics. The company thrives today, as students of baseball and some other sports realize through data attributed to the company that often appears in media stories, or when the bold company logo shows up at the conclusion of a live sports event.

We were a somewhat fascinating match for each other in that I loved statistics—albeit perhaps more traditional numbers—and I could get the attention of general managers or others in baseball operations at most any major league team office, as well as the New York City headquarters and the national media. STATS did not yet have many of these relationships but coveted them. Bill James was involved with STATS, although this was years before he became the acclaimed numbers guru who can open most any baseball door today.

We used many PR tactics to get STATS known and embraced. CEO John Dewan and I would tour some of the spring training sites with the latest of STATS' prolific outpouring of books, or we would set up a meeting with a general manager and his key associates so Craig Wright could dazzle with his depth of understanding numbers as to why certain hitters were so much more dangerous with two strikes than others.

I remember one day with Houston where General Manager Bob Watson eventually signed off on a $25,000 package with STATS ($25,000 bought a lot more bats in 1991 than it does today). Manager Art Howe said one of the things we were offering that would mean quite a bit to him was being able to see his own tendencies—not just the opposition's—to determine if it was always a specific pitch count when he would use a squeeze play.

I believe the most important of all the positive developments I brought to STATS Inc. was when I got The Associated Press to use STATS box scores for its client base. Virtually every newspaper that carried boxes got them from The Associated Press. The wire service had been creating its own box scores for decades, but the challenge of meeting timely deadlines with 100 per cent accuracy was greater every year.

Once The Associated Press was on board with a handsome contract with STATS and found out how much it could rely on both the speed of delivery and the accuracy, it was not long until the more elaborate box scores we see today, with up-to-date batting averages and pitch counts and so much more, began to appear. This part of the baseball world was forever improved.

A New Venture Plus Measuring Every Home Run for the First Time

1992

My continuing relationship with Bowie Kuhn took another interesting step some eight years after he gave up the baseball commissionership—seven years after I started working for myself—when Wirz & Associates formed a partnership with he and Bob Richmond, another successful and interesting baseball man whose background was quite different from those of Kuhn and myself.

Richmond had a triple life in the sport. He was president of two minor leagues, the Northwest and the Arizona, both catering to new professionals; was part owner of a Double-A franchise in Midland, TX; and he had become arguably the best-known broker of minor league franchises.

Both Kuhn and Richmond had powerful contacts and wonderful reputations, and minor league sports—largely baseball and hockey—were on a fast track of success. There was a great opportunity for our new business, Sports Franchise, Inc. (SFI), to thrive and produce nice revenue for the three of us.

None of us was independently wealthy despite our years in baseball. While Kuhn had 15½ years as commissioner with an attractive salary and perks, he never had anything approaching the mega-financial contract Bud Selig enjoyed in his tenure. Kuhn also took a beating from a failed law firm he co-founded after leaving the commissioner's office, supposedly being hurt in a major way by a partner. His primary income, at least so it seemed to me, came from some consulting opportunities through his law and baseball experiences, as well as from speaking engagements throughout the United States.

My boss, business partner and friend, Bowie Kuhn

Richmond, who also had a law degree, had hopes we could branch into finding buyers and sellers in other sports, and perhaps get an occasional major league brokerage opportunity because of Kuhn's high-level contacts.

I had my own contacts at both the major and minor league level, as well as some from other sports, although I was largely to be the administrative glue for SFI.

Our company brochures and newsletters told great stories and lauded our ability to assist municipalities, as well as professional and amateur leagues. They talked about both expansion and relocation services, plus the ability to assist in winning league approvals, strategy and planning, and negotiating concessions agreements. All of it was true.

We had geographic issues which kept us from being together all that often, with Kuhn in Florida, and Richmond in Eugene, OR, during the summer and in the Phoenix area the rest of the year. My office, at the time in Milford, CT, was SFI's mailing address, and the location when we eventually added an executive director to manage our day-to-day operation.

It did not take long before we had identified a number of interesting potential clients. There were baseball franchises aside from those Richmond reserved for himself because of his ongoing business. We could see opportunities in Butte, MT; Harrisburg, PA; Chattanooga, TN; Charlotte, NC; and Visalia, CA. There also were East Coast Hockey League opportunities around the East and South, minor league basketball in Birmingham, AL, and Omaha, NE; the Arena Football League; and startup soccer and cycling leagues. We also were able to identify any number of investors who would listen to whatever we could offer, and we started opening consulting doors where our individual talent and experience fit.

All of us were enthused. I know I devoted a considerable amount of time, much of it trying to keep us focused.

One undertaking typical of our efforts was to assist what was to be the centrally-owned Women's Professional Fastpitch League for softball. Kuhn already was chief spokesman. The expected launch was set for the summer of 1995. Solid funding allowed for a deal to be struck with ESPN, which would televise part of an exhibition tour.

The WPF appeared to have real possibilities because of both the passion and skill of the players. Dominant pitchers were highly skilled, although that also kept scoring to a minimum, even with some newly-introduced rules. There were other difficulties, of course, with a primary one being that only a limited number of communities had any appreciable softball fan base. Those that did were largely in out-of-the-way areas. Major markets were not going to be easy.

I almost felt sorry for those pouring money into this undertaking because they did not have typical experience in running small franchises. SFI gave the WPF considerable visibility, but that was not enough.

SFI had other client success stories, although the practical matter was all three of us partners pretty much treated the new business as our stepchild. Wirz & Associates commanded much of my time and energy since I could not neglect my clients, staff, and the guaranteed revenue and expenses. Richmond's other ventures were primary for him, and Kuhn's travel schedule remained hectic.

We remained active for probably at least three years, bringing in some occasional revenue, before eventually deciding to remain friends but go our own separate ways for business.

It may very well have been a lost opportunity had we been able to establish more continuity.

One Wirz & Associates program that really started cranking up this year was IBM's sponsorship with Major League Baseball of the IBM Tale of the Tape.

The distance of long home runs has fascinated everyone associated with the game since the beginning of time. But every measurement up until recent years was an estimate. Some enterprising PR man might take out a tape measure on occasion to try for some accuracy, or an equally enterprising writer might "guess" to embellish his story. No one had a way of disputing the distance of some Ozark Ike-type clout.

IBM started putting its technology skills to work in 1987, measuring distances to every conceivable point in some of the major league stadiums, adding in trajectory factors, and coming up with how far a ball would have traveled until it struck ground if not for striking a facade or a section of the bleachers.

Based on measuring only home-team homers in some stadiums, Dave Winfield was given credit for the longest clout (among those measured) in 1988, with a drive of 478 feet against the California Angels; Nick Esasky of Boston was tops at 456 feet in '89; Andres Galarraga drove a ball an estimated 475 feet for Montreal in '90; and Chicago White Sox strong boy Dan Pasqua struck a 484-foot drive against the New York Yankees on April 27 in 1991.

By '92, every one of the 26 stadium had been charted; both home-team and visitor homers were calculated; and for the very first time, there would be some semblance of integrity to these cherished baseball feats.

My company, working for IBM, had the responsibility of putting all of the numbers together so monthly and season leaders could be revealed for both the American and National leagues. IBM sweetened the story by donating $10,000 in each major league community in the names of the players striking the three longest home runs in home games.

This was quite an opportunity for Wirz & Associates because our name was attached to every media release, and when anyone had a question, it would land in our office. I loved the fact we could let our imagination run wild with additional computations, such as determining which player, team and stadium had the longest average home run, and we could do a great deal of outreach to the media to place stories or charts. A small list or graphic would have our name associated with that of IBM.

To this day, every time a homer is struck, it is likely an announcement will be made in the stadium of the distance of a home run, followed by mentions on radio and television broadcasts, as well as many times in the next day's newspaper story.

The fun of hearing the distances is at its magic best when the Home Run Derby is held on the night before each year's All-Star Game. I remember doing the calculations the first couple of years myself, then putting out a release at the end of the competition. I can take joy in knowing my company was there when this started, even though the system has become so much more sophisticated in subsequent years.

For the record, big Frank Thomas of the Chicago White Sox, inducted into the Hall of Fame in his first year of eligibility in 2014, was credited with the longest average home run in 1992 of 405 feet, with Fred McGriff of San Diego close behind at 400.3.

Independent Baseball Debuts; I Get Heavily Involved

1993

I was blessed that so many opportunities kept coming my way, emerging because of my major league days, or through Wirz & Associates or my "network" of contacts developed through the years. They did not always turn into success stories and certainly were not always financially rewarding. I did not have the Midas touch for turning everything into a bar of gold, but then that was not what attracted me to baseball in the first place.

My early media years, the 16 years in major league baseball and the formation (in 1985) of Wirz & Associates could be labeled as my first three professional careers. Each has a special spot in my heart, but what I can easily call a fourth career was looming even though I was not looking to take another leap. Wirz & Associates was more than enough.

I had issued some press releases in 1992—I cannot even remember if I was paid—about a startup venture to be known as Independent Baseball. It was independent in that it was not linked in any way to Major League Baseball, but it was considered professional in that players would be paid at least a few hundred dollars a month.

The teams were going to bring the professional game to communities in the Upper Midwest that, for the most part, were isolated from major or minor league teams and had virtually no chance to getting a team because of the territorial rights established by the people who ran the game.

The people organizing what was to become the Northern League usually had one of two types of backgrounds; occasionally both. This meant they had experience in the professional game, at least from a managerial standpoint, and/or they were business people successful enough that they could afford to gamble on trying to have some fun in baseball and possibly, if the stars were sufficiently aligned, make some more money. They might also have sufficient renegade spirit and/or anger toward the so-called "Organized Baseball" establishment that they hoped to succeed in spite of the odds of making the concept work.

I now have the benefit of hindsight more than two decades later of knowing Independent Baseball could work, even though the failures very likely outnumbered the success stories. But I am getting ahead of myself, because I did not have any inkling at this time that I would get deeply involved for what has amounted to virtually the entire remainder of my working career, taking me from my 50s well through most of my 70s.

It certainly started innocently enough with Miles Wolff, clearly the father of the Independent game, getting me to sign on to do these media releases hailing the planned launching in 1993 of the Northern League—the first Independent league professional baseball had seen since the post-World War II days, when seemingly every community with a diamond with 90 feet between bases and at least a small grandstand had a team.

We announced that five franchises were awarded in the U.S. and Canada after a meeting conveniently held at the Minneapolis-St. Paul International Airport, with the teams representing Duluth, MN-Superior, WI; Sioux Falls, SD; Thunder Bay (on the west side of Lake Ontario in Canada); Fargo, ND-Moorhead, MN; and St. Paul, MN. The last one raised a few eyebrows because St. Paul was located across the river from the Minnesota Twins, so a major league market was being invaded. Winnipeg, Manitoba, and Sioux City, IA, were among others represented at that meeting.

We also told anyone who paid attention that the St. Paul ownership would be headed up by Marv Goldklang and

Mike Veeck. Goldklang was a limited partner in the New York Yankees and the owner of minor league teams in Fort Myers, FL, Charleston, SC, and Erie, PA. Veeck, the son of renowned major league owner and eventual Hall of Famer Bill Veeck, was president of the Fort Myers team known as the Miracle.

Those two names could set off extensive dialogue within the walls of major league offices by the very nature of having Organized Baseball people supporting this unknown, but potentially unwanted undertaking.

Sioux Falls, Fargo-Moorhead, Sioux City, Winnipeg and, yes, St. Paul, have had teams ever since, which the major league people—and likely even the Northern League founders—would never have envisioned as possible.

It worked out well that with my love affair with Sanibel Island, on Florida's west coast and near Fort Myers, I would be in that bustling area when the Northern League held its first tryout camp at Terry Park, the very spot where the Kansas City Royals of my days played their spring training exhibitions.

This was the media release I wrote for the Northern League on March 4, 1993:

Seventy Seasoned College and Pro Players Take Part in First Northern League Tryout

The first player signed hit .305 in his professional debut in the Pioneer League last summer, but he had plenty of company in impressing scouts when the independent Northern League held its first tryout camp at Fort Myers, FL Tuesday and Wednesday.

"It bodes well for the quality of play fans will see," said Founder and President Miles Wolff. "We thought this first tryout camp might not be that well attended. We know we'll get quality at our tryouts later on, especially as major league organizations start releasing players."

286

What Wolff and Director of Baseball Operations Van Schley were greeted with at the Fort Myers camp were 70 players from virtually as many colleges, as well as experienced players from 12 major league organizations.

Todd Rosenthal, the first played signed, is the epitome of what the Northern League wants to showcase in its six Upper Midwest cities. The University of Connecticut graduate, who signed with the Thunder Bay (Ontario) Whiskey Jacks, was a .338 career hitter in four seasons at Connecticut. The Scarsdale, NY, native turned professional last summer and signed with the independent Salt Lake City Trappers. Rosenthal, a first baseman, hit .305 and drove in 41 runs with his 80 hits while being named the league champion Trappers' defensive player of the year.

"I have a work ethic," enthuses the sociology major. "I'm not here for a summer job. A million guys would like to be where I am. I want a (eventual) contract with a major league organization. I think the objective is to win the (Northern) league title and play well personally. This is a new frontier. I can see it already. The league is going to be competitive."

Rosenthal's competition at Fort Myers included hopefuls such as a 1991 Division II All-American, the 1992 all-Atlantic Coast Conference third baseman, two players who were in European leagues last summer and a player who had a professional stint with the Spartanburg (SC) Phillies. Players also came from college baseball powerhouses such as Miami and Oklahoma State as well as from college teams at such schools as Auburn, Cornell, Duke, Old Dominion and Vanderbilt.

When the two days ended, five other players were selected in a mini draft and still others were told they may get a call back later. The five draftees were Duluth-RHP Paul Caccavale, Central Connecticut State; St. Paul-RHP Eric Moran, Tiffin University; Thunder Bay-OF-C Frank Mora, University of Miami (FL); St. Paul-SS Jerry

DeFabbia, Fairleigh Dickinson; Thunder Bay-3B Brad Kantor, Manatee Junior College.

Tryouts for the June 15-Labor Day league also are scheduled for April 1-2 at Municipal Stadium in Pompano Beach, FL; May 1-2 at Pepperdine University near Los Angeles; May 7-8 at Sacramento City College; May 29-30 at Triton Junior College in River Grove, IL (near Chicago); and June 4-6 at Municipal Stadium in St. Paul, MN.

Independent Baseball started here. Literally. This was the very first tryout camp, held at Terry Park in Fort Myers, FL

The Northern League did, indeed, get off the ground that season, as did a central-U.S.-based league known as the Frontier League, which operates to this day.

The Northern drew considerable attention, too, led by St. Paul, which convinced former Chicago Cubs-Cincinnati Reds stalwart Leon "Bull" Durham, 36, to play first base and DH, and because the Saints played to 97 percent capacity at 5,069-seat Municipal Stadium.

"I love St. Paul," Veeck was quoted as saying in the year-end *Baseball America Almanac.* "They've embraced the silliness, and in the process this place has already stolen a piece of my heart."

Former Los Angeles Dodgers and St. Louis Cardinals star Pedro Guerrero joined Sioux Falls a few weeks into the season, and the league sold some players to major league organizations, starting with Rochester, MN, outfielder Kash Beauchamp, whose father (Jim) had been a big-league player. Kash Beauchamp made the league's claim of being Class AA caliber look good when the Northern League batting champion (.367) hit .400 in 60 at-bats for Cincinnati's Double-A team in Chattanooga, TN.

I had one other brush with the Independents before that season ended, when I joined Kuhn; highly-successful Westport, CT, businessman David Carpenter, about whom you will hear much more in coming pages; and others in trying to place a Northern League team in my home state's capital city, Lincoln.

We topped the headlines in the *Lincoln Star* for a time, and we virtually had the city council on our side to renovate old Sherman Field, although Mayor (and eventual Governor) Mike Johanns was not a huge sports fan. It did not help that Mike Veeck took a verbal jab at Kuhn's involvement since his father and Kuhn were adversaries on some major league issues.

We never got to the point of sufficient approval and funding, and likely would have struggled for enough fan and sponsor support in an ancient stadium. However, I take a tiny bit of joy from knowing we stirred up interest. That may have helped to a degree when the city and University of Nebraska collaborated years later to build and share the very successful Haymarket Park, which is within easy view of Municipal Stadium, where my Nebraska Cornhuskers do a great job of carrying pride for the entire state on autumn Saturdays.

As it turned out, the Northern League's debut and that short-lived venture into trying to bring a team to Lincoln were only the very beginning of my journey into Independent Baseball. That journey still commands enough time today that my golf game never will amount to more than a periodic respite from the daily routine of sorting through transactions of those going up to or being sent down from major league teams, and sifting through endless websites to find the next story I can embellish with my own views on how it fits into the baseball map.

An Indy Baseball Ownership Role
And Meeting Young Derek Jeter

1994

My business continued doing well as we got into the mid-'90s, especially with the Rolaids Relief Man program, our Just For Men work, *Baseball America* duties and the IBM Tale of the Tape perking along. I want to say I was comfortable because I knew we produced really well for these clients year in and year out, but "comfort" is a dangerous term at the same time.

One never knew when the corporate clients would decide to take a new direction in their tactics, or when new personnel would come into the picture and might not like the way one combed his hair or want some new person to put his or her own stamp on what seemed like a well-oiled machine.

New possibilities were forever emerging, and they almost always were a joy for me to consider. Landing clients who were able to pay at a respectable rate seemed to be more difficult, though, probably because I was nearly 20 years removed from the Baseball Commissioner's Office and Wirz & Associates' work had almost always been with national companies or brands. I was not well-known in Connecticut; my base was national.

It may not have made the most business sense, but I was so very intrigued to think about what Independent Baseball might bring, especially as a way of possibly enjoying the game from the standpoint of a specific team. I had not experienced that since leaving the Royals nearly two decades earlier.

The final pitches of that maiden year in the resurrection of Independent Baseball had barely been thrown when I found myself exploring the possibility of getting into ownership of a team.

Now, let me be clear. I did not have the financial resources to really invest in a team, but my love of the game and my administrative experience combined with my depth of contacts, including some who were very well-heeled, all of a sudden made it plausible I could be included in some type of ownership group.

I do not remember exactly how this started to unfold, but we were not very far into 1994 when I found myself in regular conversation with Bill Terlecky, a veteran minor league operator, whose position at the time was as general manager of the Scranton/Wilkes-Barre, PA, Triple-A team, which was the top farm club of the Philadelphia Phillies.

Terlecky was trying to put a group together to run the Thunder Bay Whiskey Jacks, one of the six teams in the Northern League. Thunder Bay, as mentioned earlier, is located on the western edge of Lake Ontario. It is not a large or especially modern city, known more for its fishing and hunting camps than just about anything else. But the 127,581 fans lured to old-fashioned Port Arthur Stadium in 36 home dates that first season ranked second only to attendance for the St. Paul Saints, who had put the league on the professional map with their sprinkling of former major leaguers and a whole lot of promotional zaniness.

The Whiskey Jacks appeared to be a decent investment if Independent Baseball was more than a short-term solution to provide summer entertainment in communities shut out of professional baseball. To start with, the nickname of Whiskey Jacks and an attractive logo were drawing attention across the entire baseball landscape, even though few people seemed to realize that was the name of a Canadian bird.

Terlecky needed several hundred thousand dollars to make the deal happen, and his personal bank account was no better than my own. I became an asset because I did have a decent reputation, and I had contacts within the game. It was not totally crazy to think that some of my corporate clients might want to jump on board.

He did have a lead investor, and when I started reaching out in a whole lot of directions, I was led to David Carpenter, whose brilliance in zinc metal and related scientific fields had helped his family become multimillionaires. Carpenter, who was president and CEO of Horsehead Industries Inc., had spent some years in Pennsylvania and had a farm in Upstate New York, but what put us together was the mutual affection between my stepson Peter Matton and Carpenter's son, Jim. David Carpenter enjoyed baseball, although I believe his primary motivation may have been that Jim was still trying to get his post-college feet on the ground, and my involvement in baseball might be an asset as Jim dabbled in such fields as sports productions.

David Carpenter was among the kindest men I have ever known, with a personality that never wavered, at least for me, in nearly a decade we were unknowingly going to have together, starting with the Whiskey Jacks.

I also connected with Loren Matthews, whom I first knew when he ran promotions for the New York Mets and from whom I could occasionally bum a ride home from a night game at Shea Stadium when I had started my day by leaving my car at the South Norwalk, CT, train station for my morning commute into Manhattan.

Matthews had moved on by this time to ESPN, where his duties eventually became such that he was the master planner who had to talk major college athletic directors and football coaches into moving a game to some odd hour on a Wednesday or Thursday in order that this developing network could stretch its college football week out another day or two. Matthews cared a great deal about baseball, and, in fact, had visions of one day owning a minor league team and moving out of the rat race of network television.

With Carpenter and Matthews on board, Terlecky had his Thunder Bay ownership group prior to the 1996 season and Bob Wirz was at least a nominal part of it. What a joy that was; I was involved enough to have a hand in securing a manager or players, and I could use my public relations ability in efforts to make the Whiskey Jacks look good in their community and to help spread the word about the potential of the Independent Baseball game.

We made a bad hire in a rookie manager, Jason Felice, who was in over his head in terms of leading others even though he had been a star player in early-day Independent circles. As I recall, the league helped us find a good replacement in Jay Ward, who had some major league time and whom I had known when he played the outfield during my Denver Bears years a quarter-century earlier.

Ward was a stern disciplinarian, which was exactly what we needed, although with the terrible start, the team finished 33-51 and in last place in what was a four-team Eastern Division. Even worse, attendance really fell off to little more than 1,000 a game.

Our group eventually sold, but Independent Baseball leagues were springing up all across the country because of some really solid franchises. It seemed possible I could have a meaningful role in this sport that was so deeply etched in my blood without leaving Connecticut, which no doubt would have been necessary had I ever chosen to pursue another major league opportunity. A family move would not have been easy; besides, Wirz & Associates was thriving, even though it still commanded many hours a week from me to keep it that way.

One of my most memorable moments of 1994 for Wirz & Associates clients took place late in the summer.

I was somewhat used to working with sports personalities because I had done this for a long time. I had a respectful approach to them almost without fail, partly because I took the attitude that they deserved this treatment. Also, one never wanted to be less than 100 percent courteous since my employees and I were representing our clients. The clients often placed the athletes on a pedestal, many times because the whole experience was new to these 20- and 30-something people who loved the experience of being with the star athlete. Sometimes, this took precedence over the fact they had a responsibility for their brand or company. The athletes usually were professional, too, although some could have used better preparation.

Looking back, one task on behalf of *Baseball America* was to meet Derek Jeter and his father in the lobby of the Grand Hyatt Hotel just outside of Grand Central Station in New York City in mid-September. Derek was a celebrity-in-waiting, as it turned out. This 20-year-old from Kalamazoo, MI, had been selected as the magazine's Minor League Player of the Year for his third professional season, which had started in Class A (Tampa, FL); gone through Double-A (Albany-Colonie, NY); and finished with 35 games in Triple-A (Columbus, OH).

The thin young man had been the sixth selection—first high school choice—in the June draft two years earlier, and he was beginning to prove the Yankees correct by hitting .329 or better at each of those three minor league stops while stealing a combined 50 bases. He had 186 hits, a rarity for a minor leaguer, especially since he only played 138 games. Jeter also had cut his errors from a troublesome 56 in 1993 to only 25 this season.

"He's unbelievable," praised Columbus Manager Stump Merrill in the story *Baseball America* ran in its 1995 *Almanac*. "If he's not the full package, I haven't seen one." Jeter talked about how easy it was "to work hard."

Mark Lavrahan/Associated Press file photo

Derek Jeter poses on the dugout steps at Yankee Stadium in New York on Sept. 14, 1994, after he was named Baseball America's minor league player of the year. The 20-year-old from Kalamazoo, Mich., finished the season at Triple-A in Columbus, Ohio. Jeter will end his career sixth on the all-time hits list (3,489 through Sunday) and ninth in runs scored (1,921).

Derek Jeter before most of his fame

I can still visualize where we sat in the Grand Hyatt lobby that day, although my mind has run pretty blank on the rest of the afternoon, which obviously ended up at Yankee Stadium.

I got a little refresher in the fall of 2014 when reams of copy were being written to celebrate the retirement of the certain first-ballot Hall of Famer and The Associated Press ran a story tracing back to the '94 draft, reissuing a file photo of the nattily attired 20-year-old on the steps of the Yankees dugout, holding the silver bowl we presented him.

Losing Dad

It is difficult to write about this year, even though business remained good and I was up to my eyeballs in new projects. My personal life took a jolt because we lost dad.

Maybeth and I were on our way back from one of our work/play trips to be a part of spring training in Florida, and had stopped to see her mom, May Woolhiser, in Flemington, NJ, when I got that terrible telephone call.

While Dad had been back to Connecticut for Jeff's wedding to Antonia the previous July, he had lost ground in recent months. Still, when my sister, Bev, called with the news of dad's death, it seemed unreal that he could be gone.

I do not exaggerate when I say my father was one of the pillars of our little village of Halsey, indeed of all of Central Nebraska. It is not a stretch to say R. A. "Fat" Wirz did not have an enemy. The best example may be the fact more than 300 people crowded into the Community Hall in our village of now perhaps 100 people for his funeral. There was no way we could hold the service in our beloved Congregational church, because even with the sound piped into the basement to help serve the overflow, so many people would be left out.

Here is a portion of one obituary:

Ak-Sar-Ben Good Neighbor Award
Winner R. A. Wirz Passes Away

"Widely respected for 40 years as the rural mailman "you could set your watch to", and owner-operator of a customer-friendly grocery store in Halsey for nearly as long, R. A. Wirz passed away Monday.

Wirz, 92, died at Jennie Melham Hospital in Broken Bow after a short illness.

Known for both his community and family involvement, Wirz hosted the first meeting to discuss establishment of the Nebraska State 4-H Camp, which was built at the Nebraska National Forest at Halsey in the 1960s.

He was also the first president (1942) of the Sandhills Region Health Association, served 19 years on the Halsey School Board, managed the Halsey Town Team baseball team, and in 1965, was honored (along with his wife Marie) with the Ak-Sar-Ben Good Neighbor Award.

Robert A. Wirz was born on Christmas Day, 1902, in Nemaha County (Southeast Nebraska), one of six children of Nick and Mary (Grable) Wirz. The family, which spoke primarily German at the time, moved to a homestead one and three quarters miles north of Halsey in March of 1909.

Although he dreamed of becoming a railroad engineer, R. A. remained a lifelong Sandhills resident, primarily as a grocer and mailman.

He had two lengthy stints as proprietor of the Wirz Cash Store, where the motto proudly displayed on every annual gift for customers from yardsticks to calendars, was "A Square Deal or No Deal".

But grocery business, often seven days a week, wasn't enough. In 1946, Wirz became a six-days-a-week rural mail carrier.

The first route was a 60-mile trip, which started and ended in Halsey, with stops at post offices in Purdum, Elsmere and Koshapah (which no longer exists) plus many ranch home mailboxes in between for the salary of $2,095.00 a year. The U.S. Postal Service eventually added 26 more miles west of Purdum to the Cascade Post Office three times a week.

"Fat" broke in 30 new pickups in the 40 years he carried mail, worked with 10 postmasters, was responsible for some

12,000 trips (most of which he made himself) and filled mailboxes about 300,000 times.

R.A. wasn't the boasting type, but he was proud that his nearly one million miles were accident free, and he admitted, "I was overwhelmed" when 250 people (twice the population of Halsey) showed up July 6, 1986, at his retirement party.

What did R.A .remember most about carrying mail? "The most memorable time was the blizzard of '49, of course, because it was exactly one month between complete trips around the route. But I cherish most, the many, many friendships which Marie and I developed in 40 years."

Many a youngster...some not so young today...remember most of learning to drive at the wheel of Fat's mail truck.

While R. A. was the gentlest of people, was believed to be without enemy, and was one of the best respected of Sandhills people, his fellow postal workers did take him somewhat to task in the message they wrote for his retirement party:

"One patron has reported that you could tell who won the previous day's baseball game by the way the mail was placed in the box. If the Kansas City Royals won, the mail was in the front of the box, and if they lost, the mail was in the back."

I did not look forward to dad's spankings if I had done some foolish thing as a youngster, but he was truly as gentle as they come in everyday life. He would open our grocery store on a Sunday if a rancher needed a few items, he would be one of the first to swing into action when there was a prairie fire, and he would go out of his way by driving some distance to see that a package did not get wet when he was on his the mail route on a foul-weather day.

I had my own benefits of the kind man being my dad. I cannot remember that he helped me with homework very often, but he made certain our family was comfortable in every way in these semi-primitive years when indoor

299

plumbing and private telephone lines were just coming our way.

And I never had to think twice about who I would be riding with when parents were needed to drive several players to a basketball game or a school play. Dad (and mom) always made themselves available.

One vivid memory of dad's funeral and the burial, where he joined so many relatives and friends in the peaceful Purdum cemetery, was of an early-teen girl from a farm along his mail route cozying up to mom throughout nearly the entire proceedings. Her show of affection and grief for my 92-year-old father, which one would not expect from a 14-year-old, touched us all.

Yes, everyone loved the man.

Back to the business at hand, the Winter Meetings, this time at the Bonaventure Hotel in Los Angeles on November 30 - December 5, continued to be a staple on my Wirz & Associates schedule because I needed to provide visibility for various clients, meet with potential new ones, and say hello to tons of longtime friends whom I might only see this one time each year.

I surprised even myself at what ground I covered in four or five days when I looked back at both the pre-arranged and spontaneous activities. The major events, very typical of each year:

Friday a.m. —Attend Bob Freitas Seminar
—Visit exhibit hall, working in pre-arranged visits to Inkwell Promotions and USA Baseball booths
Friday p.m.—Meet to discuss possible involvement with National Volleyball League
    —Go offsite for meeting with Fox Sports
    —Planning session regarding role with Independent team in Thunder Bay
Saturday a.m. —Meet with Bowie Kuhn

—Attend opening session, meet up with clients from *Baseball America* and Howe SportsData

—Visit press room to distribute Rolaids and *Baseball America* releases

Saturday p.m.—Introductory meeting with Rolaids Relief Man winner and his agent

—Attend Northern League meeting

Saturday nite—Dinner with Sports Franchises partners

—Attend meetings gala

Sunday a.m.—Use treadmill (probably never happened)

—Meet Rolaids winner for pre-luncheon reception; take photos

Sunday p.m.—Present Rolaids award at official minor league luncheon

—Return to exhibits

Sunday nite—Attend Scout of Year reception

— (Personal) Meet my sister and husband for dinner

Monday a.m.—Breakfast meeting regarding National Volleyball League

—Meet with Northern League owner

—Hold National Association of Collegiate Baseball Leagues meeting

—Meet with two associates to brainstorm projects

Monday p.m.—Lunch with New Era caps

—Introductory meeting with Baseball America Minor League Player of Year Andruw Jones

Monday nite—Attend banquet reception with Jones

—Attend official minor league banquet

Tuesday a.m.—Treadmill (probably did not happen)

—Follow-up meeting regarding Thunder Bay

And so it went as a hustling entrepreneur.

The Years of Independent Team Ownership

1996-2000

My continuing affection for baseball most likely cost me against working toward long-term financial security about now, although in fairness to myself, the first decade or so of Wirz & Associate had been very demanding. I had built the business to a point where I could afford staff, and needed the people to service our accounts, but, in reality, the major demands for clients and the always-present need to search for new ones almost always fell to yours truly. That's just the way it is.

A baseball person—the same would be true in other sports—likes the action on the diamond. It was great being in publicity, but if one loved the game as I did and trusted his instincts, what would be better than a role in developing a team? That would be the ultimate.

Fred Claire went that route when he moved from the business side of the Los Angeles Dodgers to become general manager. So did Dan O'Dowd, Ned Colletti and other friends through the years.

Why do so many develop a love for fantasy sports where "I can build a better team than anyone else?"

It was almost certainly not going to happen for me at the major league level because I had stayed the course with in-house PR and then with Wirz & Associates to build both a reputation and a future, never taking the gamble to change directions by 180 degrees at a point in life where it might have been possible.

Then along came a possible chance to do the baseball team-building even if it was at a level far below the major leagues. It still had an appeal.

302

The path I was about to go down ended up dominating much of my attention for the next few years.

One of the Independent leagues that had sprung up was called the Northeast League, stretching from eastern Pennsylvania to Rhode Island and Maine. If only I could find the right city in Connecticut or nearby, this might be the opportunity to call some of the major shots. David Carpenter was having fun with his involvement in Thunder Bay; it was a nice distraction from his worldwide travels.

David and I would have loved placing a team in Stamford, CT, a city less than an hour from New York City but virtually shut out from landing an affiliated minor league team by the rules intended to protect both major and minor league territories. Stamford had both sufficient population and a nice corporate base, but it did not have a ballpark other than Cubeta Stadium, which would have needed a major facelift even if the long-entrenched youth league officials could have been persuaded that a pro team was worth surrendering some playing dates.

We also looked at Torrington, CT, but both the market and stadium were on the small side. Eventually, the once-bustling factory town of Waterbury became a possibility. The Class AA Eastern League had made Municipal Stadium work for a number of years with a variety of major league working agreements. The last season had been 1986.

The great memory of Waterbury to my major league friends was that a running track had crossed the outfield. It could not have been very well accepted in those days, and executives today would shudder at any consideration of their prized prospects having to endure such a strange experience.

The track had long been removed by the time we came along, but Municipal Stadium still only had primary seating along the first-base side of the facility. At least, chair-back seats dominated instead of raw bleachers, but it was far from having a modern look. Someone had decided to erect a

303

building behind home plate for the media with concessions in the rear portion. This prevented any realistic consideration of adding seating in this normally premium area. Third-base bleachers provided the only other seating, and it was not very attractive.

Waterbury's political leaders welcomed a team, although neither they nor the business community seemed to have any vision that a baseball team and a new stadium at some feasible future date could energize a tired, often corrupt city.

One other obstacle for a team to succeed was that the city had granted a concessions deal for any event at Municipal Stadium or the adjacent high school football field to a local family business. Frankie's hot dogs were popular in the city, but trying to negotiate even a half-decent arrangement which would give a local baseball operator much of a revenue share from concessions for the many new fans a pro team would attract was next to impossible.

Despite these obstacles, Carpenter and I decided to place a Northeast League team in Waterbury starting with the 1997 season. It would be the Waterbury Spirit—our final nickname choice after a strange challenge when we wanted to name the team the Wizards.

We hired Russ Ardolina, now a major league scout for the Texas Rangers, as general manager. He had been in the league, and was a bright, ambitious young man whose goal all along was to one day work on the baseball side of a major league organization.

For a field manager, we considered a number of people, finally settling on Stan Hough, a Texan (Waco), who had been a minor league catcher and had experience coaching in the affiliated minors. Nice man. His job was to put the roster together, then manage it, with some help in finding talent from both Ardolina and myself. Ardolina knew players who had been in the league, and I had always wanted such an opportunity and had gotten my toes wet with Thunder Bay.

It ended up that Ardolina and I did the lion's share of finding talent.

I can remember some things as clearly as if it was this morning. The team got off to a 10-2 start in our first season. I believe the Spirit came home for a day off before moving to another city to continue a road trip. Ardolina, Hough and I had lunch at the Waterbury Club, and I had some type of personnel change I wanted to consider. Hough was totally content with the makeup of our 22-man roster. Tuck that detail away for another time.

We did not keep up the early pace, of course, but had a respectable season, finishing the first half of our split season in second place in our division at 22-20, two games behind Elmira, NY, which was managed by a solid Independent field boss in Dan Shwam. We won the second half with a 24-17 record, and had the league's Player of the Year in Tom Russin, one of my finds. The first baseman drove in 75 runs in the 83 games we played. Our top winner, Ron Frazier, I also had a hand in landing. He had grown up nearby in Torrington, and at one time was a decent prospect for the New York Yankees although he never reached the major leagues.

Independent teams have the luxury of being able to plan some experiment once in a while to have some extra fun, and, of course, to draw more attention which might lure in fans who had not come to the ballpark.

Our experiment was to bring in onetime minor league pitcher Pat Jordan, a Connecticut native whose career flamed out well below the major leagues. Jordan had become pretty well known for his writing talent, often featured in the likes of *Sports Illustrated* and author of a pretty-well-acclaimed memoir called *A False Spring.*

The real novelty was that Jordan was 56 years old, which we learned would make him the third-oldest person to pitch in a professional game. We wanted the graying Jordan to

305

come up from his Fort Lauderdale home, start a game and probably pitch an inning.

He was all for it, and supposedly threw a few times each week for months to get ready for this early-August stunt. The man had a large ego, as many an athlete does, and he did not want to embarrass himself on the mound. He even had a few friends on hand, along with his wife, Sue, who greatly resembled her daughter, actress Meg Ryan.

The event went off flawlessly, with the trim Jordan facing only four batters, one of whom he walked, in a scoreless inning. He even struck out the Adirondack Lumberjacks' (Glens Falls, NY) cleanup hitter to end it. We got some extra ink locally, as well as through an Associated Press story picked up by *USA TODAY,* and many other newspapers and columns in such publications as the *New York Daily News* and *Fort Lauderdale Sun-Sentinel.*

What we did not realize was that the crafty Jordan would use this experience for a large portion of a new book called *A Nice Tuesday*, which included a picture on the back cover of him smoking a cigar while still in his Waterbury Spirit uniform.

He can tell a story, but fact-checking did not seem to be a strong point when he repeatedly spelled my name Wirsz, and referred to the father of Independent Baseball, who had a hand in helping us put this shenanigan together, as Miles Wolfe. The baseball world knows he is Miles Wolff.

Jordan even had fun in the book with the fact former major league lefty Dave Fleming, who would try a major league comeback the next spring with the New York Yankees, relieved him to start the second inning.

The Spirit were matched with Elmira for the playoffs, a best-of-three divisional championship. The Pioneers opened at home, and Maybeth and I will never forget our very first playoff game. Ed Ponte, a gritty right-handed pitcher I found out of Florida and the only player in my life who physically challenged me (some time later) in our home clubhouse, gave us a 2-0 lead, which, I believe, carried into the eighth inning.

Knowing how the game was developing, Maybeth and I drove about 25 minutes to a parking lot in Seymour, CT, where our Waterbury radio station's signal was strong enough to be heard. We sat there for what seemed like an eternity as Ponte lost his cool to an umpire, then lost the edge on his game. It was a gut-wrenching 45 minutes or so before Elmira eventually tied, then won the game.

I had known as far back as my two seasons in Denver about 30 years earlier that the toughest losses for me to endure were those I could only listen to on the radio. Losses I watched on TV while in Kansas City were somewhat more bearable; losses watched in person were difficult but somehow more easily digested.

We lost again the next night and were eliminated from the playoffs. Still, I had considerable satisfaction knowing we could compete, and I knew I could identify and often land players with talent for this league.

We drew better than many a veteran Waterbury baseball observer thought was possible, even though it was not nearly enough to stay out of some deep red ink. We were dead last among the eight teams in the Northeast League, attracting just under 33,000 fans—fewer than 1,000 per game. It was key that Carpenter was enjoying his involvement, attending virtually every home game and a few on the road, even though the president (me) had to call him with some frequency to dig further into his checkbook.

Ardolina, our small staff and myself dug in all year round, and we grew attendance above the 40,000 mark in each of the next two seasons. Still, not nearly enough, especially with our inability to wrestle the concessions contract to an appreciably better rate.

We added another divisional title in 1998, once more getting swept in a best-of-three playoff series. I was very frustrated with Hough by the end of that second season, both because of what I considered his questionable in-game managerial strategy and probably even more because he was not strong in his ability to bring in quality players. Ardolina and I both enjoyed that part of the operation, but, in all truth, we needed to devote all of our attention to trying to improve the bottom line. We would not survive long term without more revenue or encouragement from either the City of Waterbury or the State of Connecticut that a new stadium was on the horizon.

I took a bold step—one of the most difficult in my career, whether at the commissioner's office or at Wirz & Associates. I called Hough to let him know we were not bringing him back, which probably raised a lot of eyebrows since we had made the playoffs in our first two seasons.

I have to laugh when I think back to what followed in the next few years in Stan's career. He was offered—and I believe accepted—the managing position with the Texas Rangers' Class AA affiliate. Then an even better offer came along, and he became manager of Montreal's top minor league club in Ottawa, Canada. The Expos were not a power, and I could see the picture in my head where they would fire manager Felipe Alou and reach down to their Triple-A club and elevate Hough to lead the National League team.

That scenario never developed, but wouldn't Bob Wirz have looked terrible if the man he fired from our "lowly" Independent club in Waterbury had gone on to manage in the major leagues? I often chuckle at the thought of such a development. I will say this: Stan Hough is a very decent human being. I think of him as a friend to this day, and believe he has similar feelings toward me.

Our pitching coach in '98 had been George Tsamis, a Connecticut guy who spent a good chunk of one season as a left-handed reliever for the Minnesota Twins. Tsamis actually came in as both a pitcher and a coach, but his arm was giving out so he did not make many mound appearances. He was a hard worker even though his temper could get the best of him. Ardolina wanted me to give Tsamis the managing job. I was not certain he was ready, although I eventually gave in after considering a few other people. He did fit our modest budget.

We did not make the playoffs in '99, when the Northeast League became the Eastern Division of the better-known Northern League, with the second half of the season a real collapse. Tsamis could not be faulted because of the series of injuries and defections that hit us. You pretty much have to accept it in Independent Baseball if a player wants to walk out. After all, some of the players only try an Indy league when their playing ability or immaturity has cost them an opportunity in a major league organization.

We brought centerfield wizard Jimmy Piersall back to his hometown of Waterbury, CT for an evening

Tsamis, who came back for a second season (2000), has developed into one of the most capable Independent managers, leading a team every year since we first hired

309

him. He won back-to-back titles with the New Jersey Jackals, who play at Yogi Berra Stadium in Little Falls, including an extra tier of playoffs against the supposedly stronger Northern League after his team had gotten through the Northeast League playoffs. He moved on to St. Paul, won again, and has led the high-profile Saints for more than a decade.

We got Waterbury back into the playoffs for a third time in four seasons in 2000 despite an overall 40-46 record, but our playoff winning percentage remained at .000 when we lost three consecutive games to Elmira. Even more disheartening, our modest attendance started trending downward. And, with no sign of progress toward a new stadium plus health issues emerging for Carpenter, we reluctantly decided the team was not going to succeed in Waterbury.

The next step was to try selling our franchise. We pretty much knew any sale would be to someone who would place the team in another city.

The old Waterbury Spirit franchise showed up again, but not until the '03 season. Two complete seasons went by before a team known as the North Shore Spirit was developed to play in Lynn, MA, just north of Boston.

I tried everything during this period to salvage some return on the approximately $2 million Carpenter had spent for those four seasons in Waterbury. I tracked down would-be owners, and I visited cities throughout much of the Northeast. So many people wanted to get involved for the fun of being able to say they owned a minor league baseball team. But the truth is very few of these ventures pay for themselves, especially if a community cannot offer anything but a tired stadium.

The better part of a decade later, many of the towns where the Northeast or Northern League teams were based moved from an Independent league to a summer (June-July) collegiate circuit. Without paying salaries and the related worker's comp, a budget could be slashed from $1 million-plus for most any short-season Independent league to less than $200,000 to see college players with eligibility remaining gain valuable experience and get ready for the free agent draft after their junior or senior season.

My effort to get a half-decent check for our Waterbury franchise finally came to an end when Nick Lopardo, a fairly well known businessman from the financial world in Boston, and I reached an agreement for the Spirit to become a reality in Lynn, where Lopardo would pour considerable money into improving a partially collapsed stadium.

Lopardo and I first had a handshake deal for one price, which would have been considerably below what the league would have liked to get if selling a new franchise. I would have even played a role since my experience, especially in the areas of player talent and league relations, would have been useful to the new team, at least in a consultative way. Then he started insisting on changes, which were utterly unfair. He had me over a barrel, knowing that I had been trying to find a buyer for what seemed like an eternity, and that Carpenter's health issues were growing. David wanted out at virtually any cost, and, frankly, the altered terms were not going to cause a man of his wealth to lose a great deal of sleep. Personally, I could see the handwriting that working for Lopardo would be more burdensome than any joy I would get for still being part of a baseball team.

For the record, North Shore played for five years, drawing better than we did in Waterbury, although Lopardo almost certainly lost money because of the improvements he put into Fraser Field. Lynn has since gone the collegiate route, and Lopardo, to my knowledge, is out of baseball, probably to the disappointment of very few.

I thoroughly enjoyed the atmosphere of the Independent game since the guiding premise was to win games. Everyone from ownership to management to players liked to compete. I know this description may seem strange to the casual baseball fan, but the affiliated minor leagues—the 150 or so teams supported by the 30 major league organizations—are, in fact, developmental leagues.

Players try their best because they want to improve and get to the majors. Managers are basically told who to play. The top draft choices will get their at-bats or time on the mound even if they are hitting .175 or walking people left and right. Other players may have batting averages one hundred points higher or an earned run average much lower, but if they are not perceived as those with the best future, they are not likely to be in the everyday lineup.

I got David Carpenter into another sport simultaneous with the Waterbury Spirit experience. I am happy this opportunity developed.

Connecticut had long been a hotbed for softball. Fast pitch softball. I felt confident we could make a difference, me because of my sports knowledge, Carpenter with his checkbook.

This opportunity loomed because of a women's team known as the Brakettes. Actually, when we got involved, this amateur powerhouse was still known by fans at the Raybestos Brakettes, even though this sponsorship had gone away years ago.

The Brakettes had won as many national titles as the New York Yankees had won World Series. They had drawn huge crowds to their home in Stratford, CT, too, but that was years before, and now the team was in danger of becoming extinct. The Brakettes were only drawing a couple hundred people to their games and the stadium had little more than bleacher seating.What's more, Manager John Stratton and General Manager Bob Baird still had the challenge of finding enough financial support to pay for the team to travel for tournaments when they were held outside of Stratford.

Neither Carpenter nor I had much previous exposure to softball. We found out in a hurry that these women, mostly current or recent collegians, could play. I was amazed at the pitching ability many elite players had, although there were the standouts and then there were the truly world-class pitchers, those who graced our television sets whenever the USA team or the Olympics gave them exposure. I also was shocked at how many outstanding defensive players there were—people who could waive down a hot smash at third base or shortstop and still get a runner before she could travel the 60 feet to first base.

We were warmly welcomed by the softball community. Well, to a point. I could not see any reason this well-known entity could not be operated in the same fashion as a minor league baseball team. I wanted sponsors, more season ticket sales and promotions, and a vastly improved stadium.

Stratford had a well-oiled softball committee that was adept at bidding for and hosting national tournaments, and attracting a few thousand people, especially if Team USA was competing or the Brakettes were in contention for another national title.

What I soon learned was that the Stratford group wanted the Brakettes as a draw, but they did not want to alter any of their tactics to allow new operators, outsiders such as Carpenter and the change-oriented Bob Wirz, much traction. And Stratton and Baird were not very accepting of ideas that might change the way they had single-handedly run things, even if it might save the Brakettes.

Every idea seemed to be met with resistance.

Still, as months passed and turned into years, we saw the stadium, now known as Frank DeLuca Field (after the former player and mild-mannered Stratford Softball Committee leader), improved to a point where there were some chair-back seats, better bleachers and a concessions-souvenir booth. We even made strides toward developing a hall of fame or museum.

A museum would have been an important step because the feats of such brilliant stars as Joan Joyce, Lisa

313

Fernandez, Donna Lopiano and Dot Richardson could have been showcased to every young softball player, parent, and aficionado of this fast-paced sport.

One of my most memorable recollections of the time with the Brakettes was the evening at dinner when Joan Joyce, who had gone on to play on the LPGA circuit, took us stroke-by-stroke through the round where she established the all-time low of only 17 putts in a round. It was so much like listening to Joe Gordon or Tommy Henrich recall, virtually pitch by pitch, how a baseball game of years earlier had unfolded.

I also had the pleasure of playing a round of golf with Joan Joyce and John Stratton in Boca Raton, FL, where she was both softball and women's golf coach at Florida Atlantic University for many a year.

Despite what I considered to be a lot of dedication from this end, I eventually bowed out of trying to build the Brakettes, although Carpenter remained involved virtually to the end of his life in 2007. He was only 69.

The Brakettes still play every summer, beating up on the few local and regional teams that still exist, while Stratton and Baird work with limited budgets.

How Do You Spell Relief—
R-O-L-A-I-D-S

2000 Continued

If I have not already stated it strongly enough, the Rolaids Relief Man account was extremely important to the success of Wirz & Associates. It gave us—me, I suppose—a major client for credibility and national visibility, and the steady cash flow did not hurt either.

But I was equally important to the long-term viability of this program in a marketing/public relations world where expensive promotional vehicles were introduced one year and disbanded the next.

I have no idea whether there was a long-term expectation when the Warner-Lambert Company entered into this relationship with Major League Baseball's Promotion Corporation in 1976. But the Rolaids Relief Man awards caught on. Baseball did not even have an official rule for saves until 1969, and the major league leader in saves in 1975 was the Chicago White Sox's Rich Gossage with what today would be a totally forgettable 26 saves.

Relief pitching had only recently entered a phase where teams realized they needed a "closer", someone who could cement a victory in the final innings of a close game.

The scoring for the Rolaids Relief Man in those early years was very simple: Two points were awarded to every relief pitcher credited with a win or a save; one point was deducted for a relief defeat.

I first got involved on behalf of Rolaids at the end of the 1985 season, which, ironically, was the same year Hoyt Wilhelm became the first relief pitcher to enter the Hall of Fame. Even the old knuckleballer had spent part of his lengthy career (1952-72) as a starting pitcher.

Within less than three years (1988), I had successfully lobbied to add what we called "blown saves" to the scoring equation, because many of the trusted media members pretty much ignored the Rolaids program since the penalty was limited (one point deduction) when a reliever failed to do his job and turned a near-victory into a loss.

We also dramatically altered the scoring, increasing the value of a save to three points, continuing to award two points for relief victories and deducting two points for each loss in relief and two more for each blown save.

I felt this type of change was essential if we wanted the media to pick up on the neat slogan for my client, which went like this: "How do you spell relief—R-O-L-A-I-D-S". I could not claim this as my own invention, but I was in a position to keep hammering away at the idea in our year-round media releases promoting every type of relief pitching angle imaginable.

We also created a Reliever of the Decade award at the end of 1989, honoring Jeff Reardon. We staged a well-attended media luncheon in New York City, which also paid tribute to longtime Pittsburgh reliever Kent Tekulve with a Career Achievement award, as well as our '89 seasonal winners, Mark Davis of San Diego in the National League and Texas's Jeff Russell in the American League.

I wanted to see the Rolaids Relief Man in the news virtually 12 months a year, and creating new avenues was working. We formed the Rolaids 300-Save Club in 1991, proudly recognizing the five men who had achieved that milestone at a fancy event during the Winter Meetings in Fort Lauderdale. Rolaids did not own the save, but we trumpeted it like our own, surrounding Rollie Fingers, Bruce Sutter, Lee Smith, Gossage and Reardon with our newly-minted Rolaids Relief Man 300-Save Club trophy.

This set the stage for honoring every future 300-save reliever, which we did faithfully while I was involved, usually in the home city or stadium of the hurler. And our annual winners were brought into the Big Apple for the black-tie awards dinner of the New York Chapter of the Baseball Writers' Association of America. The BBWAA was delighted to have us add two more major names for its dais, we often celebrated with a media reception the same afternoon, and this became a platform for Warner-Lambert (later Pfizer) for the Rolaids brand team to rub elbows with some baseball royalty. It is difficult to describe how much this meant to some of the people. I was recognized, internally, as long as there were not any screw-ups, and I was able to get our Rolaids Relief Man winners to come by our tables for photographs with company employees.

These were some of the spotlight events, but we also had a Rolaids winner for each major league team and every minor league by this time. In addition, there were monthly awards, rankings of the hurlers with the best save percentages, those who had the most consecutive seasons of leading a team, and a list of the career-saves leaders for every major league organization.

We packaged every conceivable milestone and achievement into the annual Rolaids Relief Man Media Guide, which was well-received when it showed up in a writer's or broadcaster's mailbox or I was able to hand it out during my annual spring training trip to many of the camps in Arizona and Florida.

It was a great platform for both me and my company, and my imprint was so heavy with the Rolaids Relief Man program that I often had to remind my media friends I did not actually work for Rolaids, but rather worked on a client basis.

I took pride in many of the innovative things I did to make the Rolaids Relief Man trophy show up in newspapers or on television, or be mentioned in radio broadcasts.

On we went into 2001, the 25th anniversary of the Rolaids Relief Man awards. It was an eternity in marketing circles.

It Is an Honor to Vote
For Hall of Fame Candidates

2001

One of the most eagerly anticipated—and always controversial—moments each January is the announcement of whether the Baseball Writers' Association of America members have elected anyone to the Hall of Fame.

This is a time when baseball is dissected so much more than any other sport. The fact detailed records exist back into the 1800s (the other major sports came along so much later), along with the reality that most American men and many women played baseball or softball at some level, gives most of us a level of expertise.

Did Phil Rizzuto's ability to lay down a perfect bunt numerous times in a 154-game season for the New York Yankees have more value than Marty Marion's total offensive and defensive contributions for the St. Louis Cardinals? And was Roger Maris' incredible 61-home run season in 1961 sufficient that he should get votes for the Hall of Fame when weighed against a rival whose career never reached that epic level but lasted many more seasons?

I have always contended that if baseball decided to move the pitching mound from 60-feet, six inches from home plate to 60-feet, three inches, the debate in the media and in countless bars would last so much longer and have more intensity than if the National Football League decided to cut the distance between the goal-post uprights in half or if the National Basketball Association wanted to move the baskets a foot higher.

Think about it.

Anyway, this was the year I became one of about 550 men and women in North America with a vote for the Hall of Fame.

I did not cover major league baseball as a beat writer like most of the other BBWAA members, but there is a section in the writers' eligibility rules whereby a public relations director can be a member of the local chapter, and if he stays in that job for at least 10 years, he is eligible to cast a ballot for the Hall of Fame.

I was not aware of any of these facts in Kansas City, but I was a member of the New York chapter during my 10½ years as Director of Information in the Baseball Commissioner's Office. I was not someone to make a big deal of the fact I should now be eligible to have a vote, but I also knew there was a precedent.

Eventually, I had a discussion with Jack Lang, the longtime secretary-treasurer nationally for the BBWAA. He researched the New York chapter records and I became a voter. I was part of the Honorary Member category, but had the same voting privileges as anyone else.

I cherished this right, and took it very seriously because one never knew when a single vote or a single omission would make the difference for a candidate, whose life changes forever when he gets that telephone call from the BBWAA that he has received votes from at least 75 per cent of all who submitted ballots and will have a plaque in the Hall of Fame in Cooperstown, NY.

My voting ended with the 2015 election because of a rules change that summer which required voters to have been actively covering the sport within the last 10 years. I have no quarrel with that decision because everyone who casts a ballot should be very familiar with the talent and character of each person before voting.

You can judge how I did because my year-by-year ballots follow. (I have listed my votes alphabetically, and an asterisk denotes those elected each year.)

2001
Gary Carter
Rich "Goose" Gossage
Jack Morris
Dale Murphy
*Kirby Puckett
Jim Rice
Bruce Sutter
*Dave Winfield

2002
Gary Carter
Rich "Goose" Gossage
Jim Kaat
Jack Morris
Dale Murphy
Jim Rice
*Ozzie Smith
Bruce Sutter

2003
*Gary Carter
Andre Dawson
Rich "Goose" Gossage
Jim Kaat
Jack Morris
*Eddie Murray
Jim Rice
Ryne Sandberg
Lee Smith
Bruce Sutter

2004
Andre Dawson
*Dennis Eckersley
Rich "Goose" Gossage

Jack Morris
Ryne Sandberg
Lee Smith
Bruce Sutter

2005
*Wade Boggs
Andre Dawson
Rich "Goose" Gossage
Jack Morris
Jim Rice
*Ryne Sandberg
Lee Smith
Bruce Sutter

2006
Bert Blyleven
Andre Dawson
Rich "Goose" Gossage
Jack Morris
Jim Rice
Lee Smith
*Bruce Sutter

2007
Bert Blyleven
Andre Dawson
Rich "Goose" Gossage
*Tony Gwynn
Jack Morris
Jim Rice
*Cal Ripken Jr,
Lee Smith

2008
Bert Blyleven

Andre Dawson
*Rich "Goose" Gossage
Jack Morris
Jim Rice
Lee Smith

2009
Bert Blyleven
Andre Dawson
*Rickey Henderson
Tommy John
Jack Morris
Dave Parker
*Jim Rice
Lee Smith

2010
Roberto Alomar
Bert Blyleven
*Andre Dawson
Barry Larkin
Fred McGriff
Jack Morris
Dave Parker
Lee Smith

2011
*Roberto Alomar
Jeff Bagwell
*Bert Blyleven
John Franco
Barry Larkin
Fred McGriff
Jack Morris
Lee Smith
Alan Trammell

Larry Walker

2012
Jeff Bagwell
*Barry Larkin
Fred McGriff
Jack Morris
Lee Smith
Alan Trammell
Larry Walker
Bernie Williams

2013
Jeff Bagwell
Craig Biggio
Fred McGriff
Jack Morris
Mike Piazza
Tim Raines
Curt Schilling
Lee Smith
Alan Trammell
Larry Walker

2014
Jeff Bagwell
Craig Biggio
*Tom Glavine
*Greg Maddux
Jack Morris
Mike Mussina
Mike Piazza
Curt Schilling
Lee Smith
*Frank Thomas

2015
Jeff Bagwell
*Craig Biggio
Carlos Delgado
*Randy Johnson
*Pedro Martinez
Mike Piazza
Curt Schilling
Gary Sheffield
Lee Smith
*John Smoltz

Field Goal Kicking
And Beautiful Gymnastics

2002

I was always looking for my next sports adventure, especially in baseball, but I also found myself continually maintaining a log of possible opportunities in other sports. I loved finding a niche either tucked away in the corner of a major sport or by venturing into a sport that was far from mainstream where I could see potential.

Two possibilities really intrigued me, with one having giant potential and the other most likely largely to bring attention to a beautiful sport that is under-appreciated, especially here in the United States. They could not have been more diverse.

With the success of the Rolaids Relief Man awards and the huge interest in professional football, I felt certain I could build a program around field goal kicking. College football had some potential, although recordkeeping would have been a nightmare at that time. So, I concentrated my efforts on the National Football League.

Where I did not create the Rolaids program or the initial scoring system, we dug in on a plan. I say "we" because my friend Jack Dolan, a walking encyclopedia on sports both in Connecticut and nationwide who also did some work for Wirz & Associates, lent a hand. So did Scott Reifert before he moved on to head up the communications department for the Chicago White Sox. I hope I am not overlooking anyone else who played a key role.

The system needed to be pretty easy for both the media and fans to understand, yet truly represent both success and failure for these kicking specialists who win and lose so many NFL games. We came up with what I believe to this day was a really fair system. Someone who reads this chapter now might find a way to take it and run with a program. The reader will not be embarrassed.

These were the basics:

- One point was awarded for each yard of a successful field goal.
- Points were deducted for any failure, including blocked kicks, if the attempt was less than 50 yards by subtracting a point for each yard under 50. In other words, a 48-yard attempt resulted in a two-point deduction; a 28-yarder cost the kicker 22 points. (Misses of 50 yards or more count against the kicker's season-ending percentage, but that was not part of our program.)
- A kicker's point total stayed with him if he changed teams during the season.
- Bonus points, which could be key, were awarded in this manner: If a kick tied the game in the first quarter, the player received five extra points, second quarter 10, etc., up to 20 points in the fourth quarter. If the kick gave the team the lead, he got 10, 20, 30 or 40 extra points depending on the quarter, and it was a 50-point bonus for an overtime game-winner.

We charted every regular-season NFL game for several years as we tried to find someone to step in as the sponsor. We even issued press releases for much of the season, distributing them to the media so we could build a case for the viability of our competition.

The Associated Press was one important ally because the wire service could distribute our rankings or use some aspect of our total statistical gathering, such as the longest field goals of the season or the kickers with the highest percentages. We broke it down so many ways, including which of the playoff kickers had the longest average or the most game-winning boots.

Here was part of our season-ending release from that first year:

For Immediate Release: December 31, 2002

Atlanta's Second Year Kicker Jay Feely Holds Off Martin Gramatica of Tampa Bay To Top Field Goal Rankings

Jay Feely was a financial consultant when he attended a free agent football camp 20 months ago. The **Atlanta Falcons** placekicker's future looks pretty secure in the **National Football League** today after the second year pro held off the charge of **Tampa Bay's Martin Gramatica** and a host of other veteran kickers to finish atop the regular season NFL field goal rankings.

Feely, who had led all but once since Week 8, and Gramatica both connected on a league-high 32 field goals for their playoff-bound teams, but Feely earned a 1,354-1,313-point margin in the competition, which was developed by Wirz & Associates, an Orange, CT sports marketing company. The rankings award points based on the distance of the field goals, deduct points on misses of less than 50 yards and give bonus points for game-tying and go-ahead kicks with the bonuses increasing the later they come in a game.

Feely ended up on top by racking up a league-leading 11 go-ahead field goals, including three in the fourth quarter of games, for a dominating 310 bonus points. Gramatica put the Buccaneers ahead eight times and earned 220 bonus points. His field goals covered 1,156 yards—an average of 36.1 yards—to 1,122 for Feely and 1,087 for **New Orleans' John Carney**, who finished third in the rankings with 1,177 points. Ten kickers scored 1,000 or more points and half of them will be in the NFL playoffs.

The 26-year-old Feely, who did his college kicking for **Michigan** after a record-breaking high school career for **Jesuit High School** in Gramatica's adopted home of Tampa, wrapped up the competition by booting three third quarter field goals at **Cleveland** Sunday afternoon, including a game-tying 42-yard boot and a go-ahead 49-yard kick in the Falcons' eventual 24-16 loss.

Complete top ten follow:

R K	KICKER	TEAM	FG M	-	FG A	TOTAL YARDS	BONUS POINTS	POINTS LOST	NET POINTS
1	+Jay Feely	ATL	32	-	40	1,122	310	78	1,354
2	+Martin Gramatica	TB	32	-	39	1,156	220	63	1,313
3	John Carney	NO	31	-	35	1,087	120	30	1,177
4	Adam Vinatieri	NE	27	-	30	980	210	16	1,174
5	+David Akers	PHIL	30	-	34	989	115	28	1,076
6	Paul Edinger	CHI	22	-	28	888	180	24	1,044
7	Mike Hollis	BUF	25	-	33	911	190	67	1,034
8	Jason Elam	DEN	26	-	36	892	190	58	1,024
9	+Ryan Longwell	GB	28	-	34	942	140	60	1,022
10	+Mike Vanderjagt	IND	23	-	31	826	250	66	1,010

+Team is in playoffs

We worked on the field goal program for several years, including teaming up with Hall of Fame kicking specialist Jan Stenerud, who believed in the concept, although as I recall he was not high on the bonus points early in the game. What a gentleman! It was a great bonus to be able to get to know him, and to have his input.

We even went to the NFL, hoping that body might have a sponsor looking for a program that would build its value as Rolaids did with the relief-pitching award.

We were serious about the field goal program. Publicity was easy to get because it was a high-profile subject

Aside from a threatening letter from Desenex, which had a punting award for a time (punters certainly do not directly win as many games as field goal kickers), virtually every player, media person, marketer or brand manager we talked to liked our concept. But no matter how much time my staff and I put into developing ideas or how many sales calls were made by associates such as Herm Livingston, Steve McKelvey or the late Dan Jacobs, we could not find a sponsor.

It probably was one of the most frustrating efforts in all the years of Wirz & Associates because I know the program had—and continues to have—merit. To this day, my files remain full of the publicity we garnered, and the years of results we compiled.

Oh, well.

My other major new undertaking was successful although that is not to say the bank account realized a great gain.

I only knew a little about Rhythmic Gymnastics, having seen some Olympics coverage and an occasional story or video clip elsewhere. It is such a beautiful sport, dominated by European women, who sometimes earn major fame and remuneration in their home area.

To be a successful rhythmic gymnast, at least on the international stage, young ladies need to be very athletic. Flexibility is one key, and it does not hurt if the performers are easy on the eyes.

I found out the reigning United States champion was Jessica Howard, who certainly met the basic criteria. She had missed the most recent Olympics by the tiniest of margins, and many would say it was only some of the European prejudices that kept her out. This determined Jacksonville, FL product won three USA championships in all.

I contacted Jessica's family, and finally met up with them as she trained while I was on one of my regular trips to the Sunshine State. Neither of us had great resources we could put into trying to line up sponsors or appearances for Jessica, and the U.S. Gymnastics Federation spent most of its effort on the men's and women's artistic programs, which had many times more participants. Watch any gymnastics competition in this country, and if the rhythmic championships get any time, it might be five minutes out of a two-day, multi-hour television program.

I probably devoted more time to trying to build opportunities for Jessica than common sense dictated, but I truly believed in her and in the sport. We had some successes, getting her a modeling opportunity where she would be featured in a slick promotional brochure for a major gymnastics apparel company; sending her to Columbus, OH, to take part in Arnold Schwarzenegger's annual fitness event; and securing her performances as the featured halftime entertainer at a home game of both the Atlanta Hawks and the Orlando Magic.

We also connected with the famed New York photographer Howard Schatz, hoping to catch lightning in a bottle somewhere in his industry.

All of this combined may have reimbursed the Howard family a tiny bit for the countless thousands of dollars they had put into her training, costumes and travel. My payout was small, although it was worth the effort for this under-publicized, under-appreciated and eye-catching sport.

Promoting three-time U.S. rhythmic gymnastics champion Jessica Howard was a nice new challenge

While Jessica went on to display her talent in a couple of Broadway shows, including Susan Stroman's *Frogs,* I moved on to working for a time with the next USA champion, Brooklyn's Olga Karmansky. Another dedicated and lithe gymnast, Olga would show her contortion skills years later in the highly-acclaimed Broadway show *Pippin,* as well as get some commercial advertising opportunities.

Baseball did not get left out in new endeavors, either. I was named president of the Torrington (CT) Twisters, at the time in the growing New England Collegiate Baseball

331

League. It was a volunteer position in which I jokingly told friends I had neither duties nor authority. As always, I enjoyed the association because the NECBL was one of numerous collegiate leagues gaining traction around the country and producing many a player for professional baseball. The Twisters had Stephen Strasburg one summer, although that was after my stint.

Telling the Stories
Of Independent Baseball
Players

2003

Some baseball players develop late, then surprise everyone. Kevin Millar did just that. So did Daniel Nava, Tanner Roark, Tom Wilhelmsen, Craig Breslow, Brandon Kintzler, Rene Rivera, Joe Thatcher, and on and on.

These people provide rich stories, which often were not being told on a national basis. I could see a vacuum, so while still actively running Wirz & Associates, I started writing a column. I called it the *Independent Baseball Insider.* I promoted it to Independent leagues for using select portions on their websites and broadcasts; I did the same with teams, and I tried interesting major league teams, scouts and fans, all with some success.

Like everything else I had done regarding baseball dating back to my college days—perhaps earlier—I did the *Insider* with a passion. I was certain this type of information was golden, if only for a select group of people who live and die with the sport.

I would put all of the columns into a binder at season's end, embellish it with combined statistics for all of the Independent leagues, and include a master roster of everyone who had made it to the major leagues or had their contract purchased by a major league organization after playing in an Indy league.

Another book may await down the road because of so many fascinating stories through the years. I started to say wonderful stories instead of fascinating, but some of them also had a sad side when a player appeared on the brink of breaking through to the major leagues only to have some rare misfortune sidetrack his dream.

Two of those stories still jump out to me every so often even though they took place several years ago. I would not blame Brian Mazone or Tagg Bozied if they still have nightmares about their experiences, although I am pretty certain they have some great baseball memories even if they were just shy of being at the major league level.

Mazone was a left-handed pitcher out of the University of San Diego who had to work his way up through the minor leagues as an undrafted free agent even though he was 11-3 his senior year for the Toreros. He spent nearly four seasons in Independent play at St. George, UT (Western League), and Joliet, IL (Northern League at that time), and was in the Milwaukee, San Francisco and Philadelphia farm systems, eventually working his way up to Triple-A. In 2006, he was having a standout season with the Phillies' top farm club in Scranton/Wilkes-Barre, PA (13-3, 2.03).

While that record was good enough that Mazone, who had just turned 30, could have been called up for the wild card-contending Phils' stretch run, it never happened. He was not a hard thrower, a key factor that probably worked against him.

Philadelphia did pencil the 6-foot-4 Mazone in to start against Houston on a Wednesday night (September 6, 2006). His wife and their two children had driven to Philly to watch. What happened was heartbreaking. The Tuesday night game was rained out, changing the Phils' pitching plans, and he was redirected to Rochester, NY, to start for Scranton/Wilkes-Barre in the International League playoffs instead of getting into at least one major league game.

The pitcher was even snubbed for the postseason International League all-star team, even though his league-leading earned run average was nearly a run per game better than anyone else's.

Mazone pitched a few more seasons, largely in the Philadelphia farm system and for a short time at Albuquerque, NM (Los Angeles Dodgers), but that one night was the closest he ever got to appearing in a regular-season major league game. He was one rainstorm away.

Bozied was drafted out of high school (Arvada, CO) and college (University of San Francisco) by the Minnesota Twins because of his power potential as a third baseman, first baseman or outfielder. He had the credentials, including three-time All-America honors at USF, where his 30 homers led the nation in 1999. He did not sign either time he was drafted, but he did join the Sioux Falls (SD) Canaries for 57 Northern League games (.307-6-31) in 2001 before signing with the San Diego Padres, who had made him a third-round draft choice.

The right-handed hitter had pounded 54 home runs in 2½ seasons in the Padres farm system, working his way up to Triple-A. Misfortune struck one July day in 2004 when he hit homer No. 16 of that season for Portland, OR. It was a walk-off blast, and when he jumped onto home plate to celebrate he ruptured the patellar tendon in his left knee. It was a major blow.

"Bozied, before he got hurt, was the best bat prospect we had at the Triple-A level," lamented the Padres' minor league field coordinator, Bill Bryk, coincidentally a big friend to Independent Baseball to this day.

Bozied never was lauded so highly again, even though after a five-home run year in '05, he had a trio of 20-plus homer seasons in the St. Louis, Florida and Philadelphia farm systems and got some occasional looks in spring training.

"It is basically me and Albert (Pujols)" working out at first base for the Cardinals," I quoted Bozied for the *Insider* after a spring training interview in 2007. Unfortunately, like Mazone, Bozied never played a game in the major leagues.

My meticulous records kept for the column and my blog, *IndyBaseballChatter,* showed that 217 players had gone from Independent leagues to regular-season major league uniforms into the 2016 season, with only Mazone, Bozied, catcher Jose Yepez (Seattle), left-handed pitcher Tom Cochran (Cincinnati) and righties Tim Bausher (Boston) and Julio DePaula (Baltimore) failing to get into any games after being called up.

The most uplifting stories of all could well be those of Chris Coste and Daniel Nava, neither of whom would have reached the majors without first playing in Independent leagues.

Coste is best remembered as a catcher, although he was playing the infield when he finished his college baseball career, and he turned to Independent leagues in order to have an opportunity to extend his playing days. He spent portions of 1995 playing in what were two short-lived leagues (Prairie and North Central), hitting in mostly nondescript fashion.

Coste's next stop was his hometown of Fargo, ND, where he would spend four seasons of hitting .300 with the Fargo-Moorhead (MN) Redhawks of the Northern League and convert to catching when the team had an urgent need.

His gritty determination was evident in those Fargo days under Doug Simunic, but the only look he received from a major league organization was to spend March of 1999 in Pittsburgh's minor league camp. It was back to Fargo for his fourth season that summer, then after three years with Cleveland, one with Boston, another with Milwaukee and 2005 with Philadelphia. It looked more and more like Triple-A was the best he was ever going to do. Coste had gotten close, but that was all, and he was a rather ancient 33 for a minor leaguer when the '06 season rolled around.

It was great copy for me to write about Coste's masterful clutch hitting and .463 batting average in the Phillies' major league camp that spring, but devastating for Coste to learn only hours before Opening Day that a newly acquired outfielder would have the 25ᵗʰ spot on the roster.

Coste went back to Triple-A one more time.

On May 21, 2006, Coste got an early-morning call from Manager John Russell of Scranton/Wilkes-Barre, PA. Chris told me later he feared he might be getting traded or released, but it was the long-awaited news that the Phillies needed him and they needed him NOW. They had a 1:30 home game, and he needed to navigate the 125 miles from Scranton to reach Philadelphia. He talked to wife Marcia, and daughter Casey, 7, and amid all the screaming and excitement, got into uniform and signed his contract by 1:25.

What a lovely story, and when the season was over Coste had hit .328 in 65 games with seven homers and 32 RBI for the Phillies. He even played in the 2008 World Series for the victorious Phillies. I told his story in great detail in my column.

Nava's story was a great deal different than that of Coste, although it was just as Hollywoodesque, especially once he got to the major leagues and hit the first pitch thrown to him for a grand slam on June 10, 2010 for the Boston Red Sox. This is part of Nava's "back story" exactly as I wrote it in my *Independent Baseball Insider* the next week:

- He shook off being only 4-foot-8 and 70 pounds when he entered high school in the Bay Area, left Santa Clara after a season in which he was more team manager than player, ignored the fact he was left undrafted after his second stint with the Broncos and did not quit when he did not make the roster of the Independent Chico (CA) Outlaws (Golden League) on his first try.
- He became the Golden League batting champion (.371) and Most Valuable Player, led the Outlaws to the league title the next season (2007), and *Baseball America* selected him the No. 1 prospect in any Independent league.

337

- Once signed by Boston prior to '08, Nava became a steady .300 hitter, and took a career .345 average that had topped out at Class AA into the 2010 season. He still ranks No. 1 among all players at Pawtucket, RI this season in hits (58), RBI (38), runs (28) and home runs (8) while hitting .294 for the Triple-A team.
- Now, he stands as the first person who played his initial professional game in the Golden League—and only the third overall—to become a major leaguer.

Nava has been a headline-maker ever since his amazing major league debut because of his rags-to-riches success story which has included starring in World Series games for the Red Sox and battling just to stay in the major leagues.

There is no doubt in my mind the undersized (5-foot-11) and often under-appreciated Nava, as well as Kevin Millar, who came out of Lamar (TX) University without fanfare, are the two best players the non-affiliated leagues have produced, if I ignore the likes of the Drew Brothers (J.D. and Stephen) and Max Scherzer. They all spent some time with Indy teams, but were known prospects who needed to have contracts negotiated before they started affiliated competition.

Millar starred with the St. Paul Saints in that very first Independent season (1993) and went on to collect nearly 1,300 hits (1,284) and slug 170 home runs during his 12-year major league career. He is somewhat of a media star today, and Nava's determined nature will no doubt help him in his post-playing days.

It certainly has been enjoyable writing about this group along with so many other Independent players, even if most of them have not had comparable on-field success. I finished my 12th year and final year with the *Insider* in 2014, and while it did not grow as big as I might have liked in the number of people who subscribed, I take pride in the respect I know it received on a year-round basis from certain executives, scouts, players and fans.

At Least We Won a Playoff Game

2004

One more team; perhaps the last one.

If you have not gotten a clear picture by now, it should be no surprise I was ready to get involved with another startup team any time the situation appeared right to do so.

Jonathan Fleisig, a confident and wealthy young commodities trader in New York City, needed a new home for the Berkshire (MA) Black Bears he owned in the Northeast League, playing at historic (and ancient) Waconah Park in the Berkshire Mountain community of Pittsfield.

My history in Waterbury, along with my passion for baseball and my proximity (only 15 minutes) to New Haven, CT, led me to get involved in helping Fleisig work out a deal to bring the Berkshire franchise to the home of the Yale University Bulldogs, Yale Field, which technically was located in West Haven.

I seem to end up with involvements in placing teams in older "historic" sites and in areas which seem ripe for a professional team but do not have the corporate base or the political enthusiasm to make it work. Such was New Haven.

Yale University "owns" the New Haven-West Haven area in so many ways, and owns that reputation because of its high educational standards as well as its medical facilities. It does not always have a reputation of embracing sports other than its Ivy League teams, but it did show considerable respect for what would become known as the New Haven County Cutters.

Much of that cooperation might have been the mere fact Yale Field sat idle for most of the year except for the relatively short Yale baseball season, which normally ended before the area reached real baseball weather.

The stadium was full of history, including the fact it was where George Herbert Walker Bush was a decent first baseman in the days when an Ivy League team could realistically compete for College World Series honors. Babe Ruth, Lou Gehrig and many others among baseball's all-time royalty had played in exhibitions at Yale Field, and the Class AA Eastern League's New Haven Ravens had a strong run for a few years, drawing excellent crowds for a time and showing off future major league stars such as Todd Helton and Alex Rios.

The luster from the Ravens had worn off, in part because of a sour taste between ownership and many local businesses before the team departed for greener pastures in Manchester, NH. We probably would have had a better reception if the New Haven area had been without a team for at least a couple of seasons, but as it was, the Ravens did not depart until after the 2003 season, in which they were lame ducks.

We came in the next summer, so we had the multiple hurdles to overcome of the Ravens' sad finish, selling the Independent game to the media and fans used to seeing highly-regarded draft choices, and working in an aging stadium that had its history but was missing most of the amenities the public expects today.

My consulting role to Fleisig and the Cutters staff included not only helping try to woo the lukewarm media but also putting together a good product on the field.

Largely on my recommendation, Jarvis Brown was hired as our manager. Brown came with good credentials even though he did not have managerial experience. He was one of those hardworking but undersized (5-foot-7) players, virtually always needing to go an extra mile to prove himself because he did not have the type of power major league teams look for in their outfielders.

He did have benefit of being a first-round January draft choice (ninth overall) by Minnesota in 1986 with excellent speed (72 steals in the Midwest League in '88), and he worked his way all through the farm system, finally joining the parent Twins during 1991. His speed helped him to be on the 25-man roster that fall when Minnesota and Atlanta put on that wonderful seven-game World Series that was decided by Jack Morris' brilliant 10-inning, 1-0 shutout for the Twins. Brown got into four of the games, including the clincher, as a pinch hitter, pinch runner or defensive replacement. He also logged major league time with San Diego, Atlanta and Baltimore, getting into 155 games overall from '91-'95.

I met Brown in 1996 when he came into the Independent game for half a season with our Thunder Bay Whiskey Jacks, then brought him to Waterbury as a player-coach for his final playing season ('98). He made me look good by hitting .331 and stealing 25 bases in 26 attempts as the leadoff man and centerfielder on our playoff-worthy team.

It was a different story in New Haven, even though we narrowly missed winning the first half in the South Division of the Northeast League when the New Jersey Jackals somehow won five games in the last three days to edge us by a game. The Cutters struggled through a last-place, 14-32 second half when Jarvis' greenness as a manager became a fatal issue.

It was not the type of finish we could afford as we continued trying to convince the difficult New Haven market we were an appropriate replacement for the Eastern League. Our attendance lagged far behind the league leaders in Brockton, MA, and Quebec as we averaged little more than 1,000 fans per game.

We made the playoffs the next two seasons, when I helped new Manager Mike Church, who had been a catcher with our Waterbury teams, put together the rosters. The best we got the attendance was in our final season in 2007, when a skilled and dedicated young woman, Marie Heikkenin Webb, moved into the general manager's chair. We drew 82,651 fans, but that was no better than eighth among the nine teams hosting games in our league, and the team departed.

I chuckle to myself with the knowledge we earned exactly one playoff victory among the five postseason teams combined in Waterbury and New Haven, but I can remember it with some satisfaction since a talented left-hander I had brought to the Cutters, Venezuelan native Rolando Valles, shut out Rich Gedman's Worcester Tornadoes in the Massachusetts city.

I also cherish memories of many personalities (both those with considerable talent and others who might fit into the quirky mould) with whom my path crossed. It is nice to say that both Marie Webb and Rolando Valles remain in professional sports, Marie as advertising coordinator for the NBA's Orlando Magic and Rolando as a minor league coach and Hispanic advisor to the Milwaukee Brewers.

A Big Disappointment,
And Bowie Kuhn Passes Away

2005-2015

I had already celebrated my 67th birthday by the time 2005 rolled around, obviously an age when many people have already retired or are in a serious countdown toward it. I had very few thoughts in that direction, and Maybeth reminds me even a decade later "I am not cut out for it." She may well be right, knowing how restless I can get without some type of plan every single weekend, but one major jolt of reality forced me to start taking a different view of the future.

The Rolaids Relief Man program had been a very major account for 21 years, starting only a few months after I made my decision to leave the Baseball Commissioner's office.

Twenty-one friggin' years.

That equals several lifetimes with most any other promotional program when brand managers or their superiors change directions almost on a whim. I would guess I worked for at least a dozen "bosses" at Warner-Lambert and eventually Pfizer on the Rolaids account, along with so many of the company's publicists, ad managers and the like. I had gotten to the point where I only needed to make a few tweaks to the outline of how the Rolaids Relief Man program worked each time I sat down with the newest person assigned to the brand and inheriting as part of their job the relief pitching awards. The baseball world certainly knew the program, but the people assigned to trying to move the needle on Rolaids' share of the antacid market did not.

Typically, these were very bright 20- or 30-something men or women trained in marketing, but not always in

344

sports or the media. Some of them might not have known where first base was located.

But I was the hired gun who came with this program which they knew accounted for hundreds of thousands, if not a few million dollars of their advertising/marketing budget. Some of the people were thrilled to have someone roughly twice their age who could walk them through the parts of the program that were a given, which meant honoring the No. 1 relief pitcher in each major league, often at black-tie events or on-field presentations at major league stadiums. Especially in the early years of the program, the CEO or president of Warner-Lambert would want to be involved in national television promos or the stadium presentations and media conferences, so Young Mr. or Ms. Brand Manager understood that the Rolaids Relief Man awards could not be ignored.

Well, at this time, with the program 30 years old and with my two decades of involvement from a PR end, the young woman for whom I reported (her name being intentionally omitted) had her own agenda. And the brand had gone through enough ups and downs, including out-of-the-country production problems, which nearly made the product invisible on the grocery and drugstore shelves at times that she apparently did not have immediate upper-management eyes staring at her every move.

I never did get a full explanation, long believing she probably had friends at one or more agencies who she thought could step in and work with major league baseball teams and the media and maintain the Rolaids Relief Man at a high level.

Regardless, Bob Wirz and Wirz & Associates and their 21 years of service were history. It was a harsh financial reality for us. But I had to shake off my emotional involvement that had developed as I nurtured the program. It no longer mattered that I had adjusted the scoring system to keep it up with the times, issued press release after press release, and developed media guide after media guide to get the nation's writers and broadcasters to continue including R-O-L-A-I-D-S in some manner when they were talking about Trevor Hoffman or Mariano Rivera or the next exciting closer saving game after game.

We used 114 pages of small type to describe all aspects in the amazing growth in relief pitching in the final Rolaids Relief Man Media Guide in '05. It is still amazing to realize the Los Angeles Dodgers' Eric Gagne saved 84 games (2002-04) without even once stubbing his toe by failing when he had a save opportunity.

The Rolaids Relief Man awards continued in some form for the next few years, although the lingering media calls I received when someone needed facts or figures told a constant story that they did not know of a website or a person where they could turn for details.

To show this was not just sour grapes on my part, look at what Rob Neyer wrote as part of an extensive story under the heading "Kissing the Rolaids Relief Award Goodbye" for *Fox Sports* in 2014 when his exhaustive research indicated the last trophies were produced in 2011:

The 1993 American League champion Jeff Montgomery of Kansas City told Neyer of his trophy: "It's in my study. I've had it displayed prominently ever since I received it."

And John Smoltz, now a Hall of Famer, "It's a really cool trophy, and I wanted to put it somewhere it can be seen. Because of what I went through to make the transition to closing, winning that award was one of my greatest accomplishments, and that (2002) was my most rewarding year in baseball."

My 21 years with those awards are now well in the past.

I have been blessed with excellent health throughout my life. I am one lucky guy in that regard. Nevertheless, health issues strike all around us. I am not certain I have been so shockingly reminded of this as on an early-spring day in 2007 when I was on my way to Florida to write some

Independent Baseball Insider columns and soak up spring training.

Even going back to my high school days, when I could only dream about getting to spring training, that part of the year was special. A picture of someone working out would appear in the newspaper. I would start looking for the April issue of *Baseball Digest* because I knew it would have all of the major league rosters. Short game stories and linescores would creep into the paper. If I was really lucky, an exhibition game—most likely the Cardinals from Al Lang Field in St. Petersburg—would come on as I anxiously moved the radio dial from one end to the other. Any little hint of the season ahead would thrill me.

I planned this '07 trip so I could stop in Jacksonville, FL, to visit my old boss, business partner and friend Bowie Kuhn in the hospital. He had been in and out of the hospital, which was probably no more than 30 minutes from the home in Ponte Vedra Beach, FL, where he and Luisa could look out across the beautiful marshland from their gorgeous living room.

I knew it did not look particularly good for Bowie, so my plan was to stop in for a few minutes, then continue down I95. Only he and Luisa were in the hospital room when I showed up. I am not certain who was happier to see the other, the bedridden or the visitor.

Bowie seemed in darn good spirits considering he was not strong enough to be moved to a rehab facility just yet. But then that was his nature.

So the reminiscing began. Had I seen any of the staff from the Commissioner's Office days? Was there any news to exchange? How were our families, whom we both knew well?

To digress a bit, I especially remember one visit when Bowie had stayed with Maybeth and me when we lived in Norwalk, CT. I imagine Bowie and I had projects we were working on together, and he often had business with some of his well-heeled friends in nearby Greenwich, CT. I know for sure he did not come by car because he was up very early in the morning and out for a run when he found a Catholic church and attended Mass. He very seldom missed a day of Mass. I believe he was back and sitting at the kitchen table before my wife and I had gotten into our day.

I did not want to overextend my hospital visit that day in Jacksonville, so whenever a nurse would come in to attend to something, Luisa and I would step out and I would say something like: "I really should move on. I don't want him to tire." Her reply, more than once, was: "Please don't go. He has not had this good a time in a long time."

I ended up staying for four hours. If it was good therapy for him, I assure you it was at least as good for me.

I realized when I was approaching the hospital that day I had not brought Bowie anything. Flowers, candy? Nothing. Then I remembered that in my trunk I had a bag with a few gray T-shirts I had made up promoting my *Independent Baseball Insider* column. They were pretty humble, especially for this wonderful man who had spent nearly 16 years as Baseball Commissioner.

There is a postscript to this story for a little later, but I somewhat sheepishly got the shirt out and gave it to him. Ever polite, he thanked me, and it was at the foot of his hospital bed for the remainder of my visit.

It turned out this was the last time I saw "my Commissioner" and friend. I believe it was 10 days later that he was gone.

Even though it was not totally unexpected when I got the call, it was a shock. Maybeth had joined me in Florida by that time, and the next couple of days seemed much like a throw-back to when I was Bowie's Director of Information. I became the family spokesman to the media, informing them of his death and, funeral plans and answering what questions I could.

Paul Degener, the second of the two boys Bowie had raised with Luisa after their father died (they also had a son and daughter of their own), became my primary contact as we exchanged notes on who should be notified and how we might reach them.

Deneger stunned me with two heartwarming overtures. Would I be a pallbearer at Bowie's funeral in Ponte Vedra (naturally, I was honored)? And a postscript about my T-shirt. "We could hardly get it off of him," Paul told me, of the days after my visit to the hospital. He insisted the nurses would try to get Bowie into typical hospital gowns only to have his dad resist and go right back to the *Insider* shirt.

I am not certain I have been so touched with any gesture before or since.

While Bowie Kuhn was such an imposing figure in my career, no one had more impact than my parents. They did not guide me in any direction, but oh, how they supported me every step, starting with providing a warm, loving home and then with making certain I had the chance to get a quality education. They were there at every single step, and the only way I could ever hope to repay them was by making them proud.

It was so difficult when they started aging, with my sister, Bev, in California and me on the East Coast. It felt so hollow to drop in for a few days on occasion—both Bev and I shot for three trips a year—and then leave, doubly so when dad was gone and mom was in the apartment and later the nursing home.

The ultimate celebration for mom was when she was nearing her 100th birthday in September of 2007. We set up an open house right in Heritage Hall in Broken Bow, and about 100 people showed up to pay tribute, including all of the grandchildren and great- grandchildren except for Bev's loving son, Matthew, a cerebral palsy child who could not travel that distance. We finished a grand afternoon with a family dinner. We probably wore mom out, although true to her fashion, she would never utter a peep other than to show her appreciation.

We lost her 10 months later, on July 29, 2008, and our compact United Church of Christ building in Halsey was so crowded the funeral service had to be piped in via closed circuit so the overflow audience in the basement could hear everything.

I did my best to keep my remarks light, stressing how she was always immaculately dressed, and sharing fun times I remembered or had seen in pictures. For example, I reminisced about mom in her Sunday best and little Bev at her side taking some target practice with a 22-gauge rifle, and mom with dad's sister, Rosa, running the Rodocker Hotel (mom's maiden name) at the tender age of 14 while my grandparents took a trip to the Black Hills of South Dakota.

What a mother! See how lucky I was.

Compared with the last six decades, my direct involvement with baseball is modest these days, other than limited activities with SABR (Society for American Baseball Research) and my writing about Independent Baseball.

The passion never wavers, though. Watching my three grandsons play is pure joy even if it often is nerve-wracking. Oh, how they love the game, to my utter delight!

By the way, how many days until pitchers and catchers? That day cannot get here soon enough.

Index

Bench, Johnny	1973, 1976, 1991
Berke, Art	1982
Berkshire Black Bears	2004
Berman, Len	1990
Berra, Yogi	1991
Black, Del	1959
Blattner, Buddy	1972
Blue, Vida	1976
Blyleven, Bert	1973
Bonds, Bobby	1973
Boozer, Bob	1958
Boswell, Thomas	1981
Boucher, Red	1965
Bouton, Jim	1966
Boyd, Bobby	1965
Boyer, Ken	1961
Bozied, Tagg	2003
Brady, James	1981
Brakettes	1996-2000
Branca, Ralph	1950-55
Breslow, Craig	2003
Brett, Bobby	1979
Brett, George	1973, 1979, 1980, 1984
Brett, Ken	1979
Briles, Nelson	1974, 1987
Brock, Lou	1991
Broglio, Ernie	1961
Broken Bow	1950-55
Brooklyn Dodgers	1950-55
Brown, Bob	1979
Brown, Jarvis	2004
Bryant, Don	1959
Bryk, Bill	2003
Bunker, Wally	1968
Burdette, Lou	1987
Burke, Joe	1974

Burris, Jim	1967, 1968
Busby, Steve	1973
Bush, George H. W.	1989, 2004
Butkus, Dick	1990
Byland, Dick	1969, 1970
Caccavale, Paul	1993
Campanella, Roy	1975, 1981
Canseco, Jose	1989
Caray, Harry	1961
Carew, Rod	1969, 1972, 1973, 1984
Carlton, Steve	1980
Carpenter, David	1993, 1994, 1996-2000
Carson, Johnny	1958, 1973
Carter, Gary	1981
Carter, Jimmy	1979
Case, Dick	1985
Cavarretta, Phil	1949
Cecil, Dick	1963
Cerrone, Rick	1982, 1985
Cerv, Bob	1956
Chamberlain, Wilt	1958
Chapman, Ray	1971
Chase, Dave	1987
Chass, Murray	1981
Chicago Cubs	1949
Christenson, Larry	1980
Church, Mike	2004
Chylak, Nestor	1973
Cisco, Galen	1971
Claire, Fred	1996-2000
Clark, Will	1985
Clarkson, Rich	1964
Clay, Cassius	1963
Cleveland Indians	1949
Cobos, Marcus	1957
Cochron, Tom	2003

Cohn, Linda	1990
Colbert, Nate	1972
Colletti, Ned	1996-2000
Collins, Bob	1968
Conlan, Joe	1985
Cosell, Howard	1980
Coste, Chris	2003
Courtney, Clint	1968
Crandall, Del	1963
Cuellar, Mike	1969
Cullen, Blake	1977
Daniels, Bennie	1956
Dascoli, Frank	1949
Davis, Mark	2000
Day, Doris	1981
Dean, Dizzy	1972
deCesare, John	1985
DeFabbio, Jerry	1993
Degener, Paul	2005-2015
Dent, Bucky	1970, 1978
Denver Post	1966,1967, 1968
DePaula, Julio	2003
Devaney, Bob	1950-55, 1959, 1962
Dewan, John	1991
DiMaggio, Joe	1949, 1981, 1991
Dolan, Jack	2002
Dozer, Richard	1973
Drago, Dick	1974
Drury, Chris	1989
Drysdale, Don	1980
Dubiel, Monk	1949
Dumont, Hap	1965
Dunlop, Harry	1957, 1971
Durham, Leon	1993
Dusek, Ernie	1962
Dusek, Joe	1962

Ermer, Cal	1967, 1968
Esasky, Nick	1992
Evans, Dwight	1975
Fanning, Jim	1963
Feely, Jay	2002
Feeney, Chub	1975
Felice, Jason	1994
Feller, Bob	1949, 1975
Ferguson, Jim	1972, 1977
Fernandez, Lisa	1996-2000
Ferraro, Mike	1966
Field Goal Kicking	2002
Fingers, Rollie	1973,1976, 1990, 1991, 2000
Finley, Charlie	1964, 1969, 1970, 1974, 1975, 1976, 1977, 1978
Fishel, Bob	1975, 1977
Fisk, Carlton	1973, 1975
Fleisig, Jonathan	2004
Fleming, Dave	1996-2000
Fort Leonard Wood	1961
Fort Myers	1969, 1970, 1971, 1972
Fowler, Art	1968
Fox, Nellie	Pre-1950
Foy, Joe	1968, 1970
Francona, Terry	1985
Frazier, Ron	1996-2000
Friend, Bob	1987
Frontier League	1993
Gagne, Eric	2005-2015
Gagne, Verne	1962
Galarraga, Andres	1992
Gammons, Peter	1984
Garagiola, Joe	1949
Garvey, Steve	1978
Gedman, Rich	2004
Gehrig, Lou	2004

Giamatti, Bart	1989
Gibson, Bob	1961
Giles, Bill	1976
Glaviano, Tommy	1949
Goldklang, Marv	1993
Gomez, Lefty	1973
Gordon, Joe	1957, 1969, 1970, 1996-2000
Gordon, Tom	1987
Gorman, Lou	1969, 1972, 1974
Goryl, Johnny	1967, 1968
Gossage, Goose	1980, 2000
Gramatica, Martin	2002
Grassland Baseball League	1950-55
Guerrero, Pedro	1993
Hadden, Sandy	1975, 1976
Hairston, Sam	Pre-1950
Hale, Creighton	1986, 1987, 1988
Hall of Fame	2001
Halsey, NE	1950-55, 1963, 1967, 1969, 1971, 1987
Hallahan, Bill	1973
Haraway, Frank	1967, 1968
Harmon, Merle	1964
Harris, Bucky	1975
Harrison, Chuck	1969
Harsh, Len	1969
Haskins, Don	1967
Hastings, NE	1960, 1963
Hauser, Joe	1956
Helton, Todd	2004
Henrich, Tommy	1996-2000
Hentzen, Bob	1966
Herman, Billy	1975
Hernandez, Jackie	1968
Herzog, Whitey	1981

Kaat, Jim	1987
Kaline, Al	1974, 1991
Kane, Bill	1978
Kansas City Royals	1968, 1969, 1970, 1971, 1978, 1980
Kantor, Brad	1993
Karmansky, Olga	2002
Kauffmam, Ewing	1969, 1970, 1972, 1973, 1974
Keener, Steve	1986
Kelly, Mike	1987
Kelly, Pat	1968, 1969
Kentling, Bill	1964
Kenyon, J. Michael	1962
Keough, Joe	1969
Killebrew, Harmon	1969
Kiner, Ralph	1975
King, Rick	1969
Kinney, Jeff	1971
Kintzler, Brandon	2003
Kirkpatrick, Ed	1970, 1974
Klinge, Jack	1988, 1989
Koosman, Jerry	1969
Kosco, Andy	1967
Koufax, Sandy	1980
Kremenko, Barney	1968
Kubacki, Jim	1958
Kubek, Tony	1966
Kuhn, Bowie	1973, 1974,1975,1976, 1978, 1979, 1980, 1981, 1982, 1984, 1985, 1986, 1992, 1993, 2005-2015
Lamade Stadium	1989
Lang, Jack	2001
Lanier, Max	1949
Lau, Charley	1972, 1984
Lemon, Bob	1970, 1971, 1972, 1973, 1976,1978, 1981
Leonard, Dennis	1980

McKeon, Jack	1957, 1973, 1974
McNally, Dave	1960, 1969
McRae, Hal	1972, 1980, 1984
Meade, Lee	1968
Merrill, Stump	1994
Metro, Charlie	1968, 1969, 1970
Mikan, George	1968
Millar, Kevin	2003
Miller, Marvin	1975, 1976
Mincher, Don	1966
Molitor, Paul	1982
Monaghan, Tom	1984
Montague, John	1989
Montgomery, Jeff	2005-2015
Mooring, Jim	1967
Mora, Frank	1993
Morabito, Mickey	1977, 1978
Moran, Eric	1993
Morgan, Joe	1972, 1973, 1975, 1980
Morris, Jack	2004
Mullen, John	1963
Munger, Bob	1959
Municipal Stadium	1996-2000
Munson, Thurman	1976, 1979
Murphy, Bob	1990
Murray, Jim	1984
Musial, Stan	1949, 1961, 1973, 1981, 1989, 1991
National League	1950-55
Nava, Daniel	2003
Nebraska, University of	1950-55, 1956, 1958, 1960
Necciai, Ron	1957
Neal, Charlie	1965
Negro Leagues	1950-55
Nelson, Chet	1967
Nelson, Rocky	1949

Nelson, Roger	1972
Nettles, Graig	1968
New England Collegiate Baseball League	2002
New Haven County Cutters	2004
New York Giants	1950-55
New York Mets	1969, 1970
New York Yankees	1949, 1966, 1969, 1977, 1978, 1979, 1984
Neyer, Rob	2005-2015
Nichols, Max	1974
Nicholson, Dave	1969
Nicholson, Jack	1987
Niekro, Joe	1980
Northeast League	1996-2000, 2004
Northern League	1993
North Shore Spirit	1996-2000
Northey, Ron	1949
O'Dowd, Dan	1996-2000
Olerud, John	1987
Oliva, Tony	1969
Oliver, Bob	1968, 1970, 1972
Omaha World-Herald	1950-55, 1958
O'Malley, Peter	1986
O'Malley, Walter	1975
Osborne, Bo	1968
Osborne, Tom	1950-55, 1959
Otis, Amos	1970, 1971, 1972, 1973, 1974, 1980
Owen, Mickey	1949
Pafko, Andy	1949
Paige, Satchel	1949
Palmer, Arnold	1963
Palmer, Jim	1969, 1989, 1991
Parker, Dave	1979

Pasqua, Dan	1992
Patek, Fred	1971, 1973
Pattin, Marty	1974
Peden, Les	Pre-1950
Pena, Orlando	1969
Pepe, Phil	1984
Pfizer	2005-2015
Phillips, Bill	1972
Piniella, Anita	1972
Piniella, Lou	1969, 1970, 1972, 1974, 1978
Player, Gary	1963
Ponte, Ed	1996-2000
Powell, Boog	1969
Powell, John	1960
Quilici, Frank	1968
Raines, Tim	1987
Ramazzotti, Bob	1949
Reagan, Ronald	1981, 1983
Reamer, Frank	1969
Reardon, Jeff	2000
Reich, Herman	1949
Reichler, Joe	1974, 1985
Reifert, Scott	2002
Rice, Bruce	1964
Richardson, Bobby	1966, 1989
Richardson, Dot	1996-2000
Richardson, Spec	1983
Richmond, Bob	1992
Richman, Milton	1974, 1981
Righetti, Dave	1988
Rios, Alex	2004
Rivera, Mariano	2005-2015
Rivera, Rene	2003
Rizutto, Phil	2001
Roark, Tanner	2003
Roberts, Robin	1976

Robinson, Bill	1963
Robinson, Brooks	1969, 1973, 1975
Robinson, Frank	1969
Rojas, Cookie	1971, 1972, 1973
Rolaids Relief Man	1985, 1986, 1987, 2000, 2005, 2015
Roof, Phil	1973
Rose, Pete	1989
Rosenthal, Todd	1993
Roth, Braggo	1971
Royals Stadium	1972, 1973, 1980
Rudi, Joe	1972, 1976
Ruffing, Red	1981
Russell, Jeff	2000
Russell, John	2003
Russin, Tom	1996-2000
Ruth, George Herman (Babe)	1949, 1973, 1979, 1983, 2004
Rutledge, Wanda	1985
Ryan, Meg	1996-2000
Ryan, Nolan	1973, 1989
Rhythmic Gymnastics	2002
Ryun, Jim	1964
Sadecki, Ray	1961
Salvon, Ralph	1983
Sandhills Baseball League	1950-55
Santo, Ron	1973
Schatz, Howard	2002
Scheinblum, Richie	1972
Schiller, Elton	1978
Schley, Van	1993
Schmidt, Mike	1981
Schoendienst, Albert (Red)	1949
Schuerholz, John	1972

Schwartzwalder, Ben	1958
Seaton, Fred	1962
Seaver, Tom	1965, 1969, 1973
Selig, Bud	1992
Shantz, Bobby	Pre-1950
Sharpe, Tony	1958
Shea, Bill	1986
Shepard, Larry	1959
Sherry, Larry	1969
Shwam, Dan	1996-2000
Siebern, Norm	1958, 1968
Siebler, Dwight	1958
Simmons, Curt	1961
Simpson, Allan	1987
Simpson, Wayne	1972
Simunic, Doug	2003
Slaughter, Enos	1949, 1961
Smalley, Roy	1949
Smith, Claire	1984
Smith, Curt	1989
Smith, Lee	2000
Smith, Robert	1985
Smoltz, John	2005-2015
Snider, Duke	1981
Sotos, Mary	1974
Spahn, Warren	1963, 1968
Splittorff, Paul	1973, 1980
Sports Franchises, Inc.	1992
Sports Illustrated	1977
Stallard, Tracy	1969
Stargell, Willie	1973, 1979
Staub, Rusty	1960
Steinbrenner, George	1974,1975,1976, 1977, 1979
Stenerud, Jan	2002
Stern, Bill	Pre-1950

St. Louis Cardinals	1949, 1961,1963, 1969
Stone, Helen	1982
Stotz, Carl	1987
Stratton, John	1996-2000
Strickland, George	1971
Stroman, Susan	2002
Stuart, Dick	1956
Sutter, Bruce	2000
Sutton, Don	1973
Tallis, Cedric	1968, 1969, 1970, 1972, 1973, 1974, 1978
Taylor, Bob (Hawk)	1969
Tekulve, Kent	2000
Terlecky, Bill	1994
Terry, Hilda	1973
Terry Park	1970
Thatcher, Joe	2003
Thomas, Frank	1987, 1992
Thomson, Bobby	1950-55
Thrift, Syd	1970
Throneberry, Marv	1968
Thunder Bay Whiskey Jacks	1994
Torre, Joe	1963, 1973
Torrington Twisters	2002
Tovar, Cesar	1966
Tsamis, George	1996-2000
Turner, Ted	1975
Ueberroth, Peter	1984, 1985
Valdespino, Sandy	1966
Valles, Rolando	2004
Varitek, Jason	1987
Veeck, Bill	1965,1975, 1978
Veeck, Mike	1993
Ventura, Robin	1987
Versalles, Zoilo	1966

About the Author

While best known as chief spokesman to two major league baseball commissioners for more than a decade and for running his own sports public relations and marketing company since 1985, Bob Wirz has been a professional in the sports world ever since graduating from the University of Nebraska in 1959.

A native of the Nebraska Sandhills village of Halsey, Bob wasted little time when he entered the university before he started broadcasting Huskers events for the campus radio station KNUS and writing stories for the student newspaper, The Daily Nebraskan.

He later had eight years of newspaper, radio and television experience, which started during his senior year at the university as he prepared for work in the professional baseball industry. He had coveted such an opportunity since his youth. Wirz worked in the news and sports departments of The Lincoln Journal, largely covering local high school sports, and then spent a combined four years as sports director of KHAS Radio and KHAS-TV in Hastings, NE.

During this time, he broadcast up to 80 American Legion baseball games a season, including serving as the radio voice of the 1960 American Legion World Series, plus 50 high school and college basketball games a season and 20-25 football games. He also hosted weekly bowling, wrestling and sports talk shows on both radio and television. He interviewed the likes of Cassius Clay (later Muhammad Ali) and golfing greats Arnold Palmer and Gary Player. One season, prior to much live coverage of games on television, he was the play-by-play voice of University of Nebraska football games, which were shown in their entirety the day after they were played on KHAS-TV.

He later became a member of the sports staff of both The Wichita Eagle and The Denver Post, covering professional, collegiate and high school events.

His first professional baseball position was as Public Relations Director of the Denver Bears (Pacific Coast League) in 1967-68. He was the Kansas City Royals' Publicity Director for their first six seasons (1969-74), and then became Major League Baseball's Director of Information from 1974-85, serving first under Commissioner Bowie Kuhn and later under his successor, Peter Ueberroth.

It was during those years in the New York City offices when baseball started centralizing the organization of its major events, the All-Star Game and World Series, with Wirz coordinating with the host teams to accommodate the requirements of about 600 journalists who needed work space and access to the headline-makers.

He formed Wirz & Associates, Inc. in the spring of 1985, and the client base eventually included such well-known accounts as IBM, Little League Baseball, USA Baseball, Major League Baseball and Baseball America magazine. Wirz and his staff handled publicity as well as many promotions for the highly-acclaimed Rolaids Relief Man program for 21 seasons, and ran national promotions for the hair-color giant Just For Men. He authored a year-round column (Independent Baseball Insider) for 12 years and has become a major voice nationally on Independent Professional Baseball.

Wirz and his wife, Maybeth, reside in Stratford, CT. They have four children and five grandchildren.

About the Artist

Artist Laron McGinn and the *Passion* author share a bond in that both grew up in the Sandhills of Nebraska, which are depicted on the book's covers. McGinn graduated from the University of Arizona with a degree in Graphic Design and Illustration and worked in Arizona and Los Angeles, but was eventually drawn back to the beauty and open spaces of the Sandhills. He paints and works on the family homestead ranch outside of Dunning, NE, which was founded in 1870. McGinn's experiences with the cowboy lifestyle and his extensive travels in Europe are reflected in his unique impressionist style. His work is now part of The Burkholder Project in Lincoln, NE.

44527571R00209

Made in the USA
Middletown, DE
09 June 2017